THE CIVILIZATION OF THE AMERICAN INDIAN

CHEROKEE CAVALIERS

General Stand Watie

Cherokee Cavaliers

FORTY YEARS
OF CHEROKEE HISTORY AS TOLD IN THE
CORRESPONDENCE OF THE
RIDGE-WATIE-BOUDINOT FAMILY

BY

Edward Everett Dale
& Gaston Litton

Norman
University of Oklahoma Press

To the memory of
General Stand Watie
Patriot
Soldier and Statesman
this volume is
reverently dedicated

PREFACE

A FEW of the letters included in this volume were obtained from the libraries of the University of Texas and the Northeastern State Teachers' College at Tahlequah, Oklahoma. One or two were secured from the private collection of Professor T. L. Ballenger of the last named institution. Nearly all of them, however, together with some two thousand more were discovered in the summer of 1919 in a farm house not far from the former home of General Stand Watie in northeastern Oklahoma. All of these are to be found in the Frank Phillips Collection of Southwestern History at the University of Oklahoma, which purchased them from the original owner.

The task of editing and preparing them for publication has been a most difficult one. Some of them hurriedly written on sheets torn from old ledgers and account books had been exposed to the weather and after the lapse of so many years were in some places almost illegible. To trace the intricate family relationships was also at times far from easy; while to add to the difficulty, distressing gaps occurred in the correspondence at times and at others it was so voluminous as to make the question of which letters to select for publication a serious one. The matter of explanatory notes has also presented a grave problem. Since the number necessary in order to make the story clear must inevitably depend upon the reader's previous knowledge of the subject the editors have, in cases of doubt, chosen to err upon the side of too many rather than too few such notes. Such a procedure has at times involved some repetitions but it is hoped that this will not prove a serious fault.

The letters have been printed exactly as written except in a few instances where it has seemed necessary to insert a comma, period, or a word in brackets in order to clarify the meaning. Considering the haste in which many of them were written, the spelling, punctuation, and English are in most cases quite as good as may be found in the correspondence of most white people of that time—even those who had had the advantages of

ix

PREFACE

a liberal education. In the few instances where the spelling is very bad, it should be borne in mind that the writers had in all probability learned to read, write, and speak Cherokee long before they had learned English and in consequence the latter was to them a more or less foreign language.

For assistance in preparation of the volume the editors wish, first of all, to acknowledge their indebtedness to the Works Progress Administration of the United States government for a grant of funds used in having the letters typed, arranged, and prepared for editing. Our sincere thanks are also due to the officials of the libraries of the University of Texas and Northeastern State Teachers' College, as well as to Professor Ballenger for permission to copy and publish the letters in their possession. We are especially grateful to Mr. Frank Phillips of Bartlesville, Oklahoma, whose generosity has made possible the Frank Phillips Collection of which these letters are a part. Finally we wish to express our thanks to the many persons who have furnished information of great value in editing some of this correspondence and to Mrs. Rosalie Gilkey Dale for assistance in various phases of the work including the reading of proof and other details incident to publication.

EDWARD EVERETT DALE

GASTON LITTON

Norman, Oklahoma

CONTENTS

ILLUSTRATIONS

INTRODUCTION

THE Cherokee Indians formerly occupied a large area in Georgia, Tennessee and Western North Carolina. Even before the American Revolution, however, they had ceded much of their land to the whites and after independence had been won by the Colonies they surrendered a great deal more by treaty. As a result, by the beginning of the nineteenth century they felt that they had left no more than barely sufficient land for their own needs.

In 1802 Georgia ceded to the United States her unoccupied western lands comprising what is now the states of Alabama and Mississippi. This was done by what is known as the "Georgia compact of 1802" which also provided that as part of the consideration for this cession the United States should, at its own expense, remove the Indians from Georgia "as soon as it could be done peacefully and upon favorable terms."

The purchase of Louisiana the following year gave a vast territory which might be regarded as a suitable home for any Indian tribes east of the Mississippi who might be willing to migrate to it but the Cherokee were very reluctant to remove. In consequence it was not until 1817 that a treaty was signed by which about one third of the Cherokees agreed to give up their lands east of the Mississippi in exchange for a new grant in Arkansas between the Arkansas and White rivers. With the removal of this group the Cherokee Nation was divided into two parts: the "Cherokee West," numbering about seven or eight thousand, residing in Arkansas; and the "Cherokee East," about twice as numerous, who still resided in Georgia and Tennessee. As a matter of fact, many of these Western Cherokees had gone to Arkansas some years in advance of the signing of the treaty of 1817, attracted by the superior hunting and fishing of that region. To these the treaty merely confirmed the title to lands upon which they had already settled as squatters.

It was not many years, however, until the Cherokee West discovered that they had not gone far enough if they expected to escape the rapacity and oppression of the land-hungry whites. A number of whites had already settled upon the Arkansas lands granted to these Indians. These refused to leave, or if they were removed, quickly returned bringing others with them. Still other white people settled along the border of this Indian country, killed the game and allowed their live stock to trespass upon the Indians' fields. Accordingly, in 1828, a treaty was signed with the Western Cherokee by which the Indians agreed to give up their lands in Arkansas in exchange for a new grant of seven million acres in what is now Oklahoma together with a perpetual outlet to the west as far as the limits of the United States extended which was, at this time, to the one hundredth meridian. Removing to this new home the Cherokee West proceeded to build themselves log cabins, and open up and plant small farms.

In the meantime the Cherokee East had become involved in many serious and perplexing difficulties. Georgia was insistent that the compact of 1802 be kept and all Indians removed from her territory, but the United States protested that the Indians were unwilling to go and nothing in the compact compelled the government to remove them against their will.

By this time the Cherokee had made great progress in civilization. Contact with missionaries, white traders, and others had taught them much of the white man's civilization. Many of them had beautiful homes, plantations with broad, well-tilled fields, much live stock and numerous slaves. Not a few were well educated, while intermarriage with the whites had produced a considerable group of mixed bloods of rare ability in the fields of both politics and business.

Fearful that their tribal forms of government would be urged as a reason for their enforced removal from the lands they had so long occupied and loved, the Cherokee, in 1827, held a convention and formulated a written constitution and code of laws. Executive power was vested in a principal chief and in 1828 John Ross, a mixed blood Cherokee largely of Scotch ancestry, succeeded to this office and for nearly forty years largely directed the destiny of the Cherokee Nation.

Angry because the compact of 1802 had not been carried out, the political leaders of Georgia enacted a series of harsh and oppressive laws directed against the Indians with the purpose of forcing their removal. These laws eventually had their effect. The Cherokee were so harassed and mistreated that in time a small group came to believe that the only salvation for their Nation lay in surrendering their lands in the East and joining their brethren west of the Mississippi.

The leaders of this group were four men whose letters, together with those of their descendants, form a large part of this volume. They were Major Ridge, his son John Ridge, and Major Ridge's nephews, two brothers known respectively as Elias Boudinot and Stand Watie. All were men of great ability and of remarkable vision and strength of character. Major Ridge was apparently a full blood Cherokee. He had comparatively little English education but possessed great native intelligence and high qualities of leadership. John Ridge and Elias Boudinot were both highly educated. Both had attended school at Cornwall, Connecticut, where each had married a young white woman of education and refinement. Stand Watie, not so well educated as his brother, Elias Boudinot, had nevertheless received a fair education at a mission school in Tennessee. He was a man of action, a born leader, and was to prove himself a brave and hardy soldier of real ability. There is evidence that John Ridge had political ambitions and that he engaged in rivalry with John Ross for the leadership of the Cherokee. This rivalry was, upon Ridge's death, transferred to Stand Watie.

Apparently for a time John Ross bitterly opposed removal. As the contest grew, however, and he saw that removal was inevitable he favored securing as large a payment for the land as possible and seeking a new home, perhaps somewhere beyond the limits of the United States.

In opposing removal Ross undoubtedly represented the wishes of an overwhelming majority of the Nation. In 1835, however, the Ridge-Watie-Boudinot group signed with commissioners of the United States the treaty of New Echota by which it was agreed that the Cherokee would cede their lands east of the Mississippi and join the Cherokee West. For the cession they were to receive some four and a half million dollars together with a grant of 800,000 acres of land in Kansas, commonly known as the Neutral Lands.

In spite of protests the treaty was promptly ratified by the Senate and in 1838 the Cherokee were removed to what is now Oklahoma. The story of their removal constitutes one of the most tragic chapters in the history of any people. Troops under General Scott drove the Indians from their homes into stockade camps from which they were later released and started westward on the long journey over the "Trail of Tears." With the two branches of the Cherokee again united, a new constitution for the entire people was drawn up and adopted.

The Ridge-Watie-Boudinot faction, commonly known as the Treaty Party, was the object of the intense hatred of the Ross group. Greatly in the minority, the members of the Treaty Party looked about for allies and found them in the Cherokee West or "Old Settlers" who objected to seeing the Ross element come in and monopolize most of the offices provided for in the new constitution. Though still in the minority, the Ridge group and its allies maintained themselves fairly well against the majority party for a short time. In 1839, however, Major Ridge, John Ridge and Elias Boudinot were all murdered on the same day. Stand Watie, the only one of the four leaders who escaped death, now became the recognized head of the Treaty Party. These murders caused the smouldering fires of passion and resentment to flame forth higher than ever before. The Cherokee Nation was divided into two hostile camps. Reprisals took place and murder and pillage were of common occurrence. Near civil war existed and Stand Watie at one time collected a large number of armed men at Old Fort Wayne, declaring that he did so to prevent himself and his friends from being murdered, while his enemies asserted that he was seeking to plunge the Cherokee Nation into civil strife.

Disturbed conditions existed for several years in spite of the efforts of the United States to adjust the difficulties between the hostile factions. At last, in 1846, a treaty was signed which sought to settle all differences between the parties. Some years of comparative peace and tranquility ensued during which the Cherokee made a great advance in prosperity and civilization. During these years the discovery of gold in California led many Cherokees westward to seek their fortunes in the mountains of that state. Among these argonauts were several members of the Ridge-Watie-Boudinot family as well as a number of their friends. Their letters written from California not only give some interesting pictures of life in the gold fields but also reveal something of the intense love of home and country, ever present in the hearts of these citizens of a tiny republic while wanderers in a strange land.

In the meantime the period of comparative peace and prosperity in the Cherokee Nation proved all too brief. It was not many years until the gathering clouds of the War between the States began to cast ominous shadows over the Cherokee people. Once more the spectre of factionalism stalked the Cherokee hills. Again the people began to divide into two hostile groups and a spirit of lawlessness swept over the country.

The fullblood element wedded to old Indian customs owned very few slaves and some of them strongly opposed slavery. This group in many cases joined the society known as the Keetoo-wah or "Pins," an organization of conservatives deeply interested in preserving the old order and early tribal traditions. The proslavery group, many of them mixed bloods and most of them favoring education and white civilization, formed chapters of the Copperhead organization called the Knights of the Golden Circle. Superintendent of the Southern Superintendency Elias Rector and the Indian agents under his direction were all Southern men favoring slavery, while most of the missionaries engaged in work in the Indian Territory were New Englanders and bitterly opposed it.

When war actually came the Confederacy sent Albert Pike to Indian Territory as commissioner to the Indian Nations with instructions to conclude treaties of alliance with them. Pike came first to the Cherokee country but Chief John Ross declared that the Cherokee wished to remain neutral in the struggle and refused to join the South. Pike accordingly visited the remaining Nations of the Five Civilized Tribes and made treaties of alliance with them. He then visited the Plains Indians of western Indian Territory, concluded treaties with some of them, and returned to the Cherokee Nation in October, 1861. By this time, after all other tribes had joined the South, Ross had decided that it would be impossible for the Cherokee to maintain a position of neutrality and so he made with Pike a treaty of alliance. Troops were promptly raised among the Cherokee and Stand Watie became colonel of one of the Cherokee regiments.

It soon became apparent, however, that while the Chickasaw and Choctaw were virtually unanimous in their sympathy for the South, the Cherokee, Creek and Seminole each had a large element favorable to the North. War broke out between the Union sympathizers and those favoring the South and the Creek leader of the Northern forces, Opoth-le-yo-hola, was late in 1861 terribly defeated and fled north to Kansas with his followers and their families. These refugees, joined by numerous Cherokees and some Seminoles, spent the remainder of the winter of 1861-62 in refugee camps in Kansas near the military encampment of General Hunter of the Northern army. There they endured untold horrors of suffering from cold, starvation, and disease.

When spring came these Indians wished to return to their homes and two Indian regiments were formed and placed with two regiments of white troops for an invasion of the Indian country. The expedition under the command of Colonel William Weer marched south to Tahlequah and Park Hill. At the latter place they captured John Ross but he was soon released on parole and went to Philadelphia where he remained most of the time until the end of the war, or in fact until his death in 1866.

Due to difficulties among the leaders the expedition soon retreated to Kansas where the Indians again spent a miserable winter in refugee camps.

INTRODUCTION

In the summer of 1863 a second invasion of the Indian Territory took place under the leadership of Colonel W. A. Phillips. This expedition captured and held Fort Gibson from which post raiding and foraging expeditions were sent out. The Cherokee soldiers under the leadership of Stand Watie, Colonel John Drew, and others were able to maintain themselves in the field against these raids and even in many cases to defeat such groups in battle. The families of the Southern Cherokee were, however, compelled to flee from their homes and to establish themselves in refugee camps along the Red River where they endured, during the winter of 1863-64 and 1864-65, all the horrors that the Northern Cherokee had faced during the two preceding winters. Some of these Cherokee families, including the wife and small children of Stand Watie, took refuge among their Cherokee relatives living in Texas.

Early in 1863 the Ross faction of the Cherokee repudiated the alliance with the Confederacy, freed their slaves, and declared their allegiance to the United States. The Stand Watie group refused to accept this action and, claiming to be the real Cherokee Nation, promptly chose Stand Watie as principal chief. From this time until the end of the war there were really two Cherokee Nations — one under the leadership of Ross who resided in Philadelphia and the other under Stand Watie with his troops in the field.

Under the terms of the Cherokee treaty with the Confederacy these Indians were entitled to send a delegate to the Confederate Congress. Elias Cornelius Boudinot, son of the elder Boudinot, was chosen to fill this position and his letters give valuable side lights upon conditions at Richmond.

During the four years of war Stand Watie was very active, engaging in numerous raids and fighting several bloody battles. His most notable exploit perhaps was the capture of a great wagon train of supplies bound for Fort Gibson; also, largely with cavalry, he captured a steamboat on the Arkansas River. He worked unceasingly to relieve the necessities of the miserable refugees along Red River and showed at all times rare resourcefulness and courage. Before the close of the war he was made brigadier general. He fought for weeks, after the evacuation of Richmond and the surrender of Lee's army. Even after General E. Kirby Smith had surrendered the entire Trans-Mississippi Department to General Canby on May 26, he still remained in the field and it was not until almost a month later — or June 23 — that he at last laid down his sword, apparently the last Confederate officer to surrender.

At the close of the war the Cherokee Nation was in a state of utter ruin and desolation. Houses had been burned, the livestock slaughtered or stolen, and the fields untilled for four years were covered with bushes and briers. Thieves and robbers abounded everywhere and Southern refugees along Red River were in a state of destitution and afraid to return to their homes because of the general lawlessness of the entire region.

Eager to know what was to be their punishment for joining the South the Cherokee sent commissioners to the council held at Fort Smith in September 1865, where they were to learn the terms upon which they would again be brought back into the good graces of the United States.

The following summer they sent two delegations to Washington to make a final treaty of peace. One of those delegations represented the Ross group, while the other, representing the Stand Watie faction, included Stand Watie himself. Each sought to secure the recognition of the United States government. Finding that the Ross delegation was to be recognized the Southern delegation sought to have the Cherokee country divided into two Nations but without success. Bitter quarrels developed between certain individual members of the Stand Watie group and, in all probability, served to interfere with the success of its efforts.

John Ross died about the time of the conclusion of the treaty but his party still remained in power. Stand Watie returned to his ruined country and set bravely to work to rebuild his broken fortunes. It was not easy, for he was growing old and the hard years of war had taken their toll of his health and strength. He engaged in business for a time with his nephew, E. C. Boudinout, but soon gave it up. His eldest son Saladin, who had been a captain in his father's regiment, died in 1868 and this must have been a terrible blow to the old soldier. Even this he met bravely as he had met everything else during his active, adventurous life. His youngest son was sent away to school and provision made for the education of his daughters. In 1869 this son also died and there were left to him only his brave wife and the two daughters.

He worked hard to care for these and in spite of all handicaps met with a fair measure of success. Not many years were left to him. On September 9, 1871 he died and the widow and two daughters were left to carry on alone. Many of their letters, written after Stand Watie's death, have been preserved as well as numerous letters of Elias Cornelius Boudinot and others of the Ridge-Watie-Boudinot family. These give a remarkable picture of conditions in the Cherokee country from 1872 to the close of the century, but that is another story.

CHEROKEE CAVALIERS

❧ CHAPTER I ❧

REMOVAL AND THE ROSS-RIDGE FEUD

IN 1832 the Cherokee Nation was still divided into two parts. The Cherokee West consisting of about one third of the tribe resided in Oklahoma while the remaining two thirds or the Cherokee East still occupied their home land in Georgia and Tennessee. The period from 1832 to 1846 was characterized by the removal of the Eastern Cherokee to the West and the union of the two groups, as well as by the development of a bitter feud between the Ridge-Watie-Boudinot group and the Ross faction. This violent controversy was ended, or at least temporarily calmed, by the Treaty of 1846.

In 1821 Sequoyah, "the Cherokee Cadmus," had completed his syllabary or form of written language for the Cherokee. This soon came into extensive use and shortly after the adoption of the Cherokee constitution the National Council provided for the establishment of a national newspaper called the *Cherokee Phoenix*. Elias Boudinot was made editor of this paper which was printed in parallel columns, one in Cherokee and the other in English.

Among the laws passed by the State of Georgia which the Cherokee regarded as oppressive was an act prohibiting any white man from residing in the Indian country unless he were a citizen of Georgia and had received a permit from the Georgia authorities to do so. Two missionaries, Reverend Samuel A. Worcester and Elizur Butler, had been for some years residents of the Cherokee country. They were both citizens of New England and neither would apply for a permit to live within the limits of the Cherokee lands. They were accordingly arrested by Georgia officials, tried in the state courts and sentenced to four years imprisonment at hard labor in the Georgia penitentiary. Their case was appealed to the Supreme Court of the United States on the ground that the Cherokee country was not a part of the State of Georgia and, in consequence, that state had no authority to make laws concerning it. This con-

3

tention was affirmed by the Supreme Court in the case of Worcester v. Georgia.

Soon after this decision the Ridge-Watie-Boudinot faction and the Ross party became engaged in a violent controversy over the question of removal. When the former group signed the removal treaty of New Echota in 1835, it incurred the bitter hatred of a large majority of the Cherokee people and this bitterness was perhaps intensified by the suffering endured in the journey westward over the Trail of Tears.

The murder of Major Ridge, John Ridge and Elias Boudinot which occurred on June 22, 1839, caused the Ridge-Watie-Boudinot group to believe that a wide-spread plot existed to destroy them all. Stand Watie became the recognized leader of the group and eventually collected a body of armed men at Old Fort Wayne. Murders and other lawless acts were common; it seemed that civil war was imminent. For a time the government of the United States vainly sought to restore order and adjust the difficulties between the two parties. At last the efforts met with a degree of success and comparative peace and quiet were restored by the Treaty of 1846.

◆§ Elias Boudinot[1] to Stand Watie[2]

Boston, March 7, 1832

MY DEAR BROTHER,

You will, before this reaches you, have heard of the decision of the Supreme Court of the United States, in favor of Mr. Worcester[3] and Butler and against the State of Georgia. It is a

[1] Elias Boudinot was the son of David OO-Watie, the brother of Major Ridge. He was born about 1802 and given an Indian name meaning stag or the male deer, which accounts for his being known during childhood as Buck Watie. As a youth he was befriended by the Philadelphia philanthropist Elias Boudinot. He in consequence took the name of his benefactor, which explains the origin of the name Boudinot borne by this branch of the Watie family. While in school at Cornwall, Connecticut, he wooed and married Harriet Gold, daughter of a prominent family of that town. Upon his return to his home in Georgia he became editor of the *Cherokee Phoenix*.

[2] Stand Watie, brother of Elias Boudinot, was born in 1806. He attended Brainerd Mission School in Tennessee and received a fair education, though

glorious news. The laws of the State are declared by the highest judicial tribunal in the Country null and void.[4] It is a great
triumph on the part of the Cherokees so far as the question of
their rights were concerned. The question is for ever settled as
to who is right and who is wrong, and the controversy is exactly where it ought to be, and where we have all along been
desirous it should be. It is not now before the great state of
Georgia and the poor Cherokees, but between the U.S. and the
State of Georgia, or between the friends of the judiciary and
the enemies of the judiciary. We can only look and see whoever prevails in this momentous crisis.

Expectation has for the last few days been upon tiptoe —
fears and hopes alternately took possession of our minds until

---

considerably less than that of his brother. His early life was conspicuous chiefly for his participation in the negotiation of the removal treaty of New Echota.
After the murders of 1839 he took a more active part in Cherokee affairs and
became the virtual head of his party. He was married to Sarah C. Bell in
1843. In the years that followed he was elected several times to the National
Council but was primarily a man of action. Stand Watie possessed great courage and strength of character. He was an excellent soldier and before the close
of the War between the States he attained the rank of brigadier general in the
Confederate Service.

[3] Samuel Austin Worcester was born at Worcester, Massachusetts, in 1798.
He was educated at the University of Vermont and Andover Theological Seminary. He was ordained a minister in 1825 and immediately departed for
Brainerd Mission in the Cherokee country. Two years later he returned to
Boston to supervise the manufacture of type for printing in the Cherokee language the *Cherokee Phoenix* which he had helped to establish. Returning to
the Cherokee country he established himself at New Echota, Georgia, where he
assisted Boudinot in publishing the *Phoenix*. He also translated portions of the
Bible which were printed in the Cherokee language upon the *Phoenix* Press.
In 1831 he was arrested by officers of the governor of Georgia for residing in
the Indian country without a permit and was sentenced to four years imprisonment in the Georgia penitentiary, but was released in 1833. In 1835 he joined
the Cherokee west of the Mississippi where he established the Park Hill Mission, which became one of the most important mission stations in the Indian
Territory. In addition to his translation and publication in Cherokee of the
Bible and numerous tracts he also established the Cherokee Temperance Society and the Cherokee Bible Society, both of which had great influence. He
died at Park Hill in 1859. For an account of Worcester's life see Althea Bass,
The Cherokee Messenger (University of Oklahoma Press, 1936).

[4] The decision referred to was the case of Worcester *v.* Georgia (6 Peters,
515-97).

5

two or three hours ago Mr. John Tappan came in to see us, and asked us whether we could not dine with him to-morrow. He said his brother had just arrived in the city from Washington, and he supposed we were prepared to hear bad news — (a chill went through my heart). Mr. Ridge[5] observed, "No, we are not prepared." He then told us of the true state of the case, and produced a paper which contained an account, and tried to read to us, but he was so agitated with joy he could hardly proceed. A few minutes after Mr. Anderson came in to congratulate me on the happy news. Soon after Dr. Beecher came — I asked him whether he had heard the news from Washington. He said, "No, what is it?" I told him the Supreme C. had decided in favor of the Missionaries. He jumped up, clapped his hands, took hold of my hand and said, "God be praised," and ran right out to tell his daughter and his family.[6] These little incidents manifest the feeling, the intense feeling, on that question. And I will take upon myself to say that this decision of the Court will now have a most powerful effect on public opinion. It creates a new era on the Indian question.

Your letter found me very feeble. I am better now, although I have not been out of the house the last four days. In consequence of my illness I have been obliged to give up my appointments at Salem and Newburyport. Nor was I able to attend a meeting held in this city last evening. I understand it was a very full meeting.[7]

Brother Franklin Gold has come all the way from New Hampshire to see me.[8] He came in last evening from the meeting — will be in this morning and go with me to Salem.

I am sorry, I grew to think many of our countrymen are betraying our country. Let us hold fast to our integrity.

[5] This was John Ridge, cousin of Elias Boudinot and Stand Watie.

[6] This was the Reverend Lyman Beecher, father of Henry Ward Beecher and Harriet Beecher Stowe. The Reverend Beecher had been pastor of a church at Cornwall while Boudinot was a student there.

[7] Boudinot was giving lectures in the East which accounts for his presence in Boston at this time.

[8] Franklin Gold was the brother of Boudinot's wife, Harriet Gold Boudinot.

6

Tell Harriet I have written to her almost every week — and generally very long letters.[9]

Publish nothing in regard to the Presidential election — about Clay or Jackson, and copy little of what is said about the S.C.[10] A great deal will be said but let us only look on and see — I shall write again soon. Tell H. I *do* behave myself.

ELIAS BOUDINOT

⥽John Ridge[11] to Stand Watie

Washington City

Mr. Stand Watie April 6th, 1832

DEAR COUSIN,

Your favor of the 23 ult. has reached here and it is truly acceptable and I now hasten to answer it. That it has been a day of rejoicing with patriots of our Country on hearing of the glo-

---

[9] Boudinot's wife Harriet, to whom he here refers, died in 1836. The following year he married Delight Sargent, but no children were born of this second union.

[10] Stand Watie had been left in charge of the *Cherokee Phoenix* during Boudinot's absence. This presidential campaign was the election of 1832 in which the re-charter of the Bank of the United States was the chief issue. Boudinot evidently did not wish to see the Cherokee involved in this political struggle.

[11] John Ridge, son of Major Ridge, was educated with his cousin Elias Boudinot at the mission school in Cornwall, Connecticut. There he met and loved Sarah Bird Northrup, daughter of a prominent citizen of Cornwall in whose household young Ridge lived while in school. Her parents strongly objected to the marriage of their daughter to the young Cherokee, especially since Ridge was suffering from a hip disease. At last they agreed that if he would return to his home and come back a year later without his crutches they would withdraw their objections to the marriage. After a year had elapsed Ridge returned, entirely well, in a magnificent coach drawn by four white horses driven by a negro coachman in livery. He was accompanied by his father, dressed in the finest of broadcloth, who greatly impressed the people of the little village by his stately form and aristocratic bearing. Young Ridge took his bride to the Cherokee country where they lived in a beautiful home on a large plantation which was cultivated by his numerous slaves. John Ridge, one of the ablest and most influential of the Cherokee leaders, was chiefly interested in the welfare of his people. After affixing his name to the treaty of New Echota he is reported to have said: "I know that in signing this treaty I have signed my own death warrant." Apparently he foresaw his own assassination which occurred four years later.

7

rious decision of the Supreme Court, I can readily perceive and congratulate them upon the momentous event.[12] But you are aware and ought to advise our people that the contest is not over and that time is to settle the matter either for us and all the friends of the Judiciary or against us all! We have gained a high standing and consideration in the interests and best affections of the community from which we can never be removed. But Sir, the Chicken Snake General Jackson has time to crawl and hide in the luxuriant grass of his nefarious hypocracy until his responsibility is fastened upon by an execution of the Supreme Court at their next session.[13] Then we shall see how strong the links are to the chain that connect the states to the Federal Union. Upon this subject the Union pauses and stands still to look upon the crisis our intellectual warfare has brought them and the Cherokee question as it now stands is the greatest that has ever presented itself to the consideration of the American People. Upon the shoulders of this body politic, if there was a proper head, the friends of the permanency of the general government could look upon this decision undismayed as to the results of the menacing attitude which the foolish Georgians have assumed.

Now before the explained laws are carried into effect, it will, I fear, first be necessary to cut down this Snake's head and throw it down in the dust. From the newspaper editorial remarks, you will be afforded the opportunity to see the operations of this affair and the length of the rope that Georgia has to browse upon the rights of the Cherokee Nation. The remarks I have thought called for on this occasion, that we as a whole and individually, may not sleep upon our post, but as good soldiers watch thoroughly every avenue through which the enemy may approach.

12 Worcester *v.* Georgia.

13 When the Court decision was rendered President Jackson is reported to have said, "John Marshall has made his decision; let him enforce it now if he can." Whether or not this is true, it seems that Jackson had little sympathy with the desire of the Cherokee to remain in Georgia, and approved the hostile measures of that state toward them.

Mission School at Cornwall, Connecticut

The Secretary of War[14] is exceedingly anxious to close a treaty with our Nation upon the basis that will secure to us the sovereignty and fee of and over the soil west of the Mississippi and money enough to make every friend to his country rich with the addition of a perpetual annuity for the support of public institutions. I feel disgusted at an administration who have trampled our rights under foot to offer new pledges from their rotten hearts. He says that Jack Walker and James Stark have informed him that there is a majority in favor of a treaty on the Tennessee side of the Cherokee Nation and that they believe they are also in the majority in the limits of North Carolina of this description. The Secretary says that if so, they will treat with them or any of the other bands who shall prove to be in the majority there. I told him that it was false and granting for the sake of argument that the Government succeeded in making a treaty with a fraction or faction of our Nation, he knew very well that it would never be ratified by the Senate constituted as it was, as we assuredly would protest against it and defeat it.

In view of these facts, have I not said well when I said you should be on your guard? As to the Arkansas delegation[15] they can never do hurt and their greatest hope is to cling fast to our friendship and to reunite with us. If the time ever should happen to come when we thought best to make a treaty, we should do so. This is their language. Rest assured, dear Cousin, that we have the advantage and let this question result which way it may. As I have said before, we shall live to tread on the necks of traitors. It may well yet be a fearful time for them if they have hearts for reflection to know that they have only been false and done mischief to themselves.

I wrote to you from Hudson. I have not seen the Phoenix for some time. Allow me to suggest the propriety of presenting all you can of what is in the minds of the whites and en-

---

[14] The Secretary of War was Lewis Cass.

[15] Ridge's reference to the Arkansas delegation is to representatives of the Cherokee West at this time living in Oklahoma. Leaders of this group later joined with the Treaty Party in opposition to John Ross.

couraging our people to communicate the facts to you from various quarters by letters which you can publish. The reason why the National Intelligencer has not been sent is that the subscription for it had expired, but which I have renewed for the Phoenix. Of the National Journal, there is a stronger reason — it is defunct.[16]

From the strain of this letter, you will perceive that it is not for publication. "United we stand, divided we fall." Since the decision of the Supreme Court, I have felt greatly revived — a new man and I feel independent. I am hoping you all do too. How much of gratitude do we owe to the good men Mr. Worcester and Dr. Butler. You did not mention my son, Rollin.[17] Present my best respects to Mrs. W. and Mrs. B. and Miss Sawyer. I shall, you know, always be glad to hear from you.

Ere this reaches you, you will have heard of the foolish Creek Treaty.[18]

Yours, etc.
JOHN RIDGE

✑ Elias Boudinot to Stand Watie

Washington, Feb. 28, 1835

MY DEAR BROTHER,

For a few days back we have been trying to obtain the best stipulations that we can to be sent to our people — for them to accept or not to accept as they choose. We find the greatest difficulty to be in satisfying those who are determined to stay.[19]

---

[16] Ridge is apparently referring to a newspaper received in exchange for the *Cherokee Phoenix*. The latter was published continuously until May 31, 1834.

[17] This was John Rollin Ridge, later to become a newspaper man and poet of some note in California.

[18] This was the Creek treaty of March 24, 1832 by which the Creeks agreed to cede their lands east of the Mississippi and remove to Oklahoma.

[19] Some of the Cherokee were unwilling to remove under any consideration. A number of these fled to the hills and mountains at the time of removal in 1838. Lands were later purchased for them in western North Carolina where their descendants, known as the North Carolina Cherokee, still live.

Our proceedings have finally so frightened Mr. Ross[20] so that he made several propositions lately, all of which have been rejected promptly except the last, which is, to agree to take the gross amount in money which the Senate shall say will be sufficient. He has this day given a written obligation to that effect. His intention is to get the money and hunt out a country for himself.[21] This the President is willing should be laid before the Cherokee people, also a proposition giving the same amount if they will go to the west. The question is to be submitted to the Senate to-day. I have not time to enlarge — but I can tell you our rights are fully secured. I am sure the Cherokees, when they find out that they are to remove at all events will not think of going to a Country of which they know nothing. Where will Ross take them to? But here is a country to which they can go with the same pecuniary advantages — a country already obtained and near by. Besides the president has agreed to add the Neutral Land — which is a most excellent country. [22] We have now some prospects of a speedy termination to our perplexities. Be firm to our cause and we shall yet succeed in saving a majority of our people.

I hope you will not be disturbed in your possessions — if

[20] John Ross, born in 1790 near Lookout Mountain, Tennessee, was one-eighth Cherokee, the son of a Scotch father and a quarter blood Cherokee mother. He was educated by private tutors and at Kingston Academy, Tennessee. Ross assisted in drafting the Cherokee constitution of 1827 and the following year became principal chief. He held this position until his death, although for a brief period during the Civil War his right to it was disputed by the Southern wing of the Cherokee and the government of the United States. For a time he strongly opposed removal westward, but finding it inevitable he organized the migration and led his people to their new home. Here he helped make the new constitution of 1839 uniting the Eastern and Western Cherokee. At the outbreak of the Civil War Ross sought to remain neutral but, in October 1861, he signed a treaty of alliance with the Confederacy which was repudiated in 1863. Taken prisoner by Union troops in the summer of 1862 he was soon released on parole and went to Philadelphia where he remained until his death in 1866.

[21] Ross probably planned to settle outside the limits of the United States which was contrary to the wishes of the Ridges and Boudinots who wanted to join the Cherokee West.

[22] As stated in the Introduction, the neutral land was a tract of about 800,000 acres located in Kansas.

11

you should be never mind — we shall make provisions for all such.[23] We are well, and at this time in high spirits. Give love to all — in great haste.

Yours,

ELIAS BOUDINOT

⌘ John Ridge to Major Ridge[24] and Others

Messrs. Major Ridge, Wrinklesides,   Washington City
     Charles Moore & David Watie   10th March 1835
         & others of Cherokee Nation

MY DEAR & RESPECTED CHIEFS,

I have delayed this long in writing to you in the consequence of the hard struggles I had to make against John Ross & his party. At the outset they told Congress that our people had decided that they would choose to be citizens of the U. States [rather] than to remove. We contradicted this & he has failed to get an answer from Congress. From various indications we ascertained that he was going to act falsely to his people & sell the Nation either by getting Reservations of land or taking the whole in money on pretense of going out of the limits of the U. States. We protested against this & we have succeeded to get a treaty made to be sent home for the ratification of the people.[25] It is very liberal in its terms — an equal measure is given to all. The poor Indian enjoys the same rights as

[23] Lawless whites constantly encroached upon Cherokee lands destroying or carrying off property. Recompense was later made for such losses.

[24] Major Ridge, born about 1771, served with credit in the United States army in the wars against the Creek and Seminole, attaining the rank of major. He was called "Ridge" by the whites, this being the briefest possible English interpretation of his Cherokee name which signified "walking the mountain tops." Major Ridge was apparently a fullblood of great wealth and influence among his people. In 1792 he married Susie Wickett who bore him three children, John, Sarah and Walter, some of whose letters appear in this volume.

[25] The terms stated indicate that this was a preliminary draft of the removal treaty of New Echota which was signed by the Ridge-Watie-Boudinot group nearly ten months later, or December 29, 1835.

12

the rich — there is no distinction. We are allowed to enjoy our own laws in the west. Subsistence for one year, $25. for each soul for transportation, fair valuation for ferries & Improvements, $150 for each individual, more than forty thousand dollars perpetual annuity in the west, & a large sum of money to pay for the losses of the Cherokees against the white people. In fact — we get four milions & a half in money to meet all expenses & large addition in land to that already possessed by our brethren in the west. John Ross and his party tried hard to treat & get the whole in money & go as they said out of the limits of the U. States, but they have failed. Jackson said that he would not trust them with the money of the people. The Indians here under his care wish that he would refer the whole to the people. Ross has failed before the Senate, before the Secretary of War, & before the President. He tried hard to cheat you & his people, but he has been prevented. In a day or two he goes home no doubt to tell lies. But we will bring all his papers & the people shall see him as he is.[26]

We have thought proper to send two of our Delegates to go to Arkansaw that Jolly[27] may send four of his Chiefs & attend our great Council. General Jackson will send a just man, a minister of the Gospel from New York with this party, it is to be refered to every man in the Nation.

The Congress has allowed money enough to pay the expenses of our Councils while the people are signing this treaty if they approve it. We are all well. I shall go to the north & see my wife's parents & in great haste will return to you. Stand, stay. All will be right. The U. States will never have any thing more to do with John Ross. Thus it becomes of selfish men. Maj. Currey will have five hundred copies printed by order of the President of this treaty for the use of the people. He will

[26] This letter shows the intense rivalry between John Ridge and Chief Ross and the growing bitterness between the two groups. The attitude of President Jackson toward Ross probably caused Ridge to revise the opinion of the President he expressed in his earlier letter. This is evidenced by the fact that his youngest son, born about this time, was named Andrew Jackson.

[27] This was John Jolly, principal chief of the Western Cherokee.

give you the Particulars before I could. I shall write to our friends Charles Vann & George Chambers.

I am yr. friend

JOHN RIDGE

◄§ W. M. Thompson to Elias Boudinot

Cassvill georgia

November 5th 1838

Mr. E. Budinote

DEAR FRAND

Onst more at home and tolerebell well rested. I left the agensey[28] on the 24th of last month at 12 o clock and had been thare a month at thate time. I will try and give you an oute line of matters at thate plase — John Ross has maid a moving Contract with general Scott at $66 per had[29] — the indians is divided into twelve detatchments haided as follows: Elijah Hicks[30] first detatchmente started aboute the fifteenth of september to catch detatchment. thare is an asistent Conducter, three manigeres, wagons masters, an asistent, a Comesarey and an asistent a fairer an asistent and 20 persons to each wagon.

Hair of Candeys Creek[31] Conducted the 2 detatchment. by some mens he was removed and Thomis Foreman became its Conducter. the 3 was Conducted by Busheyhead.[32] the 4th by Jones the Baptest pretcher from valley towne.[33] the fifth by Steephen Foreman. the treaty party by John Bell under the

[28] Thompson was probably referring to the old Cherokee Agency on the Hiwassee River near Calhoun, Tennessee.

[29] Finding that the Cherokee must go, Chief Ross made a contract with General Winfield Scott by which Ross was to have charge of the removal.

[30] Elijah Hick's detachment consisted of about 850 people. When they reached the Indian Territory early in January, 1839, this number had decreased by about a hundred.

[31] Hair Conrad started with about 850 people. The number had been reduced to about 650 when they reached the Indian Territory early in January.

[32] The Reverend Jesse Bushyhead, conductor of the third detachment, started with 950 Cherokee and reached Indian Territory early in February. There were six births and thirty-eight deaths during the journey.

[33] The Reverend Evan Jones' detachment departed October 15 and reached its destination February 2. During the journey the number was reduced from 1250 to 1033.

14

athorety of govern[men]t and the rights of the treaty. th[e] move all started [whe]n I left the agensey. Tayler[34] Conducted a party, Brown aparty, Bud Watt of dear a party, Gorge Hicks[35] a party, Gorge Stell a party, petter Halter brand[36] a party, Wafferd from north Carolina aparty. this I have given you the Conducters names. the eyday is there are the represantations of the 12 tribes of Iserel on thare way from the land of bondadg and thare has dyd something over a thousand sants. thay was in Camped ner the agensey. the Hightower indians is in Steven Foremens and Balls divashion — we hope that matters of diveshen as to the afars of the governments of the nation will bee managed with sutch prudens as will not involve the intrest of the people. this is in relation to the Chiefs them selvs. try and obtain a filling of ofises by the voise of the people as sone as practibell and that will give the Common people to feel thare rights is restored.

asto the man hoo may sattle the maters of your improvements and spoilation money matters is like wise of great importens.[37] the Commisheners hoo have acted at the agensay on[e] is by the name of Jams Little from gorgea aworthey and business dooing man and has the Confidents of every person as an honest and worthey man.

Thommis Wilson from north Carolinah is a man of buisnes and is thorou[g]ly aquanted with these matters. these man will be better prepared to finnesh this matter at the most than aney strangers Can bee on a Counte of thare long trades and aquantens with all the matters. as far John C. Cannedey hee is 0000 from 0000 and 0000 [from] 0000 remains a nusens to sosiety and opposit to all good. thare is a Coln Joseph McMillen from the Tennessee sid hoo is one of the vallueng age[nts]

34 Richard Taylor's party of 1029 reached the new home with 944.

35 George Hicks conducted one of the last parties to leave Georgia. He arrived with 1039 out of the original number of 1118.

36 The writer was referring to Peter Hildebrand, whose detachment of 1776 had been reduced by more than three hundred when it reached the Indian Territory.

37 The Cherokee had many individual claims against the United States for improvements and property lost or destroyed during the period of removal.

that is [acq]uanted with all the locations of [the] Contery [hoo] would be asutibell asistent. I [am] Candet in my remarks and I think you will doo well to in forme your salves on this vary importent matter. your application to the Cerketterey of war in time may secure thare asistens and thay will Caroue oute the treaty to the satisfaction of the treetey partey. as to the matter of John Shooboot thare has as yeat nothing been don. Nathaneal Smith says he must bring him back and he has wrote to him to thate afacte.[38] this is all business in the dark to me. the spoilation bill of six hundred dollars for Aggey is not on the spoilation Book as Candy told the Clerks all tho Canedy says he has the bill that past the Committee. as I have no Commission on thate matter I cannot urge it tharefore the matter as to the freedman of John and the spoilation bill for Aggey[39] is in afare way both to bee lost. if Lissey and polley will otherise me as thare lawfull agent to act in the matter as to the rolles of John and the expanses to bee paid oute of this spoilation [money] I will lay down all other business and aten[d] [to] this matter. whate is don must be done soon. I will awaite your answer before I can proseed. you now whate kind of an instruments it must bee. delays may be dangerous in a matter of so grait importens.

my famely is in good halth. we have another daughter aboute 6 weeks old. I m[ight get others down] against on this matters. [wright me when con]venent. I wish to heere from all my frands in that Nation. I got a letter from Jack hockens and Nansey a goint latter the kindnes of whitch is grate fulley acnoledged. gave my respects to all your fathers famely and Majer Ridges [and] John Ridg. thare names Crowds on my mind whan I think of all. take my bast respects

W. M. Thompson

lat us larn your prospects of Crops [prom]ise of provesion P. C.

---

[38] This was probably General Nathaniel Smith who became emigrating agent in 1836.

[39] This refers to slaves lost during the removal.

◄§ Andrew Jackson to John A. Bell[40]
and Stand Watie

Hermitage
Octbr 5th 1839

GENTLEMEN:

My health will not allow me to visit Nashville today as I expected when you left me. You will find enclosed the papers left with me & a letter to the president of the United States in as strong language in your behalf & that of your friends as the facts and the outrageous & tyrananical conduct of John Ross & his self created council would authorize, & I trust the president will not hesitate to employ all his rightfull power to protect you and your party from the tyranny & murderous scemes of John Ross.

I hope peace and friendship among your whole people may be restored by peacefull & just means. Should this not be the happy result then, when oppression comes and murder ensues, resistance becomes a duty and let the arm of freemen lay the tyrants low & give justice & freedom to your people — but before this stand against oppression is taken, you must appeal & resort to all peacefull means to obtain justice & if the murderers of the two Ridges & Boudenot are not surrender[ed] & punished and security for the future gurranteed, then & not until then will the great and good Spirit smile upon your exertions by force to obtain justice by freeing yourselves & people from oppression.[41]

I remain respectfully yours

Messrs Bell & Waity   ANDREW JACKSON
   Cherokee delegation

---

[40] John Adair Bell, who was later to become a brother-in-law of Stand Watie upon the marriage of the latter to Sarah Caroline Bell, was one of the signers of the Treaty of New Echota.

[41] This letter is included through the courtesy of the owner of the original Professor T. L. Ballenger of Tahlequah, Oklahoma.

✌§ E. Moore and John Watie[42] to Stand Watie

Honey Creek Cherokee Nation
March 31 1840

DEAR SIR:

We take this time to write a few lines to you to inform you that the times are not much better than they were when you left us.[43] For not more than four days ago Jack Hawkins came very near being killed by a member of the Ross party & when the party that came to kill him found he had escaped, carried off a trunk containing nearly all that he was worth, for a few days before that they had taken his provisions and his horse so the man is almost destitute of clothing & food.

We hear that Ross & his party are not received by the Government as delegates.[44] We hope that sufficient evidence may be obtained against Ross of having been the sole cause of the murders that has been committed by his tools.

Some few of his party has been wise enough to know what he was & what his intentions were.

We have heard it said about among the people that Gunter[45] stated in his letter to some of his friends that if he did not effect none of his objects at Washington, that when he returned the times would be as bad as they were before. You and the rest know him, you know his character. He is an enemy to the Treaty party, to the U.S. & a man that has gone as far as he has in destroying his Nation can go a great deal farther

We feel very anxious to hear from you & the other friends at Washington City.

[42] John Alexander Watie was a younger brother of Stand Watie.

[43] The murder of Major and John Ridge and Elias Boudinot on June 22, 1839 had thrown the entire Cherokee Nation into a state of turmoil and near civil war. Stand Watie had gone to Washington to present his party's side of the controversy.

[44] The delegation to Washington headed by John Ross was not received by the Secretary of War, who indicated his belief that Ross might have been in part responsible for the murders of 1839.

[45] Probably Edward Gunter, member of the Ross delegation.

The Troops are all Lying still & doing nothing toward arresting the murderers.[46] But we hope that it will not be the last of it.

If the murderers have to be arrested we have no doubt but that the Cherokees themselves could make the quickest work of it.

You must write to us as soon as you receive this & tell us the news whether they are good or bad.

We remain your friend &c.
E. Moore
John Watie

~§ Stand Watie to T. Hartley Crawford

Globe Hotel
Washington City
15th April 1840

To T. Hartly Crawford
Commissioner of Indian Affairs

Sir

I am requested by Mr. John Fields one of the Cherokee Indians to call the attention of the Department to certain claims which he sets up against the government of the United States.

The first is a charge of $60. against the government for services rendered under the direction of General Nathaniel Smith emigrating Agent, for collecting a detachment of Cherokees at New Echota, in the spring of 1837 and transporting them to Ross Landing on the Tennessee River. Mr. Fields, not having the regulations on the subject, failed to have his accountes allowed by Genl. Smith, and Genl. S. having left the county he is unable to procure the certificate of Genl. Smith. Allow me to inquire if this proof for his services may be substituted and his claim allowed.

The next claim is for "Spoilations," in having some negroes taken from him one which he entirely lost. He informs me that the committee, organized under the Twelfth Article of the

---

[46] Federal troops from Fort Gibson sought to maintain order in the Cherokee Nation following these murders.

Treaty of the 29th December 1835, decided upon Six hundred Dollars in his favor which has never been paid.[47] Allow me to enquire if this demand may not be directed to be paid at the proper time & place.

He likewise asks me to call the attention of the department to two claims which were placed to his credit by the commissioners under the 9th Article of the Treaty above referred to — one against Kah-he-na-hee for $110.00 and one against To-morrow for $25.00.[48] These accounts he wishes transmitted to the proper Disbursing officer with directions where & when he may apply for their payment. Your attention to his request would much oblidge your humble & Obt. Sevt.

STAND WATIE

Memorandum:
> Letter to Comm[r]
>   Ind[n] Affairs
>   Subject a/c Jno Fields.

❧ S. B. N. Ridge[49] to Stand Watie

Osage Prairie

Mr. S. Watie   Oct 22, 1844

DEAR SIR,

I expected you here last week for several days, but Now I presume you must have returned from Flint some other way. I was desirous to have some conversation with you on business while you was here but had no good opportunity, so I hoped you would return this way, as partly promised to do. I wish to see you very much so that we may have a settlement of our

---

[47] Article Twelve of the Treaty of New Echota provided for the appointment of a committee of leading Cherokee to transact all business on the part of Indians, which might arise in connection with the treaty.

[48] Article Nine provided for the appointment of suitable agents to make fair valuation of the improvements of the Cherokee or other property from which they had been dispossessed in a lawless manner.

[49] Sarah Bird Northrup Ridge was the widow of John Ridge. After the murder of her husband she remained in the Cherokee country, probably to make certain that her children should share in the lands and other properties of the Cherokee Nation.

business & have a perfect understanding between us. I find I can not get any corn in this neighborhood, so of course I shall be greatly pressed in providing provision for my family consumption.

I sent Peter & Phil after corn & shall endeavor to keep them hauling until they bring all I can get from you. The wheat you have used of mine I shall be under the necessity of requiring the same quantity to be returned to me again in wheat if possible & if not in corn. If John can get some of Charles More & Mr Huss, or any others in that neighborhood who are in debt to the Store, I wish him to engage all they have to spare. I wish him to let me know soon, so that I may make other arrangements if I fail there. I must be actively engaged in procuring corn or we shall starve before another fall.

If Mr. Kell has not yet brought the mules & horses he promised to deliver to you on the first of this month I wish you or John to see that he brings them soon. I need the mules now.

Phil told me you had heard who had Brag who was stolen from me some two or three years since — if you know anything respecting her I wish you to let me hear by Peter & by what means I can get her in possession. I wish for my large table if you can spare it. I sent word by John that I should soon want it. I have so much work to do that it will be impossible for me to visit you soon. I wish you to come up soon & bring some or all your family with you — with kind regards to Sarah & Elizabeth,[50] I am   Affectionately yours,

S. B. N. Ridge

✑ Elinor Boudinot[51] to Elizabeth Webber

Washington, Dec. 9, 1845

Dear Aunt,

I was made happy indeed, I assure you, a few nights since by receiving a letter from *you*. I had been wishing all day I

---

[50] Stand Watie's wife and his married sister, Elizabeth Webber. He had married Sarah Caroline Bell in 1843.

[51] Elinor Boudinot, who must have been about eighteen at the time this

could receive a letter from some of my friends in Arkansas; it is the first one I believe I have received within four years. I had begun to think you had all forgotten me.

It is Tuesday evening 7 oclock, and I am sitting by a warm fire in our sitting room with uncle and aunt Brinsmade; cousin Abbey is out im[prov]ing the sleighing. I need not tell you how I s[hould] enjoy it could you be here, and we could see [each] other and I could talk with you. I [think] it would be much pleasanter and easier than writing, but it is great pleasure for me to sit down and con[verse] [wi]th friends away here in this way. I have written several letters to friends in Arkansas but have not received one answer, perhaps they have been miscarried. Charles and uncle John both owe me a letter why dont they answer them.[52] If they knew how happy it makes me to hear from them they would write often. I am looking for a letter from Rollin every mail now, in answer to one I wrote him a month or two since.[53] You said you heard by a letter Rollin received from William that Sarah was very sick, she was sick a great while, but we hope now she is at *rest* and perfectly happy, with Pa and ma in heaven; she was willing to die and seemed to be entirely resigned to the will of God whatever it might be, she looked forward to death and spoke of it with as much calmness as if she had been thinking of visiting her friends at a distance.[54] About 7 weeks before she died she started to come to Washington, thinking it would benefit her health and at best be the means of her entire recovery. Mr. Frank and William came down with her, she bore the journey remarkably well and she seemed to grow better for awhile, but after three or four weeks she began gradually to fail till a few days before s[he] died when s[he] was taken suddenly a great

---

letter was written, was the oldest child of Elias Boudinot. After the death of her father her step-mother, Delight Sargent Boudinot, removed with the children to New England. Elinor was at the time of this letter residing in Washington, Connecticut, with her uncle and aunt, General and Mrs. D. B. Brinsmade.

[52] Stand Watie's brothers, Charles and John Watie.

[53] John Rollin Ridge, son of John Ridge.

[54] This must have been Elinor's sister, Sarah Parkhill Boudinot.

deal worse, it [was] ... night, after that she could not eat any or [speak] but a very few words, till Friday night when [the] gentle spirit took its flight, to join Pa and [ma] and *all* the saints in singing the song of [redee]ming love for ever and ever, and if we would [live] again we must prepare to *die*. But I must not talk of her too much for it makes me very sad, all that we can say of her now is that *she is gone;* it is hard to real-ise, how soon the rest of us may be called or who first is un-known to any of us, the great thing is to prepare for death.

Lou wrote that uncle Stand talked of coming here this win-ter, I do hope he will, how glad I should be to see him and all the rest of you too; you and uncle John and Charles thought when we left you you would come and see us in two or three years, but it is 6 years now and none of you have we yet seen, there have been a great many changes there since that time. Grand Pa and aunt Mary have died, you are married and have two children, uncle Stand is married and has one son,[55] uncle John too married; since you all have families to take care of, I presume it will be needless for us to expect you to visit us. I dont see why Charles cant come. I wish I could see him, I pre-sume he has altered very much, and [I] [sh]ould not know him should I see him.

William is in Philadelphia engraving with a cousin [of] ours, we had a long letter from him last Saturday night, he wrote he likes his business much, and [seem]s to enjoy himself well, we think he is [doing w]ell.[56] Mary, Cornelius and Frank are with ma in [M]anchester Vermont.[57] I am as you know at [uncle] Brinsmade's. Cousin Mary is at school in [Massachus]etts, cousin William is in business there also. [Cou]sin Frank is married and lives just across the garden, he has his second wife, the first wife died about two years and a half ago and left two little children, Isabell the oldest three

---

55 This was Saladin, Stand Watie's oldest son.

56 This was Elinor's oldest brother, William Penn Boudinot.

57 These were Elinor's sister and two brothers who were with their step-mother, Delight Sargent Boudinot, referred to here as "ma."

years old, and Sila the youngest a fortnight; he has another child by his present wife.[58] She was sister to his first wife, they were Mr Samuel Learitt's daughters, perhaps you remember them Selence and Elizabeth.

Franks children are the three prettiest I most ever saw. Grand Pa and Grand Ma are still alive.[59] Grand Pa fails very fast, and we think he [will] not live through another cold season. Grand ma seems as well as ever, she does not appear to fail in the least, her judgment is as good as ever, all the uncles aunts and cousins are well as usual, uncle Swift you remember him? you see I have been quite particular telling you of my friends here. I thought you would probably remember [them] it would interest you to hear all about the[m]. We [have] grand sleighing now, and I have been out two evenings this week improving it, it is delightful riding these beautiful moonlight evenings. You spoke of having the tooth ach a great deal, I can sympethise with you for I have been troubled with it almost constantly the past summer and fall. I think it a kind of pain hard to bear, I loose all patience when my tooth achs.

My health was quite poor last summer and I lost 20 pounds, but I am now very well and have nearly gained as many pounds as I had lost.

You give my love to all my friends, ask them to all write to me. I intend to write to aunt Nancy before long. I hope you will answer this soon as possible. I have about filled my sheet, all send a great deal of love, and aunt Mary says tell her I would write if I was not so very [tired] this evening. It is half past nine now and I am [all] alone, uncle and aunt Brinsmade are gone to bed. I shall sit up till cousin [A]bbey gets back. I have no more room so good night, and write very *very* soon to your

Affect. niece
ELINOR

[58] Mary, William and Frank must have been the children of D. B. Brinsmade.

[59] Colonel and Mrs. Benjamin Gold.

24

⇜George Lowrey[60] to Stand Watie and Others

Park Hill, Feby. 10th 1846

Sirs

A sense of official duty impels me to address you at this time.

The continued combination of so many armed men at "Old Fort Wayne" is a subject of general and just complaint.[61] Under any circumstances such a movement is calculated to create no little apprehension, but it is more particularly so since the country has resumed its accustomed tranquility. I feel compelled, therefore, to remonstrate with you against the course pursued by you and your associates and to urge the propriety and necessity of its discontinuance. It is not only contrary to the laws of our Country, but is uncalled for and calculated to keep up a state of distrust and apprehension in the public mind.

I do therefore hope that you and your associates will take these things into consideration and break up without delay your present organization, return to your respective homes and countribute whatever may be in your power to the promotion of order and harmony among our people.

Very Respectfully,

George Lowrey
Actg. Pl. Chief
Cherokee Nation.

---

[60] George Lowrey, prominent Cherokee statesman, served for a number of years as assistant principal chief. He was acting principal chief at this time during the temporary absence of Chief Ross.

[61] The disturbed conditions in the Cherokee Nation eventually caused Stand Watie to assemble a body of armed men at Old Fort Wayne in the Cherokee Nation near the Arkansas border. Stand Watie justified this act by declaring that it was necessary to defend themselves against the aggressions of the Ross party.

⇜R. Armstrong and N. R. Harlan to Stand Watie

Colonel Stand Watie Beatey Prairie 20th March 1846
Washington

DEAR SIR

We had the pleasure of seeing Mr. Bradley this morning who informed us that you left Bentonville on Monday last for Washington City.[62]

Your Brother and Lt. Johnson with a Command of the 1st Regt of Dragoons as We are informed left Fort Wayne on Wednesday to attend the trial of Robert Squirrel, Muskrat Thompson & Wm Wicket taken on suspicion for the murder of old Samuel Martin. News has just reached us that Thompson is acquited and Bradley has gone down as a witness on behalf of Wicket and from what we can learn he will come clear of the charge made against him. What will be the result of Squirrel we are at this time at a loss to say, but his chance is bad.

A few days ago two Creek Indians killed One White Man and wounded another who were on their way with a Wagon laden with Goods for the suttler at the post of Fort Gibson, they plundered the Wagon and took the team. The murderers passed through Fort Gibson and have not been heard of since the deed was committed.

Information reached us on Tuesday last from Judge John T. Adair who called at the house of James A. Thompson on his way to Court and stated that Alexander Foreman, Whitepath, and a Cherokee name unknown to us but said to be a member of the National Council for Illinois District was all three killed at Foremans Landing mouth of Illinois.

The men under the command of your Brother are doing well, very few of them have visited this place since you took

---

[62] When Stand Watie had departed for Washington to present his side of the controversy to the officials of the United States government his brother John was left in command of the men at Old Fort Wayne.

departure. They have Picketed in the fort and are now secure from any attack that may be made against them — the information we now give you you may rely is correct and should you see cause to communicate the same to our delegation in Congress well and good. Will you purchase for R. Armstrong from Mr. Taylor, Bookseller in Washington the British & Naval Army & Navy Lists for Jany 1845 and get Gov. Tile to frank them for me as in them I will receive some information that will be to my advantage.

You may rely on hearing from us every week and we shall expect you to write us as often as convenient.

Your family are well, tender our best respects to J. A. Bell, J. M. Lynch, L. Bell and the balance of the Treaty Delegation — and except our best wishes for your health happiness & prosperity & Believe us to be your real & Sincere friends.

R. Armstrong[63]
N. R. Harlan

✑R. Armstrong & N. R. Harlan to Stand Watie

Colonel Stand Watie   Beatey Prairie
Washington   27th March 1846

Dear Sir

We done ourselves this pleasure on the 2oth Inst. We regret that we have to recall part of our last on the subject of the murder of Alex Foreman, White Path and another Indian said to be of the National Council from Illinois district. This information coming from Judge John T. Adair every one considered to be correct, but Starr Bean has just returned from Evansville and it is generally understood that nothing had befallen those persons and that the same was got up for a bad purpose. You

[63] Armstrong and Harlan were members of the Treaty Party and close friends of Stand Watie. Their two letters picture clearly the disturbed conditions in the Cherokee country at this time.

will Please contradict the first report at the Seat of Government as it will go to show to the Heads of the Departments the duplicity used by the Ross party. Since our last Wm Wiket & Robin Squirle were honorably acquitted by a jury of their country for the murder of S. Martin. Those individuals may thank Lt Johnson for going to court we believe that his appearance at court gave them to understand that his intentions were that the prisoners should have a fair and impartial trial; Your Brother John, & Elijah Moore deserve credit in attending to the management of the prisoners and it is generally believed in the Nation that with their skill these men were acquitted or at [least] Robin Squriles case was considered a very doubtful one.

The two creeks who killed & wounded the men who were in charge of the Sutlers Wagon have been surrendered by Col Logan to the Cherokee Agent and Col John Walker U.S. Depty Marshall left here yesterday to take them in custody and deliver them over for trial to the authorities at the Rock [Little Rock, Arkansas].

Your Brother held a military council with the officers under his command on Monday last when they came to the determination to abandon Fort Watie[64] until a certain day in next month in order that the men might have an opportunity of supplying themselves with clothing &c. — and if it was deemed expedient to reorganise the Company due notice would be given for them to reassemble. Various opinions are found for abandoning the fort, among your friends they consider that your Brother has pursued a prudent course as the men were geting induely destitute of clothing and no possible chance to be furnished with goods unless by Harris at 12½ cents pr dollar. this sacrifice they could not put up with, several of the men belonging to the company began to murmur at such gross imposition and determined to leave in order that they could furnish themselves on better terms. Would it not be adviseable for your Brother, Mr. Harlan and myself to have the Pay Roll and all the amounts made out and forwarded with the original

[64] It seems that the men designated their stockade at Old Fort Wayne as Fort Watie.

28

copy of the Resolutions passed the 25 & 26 Decr last in order that you could exhibit the same to the Honble Secty of War when we have no doubt he would place you in funds to pay off all claims due to the men and individual contractors.

Should you see Gov Yell[65] say to him that his friends held a meeting and nominated Col Walker for the Senate & W. J. Howard for the house of Representatives and those Gentlemen will be elected and will stand firm as friends of the Governor's. You will please write us as often as you can as we will not leave a stone unturned to act as Your sincere friend

Robt. Armstrong
N. R. Harlan

H. L. Smith to Stand Watie

Beaties Prairie, Arks.
4th April 1846

Dear Sir

I should have wrote to you sooner but having nothing to write I waited to hear all the News I could before I commenced. Giving you what is going on, in the first place your family is in good health and doing as well as they can. Elizabeth Weber is with Mrs. Watie. Major Bradley has 2 acres fenced & cleared ready for a Garden. The weather has been and is yet quite cool and vegetation very little out. The health of the country is Tolerably good. John Waties forces left the Post about Two Weeks since and agreed to meet again the 20th of this month or Earlier if necessary. Nothing new in the Nation has Taken place in this vicinity; but a great many things in other parts of the Nation. Robert Squirrell, Thompson Musrat & William Wicket have all been Tried and *acquited* for the Murder of Saml Martin. Wheeler Faught was hung on the 23rd of last month for decoying *Stand* out when he was killed.[66] Two others were to be tried this week for the same offense,

---

[65] Governor Archibald Yell of Arkansas.

[66] Stand Daugherty, a prominent member of the Ross party, was apparently killed to avenge the murder of James Starr which occurred in 1845.

have not heard how they came out, it is said Faught made a long confession dont know what it was. Several persons have been *killed* since you left. Dont Know Them, except old *"Corn Tasel"* who lived in Flint he was killed at home and a negro boy taken off. Some persons Stole Two Negro boys from Wes. Creek, and Two *Mules,* got away with them. M. Simon & others is charged with it. I heard today that five or six Negroes and several Good Horses had been taken from Flint. Two Horses from Washington Adair. Great excitement prevails about Evansville. the Citizens in Washington County in that vicinity has petitioned the Governor to have the Cherokees removed from the State who move as war.[67] —Lewis Rosses negroes had been collecting *amunition & Guns* and a few days since he discovered it and found several fine guns & considerable quantity of powder & lead. He Could not make them confess what they intended doing with these guns & ammunition. *Shores* who purchased negros from S. Bell, L. Lynch and some others in the Nation has lost four or five, got none of them yet thinks never will. The one he got off L. was shot by Morris, & when Shores sent for the negro Morris would not let him have the negro until he would pay $150.00 to J. M. Lynch.

Tell Lynch I saw his family a few days since they were all well and puting in Crop. All his friends well. *Saml. Bell,* Racheal and the children are well and doing well. J. C. Price I saw. J. Parkes family all well and getting along well; no disturbance. R. D. Blackstone family well and doing as well as they can. Mr. England moved to his place. G. Wards family well two days since and doing well, puting crop, nothing from them worth writing. Tell Rogers I heard from your family a few days since you & J. M. B., [left] all well.[68] your Brother Charles & Nelson has moved back to Grand River with their mother; Mr. Huss family well. I saw Charles a few days since, John Watie well yesterday. I have not heard from Brill Martins family for sometime. Esqr. Ward & Samul Tagert *fought*

---

[67] A number of Cherokee lived just outside the Cherokee Nation in Arkansas, and continued to take part in the conflict raging across the line.

[68] J. M. B. refers to James M. Bell, brother-in-law of Stand Watie.

the other *day, both drunk,* no harm done. Tom Davis and Ben May *fought* yesterday not hurt. *Dave Knight* Kiler cut Jesse Buffington bad with bowie knife. Tom Clark whiped Wallace Capwood, not bad, both drunk. S. H. Putner & wife gone to Fayetteville to stay; Brett B. Nicholson at home. Stan Adair came home from Evansville a few days since, says John West family well. — I have nothing of importance more to write. I think from what I can Gether there is a *company forming* on both sides of the line to *arrest* these men that is killing and stealing negroes and horses.

Say to Jo Lynch if he can Get any money for me I want him to forward me some by the first chance for I an in Great need — Jo. must write me without fail. A. B. Cuninghams health better. June Miller tolerable. Tell D. Bell not to *smell a wolf* while he remains in Washington. I shall expect to hear from all of you who I have named, and let me know what your prospects is for settling your Difficulties. My Respects to John A. Bell and William Holt, Preston Starrett. Joe Starrett is well. *Stand* remember me to all of those I have named. Write as soon as Convenient.

Your friend & C

H. L. Smith

Stand Watie & others

P.S. to J. M. Lynch: Moss Fields William Blyth with the other Heirs of Richard Fields has given me a power of attorney making me their agent.[69] To bring suit for their claim of land in Texas and I want you to make some Enquiry about the claim of Gov. Houston & Genl. Rusk. The Heirs is willing for you to go in with me and if the Claim is a good one we can Get an *Equal* part with the heirs for our services. Write me what information you get from G. Houston & Genl. Rusk immediately, perhaps I may go to attend to it before you get home un-

---

[69] Richard Fields was one of the leaders of the Cherokee who settled in East Texas about 1819. Twenty years later the Cherokee were driven out of Texas and the claim referred to was for the lands they had been forced to abandon.

less you promise me that you will go with me when you come home.

H. L. Smith[70]

৺§John Candy[71] to Stand Watie

Park Hill, Cherokee Nation
April 10th 1846

Dear Sir,

I promised to write to you every time anything of importance took place. After I came to the place I found out that it would hardly do to mail letters at this place, and I have had no opportunity of sending letters to another Post office.

You will doubtless recollect that Stand the murderer of James Starr was killed and scalped and that Faught was caught for decoying him and has since been hung. Since that time Old Cornsilk has been killed & robbed of a negro. Mrs. Pack has had some negro children kidnapped. Barrow Justin has been caught, tried and was hung yesterday. Ecoowee became States witnes against him. Bug John Brown & his company caught a horse thief and they have killed him. It is now rumored that he and his company (that is Brown) have cut up another man in Flint in his own house. Bug seems to be the Constitution, law, Court, & Executioner, Yet our Editor Can't see him in any other light than a *decent & clean* man, all facts to the contrary notwithstanding.[72] I forgot to mention that another man was killed at Ellis Hardin's. This man, it is said, was one of the company in Downing's gang on the mountains. He was scalped.

I think there is now to be no end to bloodshed, Since the Starr boys & the Ridges have commenced revenging the death of their relatives. A dozen or so are implicated and I am afraid that some of them will be more desperate than the first ones.

---

70 H. L. Smith was evidently one of Stand Watie's close friends.

71 John Walker Candy had married Stand Watie's sister, Mary Ann.

72 Candy was referring to William Porter Ross, nephew of Chief Ross. He was editor of the *Cherokee Advocate* which had succeeded the *Cherokee Phoenix* as the official newspaper of the Cherokee.

Murders in the country have been so frequent until the people care as little about hearing these things as they would hear of the death of a common dog. The question may be asked — Who first began the troubles in the Cherokee Nation? The answer is obvious. We know it well.

JNO. CANDY

We are very anxious to hear the news.

❧R. M. McWilliams[73] to Stand Watie

Honey Creek, C. Nation
April 13, 1846

DR FRIEND

Sir I will write you a few lines to let you know that we are all yet alive and well, though somewhat confused on account of the recent arrests and executions in the Nation. Faught the person accused of decoying Ta-Ka-To-Ka into the hands of the Starrs has been hung. Also a man by the name of Barrow, by the evidence of Ecoos his former friend and companion who was also under arrest, and turned States evidence, and has I understand implicated all of the leading men of the Treaty Party in all the recent murders of the dominent party in the Nation.

You will perhaps as this reaches you have heard that we on the 23 of last Inst separated to meet on the 20 of the month. But owing to the late excitement and the arrest of our men, Big David Nightkiller and Billy Cudjor By the Sheriff, we have this day met at Charles Moors and Resolved that we will remain together and have sent out a committee to select a place for our people to stay. The selection of which should be some where on this Creek though there would be a considerable split in our ranks some are in favor of going back to Ft. Wayne, and you have no Idea how much we need your council and Influence at this time. Though I hope the boys will all feel willing to stand up to the good cause in which we have enlisted

[73] R. M. McWilliams, a friend of Stand Watie, was, a few months later, a soldier in Taylor's army in Monterey, Mexico.

and remember yours and Mr. Huss's good advice when you left us. Mat Bags son is to be hung on friday next for Rape intent to Kill &c.

The weather has been uncommonly cold here this spring, we have not had 3 days of good weather at a time since you left; there has been a great deal of rain, the streams are all flush, we had a considerable fall of snow on Saturday last with sleet and rain, the peaches are all killed, People are very backward with their farms, no corn of any account planted yet.

Maysville is yet unconsumed though not I think because there is ten righteous in the place, the spring fights has not yet closed.[74] Tom Clark whipped Wallace Caywood a few days and was arrested took before Esqr Ward for trial, and whilst the Warrant was reading sliped out of the office and crossed the line and has not been in town since.

Tom Davis & Ben May had a fight neither was the best man though Ben said that if they had not parted them Tom would have whopped; and last though not least [of the fights] Old Tagart and Esqr Ward made a piched battle; went over on the Cherokee side to fight, and 'tis said that the first blow old Sam knocked the justice back into the State and gave him a right respectable whopping but the funniest part Ward was arrested, while old Sam [was] let alone, he having stood in the Nation and whipped the Esqr in the State.

Our committee to select a plan for our Fort has returned and have purchased Hillard Roger's house &c and we will commence work tomorrow.[75]

Old Mrs. Ratliff is no more she died on last Friday.

Your family are all well I was their a few days since. Old Maj. Bradley is their making a fine Garden &c. Your friends are generally well and wish you well, and all the Boys are coming to me while I write, to say, send my love to my friend

[74] Maysville, Arkansas. Conditions among the whites in this western frontier region were almost as rough and lawless as in the Cherokee country.
[75] Shortly after the abandonment of Fort Wayne, the Treaty Party made plans to construct a new stockade in order to be prepared for any emergency.

Stand & Mr. Huss and all the other Delegation. Remember me to Mr. H. and all of our friends in Washington and dont forget to write to me on the receipt of this.

pleas excuse my bad penmanship and blocking. I write sitting on a log writing on a board.

I remain your true and affectionate friend

R. M. McWILLIAMS

Stand Watie Esqr

ᎤᎦ John Rollin Ridge[76] to Stand Watie

Fayetteville, Ark. April 14th, 1846

DEAR COUSIN STAND:

A number of weeks have passed since you left for Washington, and as I know from the papers that you have arrived at that city, I wish to write to you and request all the information you have on hands with regard to Cherokee interests.

No very important transactions have happened since your departure, except the killing of five or six Indians of the Ross party, including Old Ta-ka-to-ka, by Tom Starr and his confederates. Caleb Duncan was way-laid, a short time ago, by several of the Wards who snapped a pistol three times at them; when about to be surrounded, he wheeled his horse and escaped by flight.

I have been in town here ever since you left pursuing the study of Law and will remain for a considerable while, so when you write, as I hope you will do immediately, please direct to this place. One thing in particular I wish to know, and that is, when (if ever) John Ross designs to return, and by what rout

[76] John Rollin Ridge, son of John Ridge was born in 1827 in the Old Cherokee Nation in Georgia. When his father was murdered, his grief stricken mother removed the children to Fayetteville, Arkansas. Young Ridge was educated there and at Great Barrington school in New England. Because of ill health he was obliged to give up his schooling in the North and return to his home in Arkansas. This letter indicates that he had some thought of attempting to kill John Ross as the latter returned from Washington to the Cherokee Nation.

he will probably come. A great degree of interest is manifested here concerning him and I desire to be acquainted with his movements on our particular account, which, when summed up and determined, will satisfy me. I hope that claim of ours is in a fair way to be settled — I would like to have you inform me how that stands.

My love affairs in Osage Prairie are drawing to a close — I am borne down by superior parental authority and must look else where for the delights of human existence, in the line of youthful affection. The circumstances, however, has not torn my heart nor rent it to shivers; neither am I about to destroy my life or throw myself away — nothing of that sort, for I am as happy as a sky-lark, "with the dew on his wings." I look forward to the future with hope and pride. I am boarding now at Old Oustots, where there is living a prettily shaped girl, of about 16 or 17 years, who is very friendly and gives me a quantity of enjoyment in her company, whenever I get tired of dusty pages and legal technicalities. Ought not I to be satisfied to some extent? Who should complain simply because one maiden is debarred from his presence and society, when there are thousands of other soft breasts, gentle eyes, and slender waists in the world? I would like to be in Washington at this time to see some of the beauties who enchant the vision, as they glide by or exhibit their charms on sofas and couches! I saw a week ago the speech of John C. Calhoun on the Oregon question, and like his views in regard to the subject and the course to be pursued by the Senate better than those of any other member in that body. I suppose you heard him deliver that speech. It was not equal to the efforts of his younger days, which I have read, in point of burning eloquence, but it was a sensible and just view of all the points involved in the Oregon controversy.

I have nothing more of any interest to communicate & will therefore make my Finis.

Your affect, Cousin

JOHN R. RIDGE

Fayetteville
April 17th

⋗ Sarah C. Watie[77] to James M. Bell

April 16 1846
Aks Benton county

MY DEAR BROTHER

I have no doubt but you would like to have a letter from you sister. I have nothing worth much to say. the police have taken David Knightkiller and run Eli Raper off and several others. I have not heard what they have done with david and them but there is no doubt but what they will either whip or hang him. Several have run over the line for reffuge. Walter Ridge has just come in from honey creek. he says John Watie has collected his men to gether again and is now building a fort at hiliard Rogers place. I wonder what they will do next. I expect they all be scalped before long. I have not heard of the Starr boys in some time but I rather think that Joseph Raper has gone to flint to joine them but this is only a thought of my owne. that boy that they whipped for steeling is dead. I have not seen the last Cherokee advocate but I have heard people say that it implicated Joseph Lynch and Clem Thompson in the burning of Megs house but you know that wont do. they hung Wheeler Faught for having a hand in killing Stand Dority. they say he made a long confession but I dont know what it was Rachel has gone on to grand river. I did not know she was going down untill she was gone. you must write to me soon. I am so anctious to hear from you all but I do not expect you cast one thought on me since you left. you must not drink any while you are gone. I want you to write to me soon. I am allmost crazy to hear from you all, some times I sit down and cry my eyes out but it all dont do any good but it dont make business any faster. Major is well and tryes hard to stand alone he will walk soon.[78] I would wright more but the baby is cry-

---

[77] Mrs. Sarah C. (Bell) Watie, wife of Stand Watie and a sister of James M. Bell, was born on March 11, 1820 in the Old Cherokee Nation east of the Mississippi.

[78] Saladin Watie was probably called "Major" in honor of his great uncle, Major Ridge.

ing and I must stop. I have to send this right of [to] the post office or else I would fill it.

Tell Sarah Paschal[79] that her mother has just sent for E to come down; [and] write a letter for her. tell my brothers that I think of them often and I wish them all the success in the world.

I have not heard from flint in a great while

from your affectionate sister

SARAH

Major Bradley says the people are running to hell and damnation I dont know what that is I have made a few mistakes but Walter Ridge[80] has talked all the time you must write and tell me if the ticets will be good[81] write soon.

⋐§John Rollin Ridge to Stand Watie

Fayettville Arks., April 17th, 1846.

DEAR COUSIN STAND:

I wrote you only a few days ago, and told you all that I desired to say, except of an article which I wish extremely that you would get for me, that is a Bowie knife. I would like one not very large, nor very small, but rather small than large. You would oblige me very much indeed by doing so. I would ask Paschal[82] but I know he would not be willing to do me that much favor. I heard from your family a short time since and they were all well. I saw a man this morning from Boonsboro who had seen Tom Starr and Sam'l McDaniels they were in fine health and spirits. Those fellows, especially Tom Starr, are talked of frequently and with wonderment about here. He is

79 Probably Sarah Paschal Wheeler, niece of Stand Watie.

80 Walter Ridge was Major Ridge's youngest son.

81 Cherokee finances were at this time in a very deplorable condition. The tickets referred to were coupons issued by merchants or other prominent business men.

82 Probably George Washington Paschal, husband of Sarah, youngest daughter of Major Ridge.

considered a second Rinaldo Rinaldina.[83] Robberies, House-trimmings, and all sorts of romantic deeds are attributed to this fellow, and the white people in town and around say they had rather meet the devil himself than Tom Starr!

I must reiterate my request for you to write soon and often

Your sincere friend and Cousin

JOHN R. RIDGE

✑S. Rindly[84] to Stand Watie

Maysvill Apl 30, 1846

MY DEAR SIR

Since my last the Company formerly under you have assembled at their new location at Hilliard Rogers where they have built a good stockade and are well supplied with bacon meal &c but as croping time is now at hand many will unquestionably prefer farming to soldering. I said to your Brother John while at the fort and as he was going to the agency to reside not to think of keeping the men together as there was no one besides him self capable of commanding or governing them. this I think to be really true but as there is many restless spirits amongs them they have assembled to the number of about twenty and will probably keep embodied untill they here from you. Your brother is at the agency, McWilliams in the Creek nation, Jn. Duncan with Mary & Binge at home and Mankiller in command. this constitus about the arrangements. Now, with them I will suggest to you the propriety of writing to them to disband and for those who are in danger of being apprehended to locate themselves on this side of the line this course will at once I think lead to good results, as there is little or no danger from the Ross party at present. you alone was the object of there Vengeance but on this subject you are the judge.

[83] Rinaldo Rinaldini, the Border Captain, was the hero of a romance of the same name published in 1797 by Christian August Vulpius, German novelist and dramatist who was a brother-in-law of Goethe.

[84] S. Rindley, a friend of Stand Watie, was apparently one of the band of self-exiled Cherokee residing across the line in Arkansas.

the health of your family as usual continues good as well as your friends generally. I learned yesterday that the police had desperately wounded Ellis Starr, James Starr and Buck Starr who now lay at Cane Hill under the Care of medical assistance and report says no hopes are intertained of their recovery.[85] at the same time *Tom* Starr in company of Mat Grasing was on the rode from Van Buren and was fired on by some of the same party, and unfortunately killed Jacob a fine negro [of] Tygeres father in law who was in company with them. this will cause a stir among the whites, as all these transactions occured in Arkansas and in Washington County. the Marshal will I think have plenty of business along the line. Ward of maysvill rec'd a letter from Bryant dated the 1st of the present month but not nothing was said of your or Mr. Hunts arival at Washington whitch creates some little anxiety about your health and would it not be well to write to some of your numerous friends and quiet their apprehensions on this score. should there be a fair prospect of a Treaty the fencing and improving your Honey Creek place will be an object to you whitch I will attend to for you if advised so to do. on this and all other subjects let me know. I shall take your filly the Sorrel to a Jack and the Black to Arguyle who now stands at Cane Hill. I have no requests to make except for y[ou to] remember in garden seeds, but Elizabeth requests me to say to you she shall expect the salt seller and from her great anxiety for this article of house keeping I am inclined to think she intends soon to marry, be this as it may her request is but small in a pecuniary point of view. your little son now stands alone & will soon walk. he if he could talk would join with your family and friends in wishing you health and all success in your undertaking.[86]

Truly Your Friend

S. Rindly

[85] These members of the Starr family had been wounded by the Cherokee police who chased them into Arkansas, where they were given protection by General Matthew Arbuckle.

[86] Stand Watie was still in Washington at the time this letter was written.

❧ John A. Watie to Stand Watie

(*Sunday*)   Honey Creek May 10th, 1846.

DEAR STAND,

I received your letter yesterday from Cumberland. I was happy to learn that you & frends were well. I also received a letter from G. W. Adair dated 6th ult. And saw one from our friend Mr Huss to his family dated 7th April Stating the death of E. Starr which I was sorry to hear. But at the same time I felt enlivened from hearing of the flattering prospects which all our friends writes us from Washington.

Our party in this part of the Nation are all listening with anxious hearts & open Ears to hear from Washington. May the Lord be with our delegates that they may succeed in getting us out of our troubles soon.

I wrote to you on the 5th inst. from Maysville giving you the particulars of the killing & wounding in the neighborhood of Greenville. I have not heard any news from that Quarter since.

An unprovoked murder was committed day before yesterday on Jack Elliot at his residence on Grand river. Arch and Jack came up yesterday Evening bringing the news &c.

They stated that they & their father were working in the field untill neare about sun set; when they left to go to the house they were fired on by some [one] conseled in the Bushes, one of the shots hitting the old man which caused his death almost instantly, another shot came very near hitting Arch which went through his horses head; the boys discovered three men making their way off. They were three Cherokees,— foot men — they were tracked to Saline Creek some 8 or 9 miles from where Elliot lived.

Mr. Elliot was with us several days in our fort. When he left he said he would return in one week he & his boys.

I have no doubt in my mind that his being with us & opposed to John Ross measures was the cause of his death for he was a man who spoke his thoughts tolerable loud in any Crowd.

41

I understood Arch & Jack to say that their sister Mrs. Sprinston said that Sprinston told her that he intended to have all the men who had been in the fort killed off.

You know Mrs. Sprinston was daughter of Jack Elliot.

We are still keeping up a small company of about thirty men, Jackson Mankiller commanding. Jno Duncan attending to his fathers Business. Most of the boys are trying to raise crops. Most of the Flint boys gone back to flint. R. McWilliams has left the diggins in a sort of a Loap.[87]

You will please attend to that claim of Richard Scott. You will find it in the promiscuious valuation to Swimmers heirs then carried to the big Book and transferred from there to the credit of Richard Scott. But it has been omitted by the clerks to register the same on the pay roll.

Brother Charles is living with me and sends his best respects to you so does Eliza send hers. Our friends in this quarter are all well. the men send their best respects to you & Mr. Huss.

Give my best respects to Mr. Huss & my friend Jim Price & tell them that their Families are well.

From your Brother
JOHN A WATIE

P.S. You must endever to make some arangements to get some clothing for our Boys in the Ft. if possible.[88]   J. A. W.

ᦆ Robert Armstrong to Stand Watie

Colonel Stand Watie   Maysville 29th May 1846
Washington D.C.

MY DEAR FRIEND

I addressed you with others on the 22nd Inst to which I beg leave to refer you. Your very kind letter of the 18th April came safe to hand for which I return you my most hearty and sin-

---

[87] McWilliams left the Cherokee Nation to enlist in the Army for the war against Mexico. He evidently considered his life in Taylor's army safer than in the Cherokee Nation at this time.

[88] Something of the unrest and outlawry in the Cherokee Nation is revealed in this letter and, in some respects, justification is seen for the establishment of the fort.

cere thanks, and as you stated it was not confidential I took pleasure in handing it to your particular friends for perusal. I am happy to see the good feelings exhibited by the President in our favor as well as those evinced on the subject by the Commissioner of Indian affairs are of the most flatering and I am in hopes that both Houses of the National Council will report favorable.[89] I notice that it is your opinion that the members of both committees are in favor of a Division of the lands and funds. Something must be done for the good of our people and that soon. The Ross party are out and adoing. They state that their intentions are to make a sacrifice of every respectable citizen belonging to the Old Settlers & Treaty Party they may fall in with and their Police Parties are all the time on the alert and doing mischief of considerable magnitude — ever since they had their Secret Council on Spring Creek. it is reported about 500 persons were in attendance. Since the meeting adjourned there has been nothing but confusion and threats thrown out by the party. Information had been rumored that the fort on Honey Creek was to be taken by Storm on Saturday eve last. Your Brother on receiving the news lost no time in making it known to the officers in command at Fort Wayne, his reply was that their had been so many flying reports and until such time as he was satisfied that an attack would be made could not leave but the moment he was in possession of correct information he would be in readiness and aid those who might be attacked. I know for a certainty that the men abandoned the fort on Sunday moving together with a number of respectable citizens with their wifes and children from Grand River & this neighborhood who have been compelled to seek protection in the state. Dear Stand you can form no idea of the situation of our distressed and unhappy people. we are it is true in the mi-

[89] Armstrong is referring to a report submitted to the President by the Commissioner of Indian Affairs on March 13, 1846 in which he justified the grievances of the Treaty and Old Settler Party and recommended a division of the Cherokee Nation. President Polk, in a special message to Congress on April 13, 1846, urged the division of the tribe or a provision for a new home for one group (See *Messages and Papers of the Presidents,* IV [1846-1849], 429-31; cf. Polk's annual message of Dec. 2, 1845, *ibid.,* IV, 411-12).

43

nority and at this crisis can only act on the defensive. A memorial was got up yesterday afternoon by your Brother to General Arbuckle communicating the situation in which our people were placed soliciting Rations, &c signed by some of the most prominent men in the Nation and our friend David Bell left last Eve as bearer of the same, upwards of 150 men women and children are under blankets near the Jas Scotts Mill in the State of Missouri and there will remain until further ordered. They are destitute of provisions and unless relieved by Genl Arbuckle God knows what will become of them.[90] Your Brother begs me to say that your letters of the 23rd Apl & 1st of May were duly received as well as the documents [for] which he begs you to except his thanks. Our mutual friend James Price has this moment informed me that the Ross police are a-way-laying this highway from Honey Creek to Prices House and the police are seen every night recruiting in the state of Missouri in search of those belonging to our party. Saml. W. David was taken prisoner by a command of the States Dragoons at the House of Mr. Dinnes and taken to Fort Wayne. The officer here is preparing to send him to Capt Been to be delivered over to the Civil authorities of Washington County. Poor Saml it was his intention to have left the next morning with Mr. Price to surrender himself and stand trial but unfortunately for him they were too fast. His worthy old father was to see him at the Fort. Poor old Gentleman he says that it is bringing his Gray hairs to the Grave, his troubles of late being so numerous. Mr Price requests me to say that he will write you and Mr. Lynch by next mail and expects to hear from you often. he got home safe and found all well. I will write you from time to time. do not forget your friends in sending papers and letters as it is a pleasure to them to receive from you any information as well. All place our sole confidence in your integrity. May the blessing of God prosper and protect you in all your undertakings is the wish of your Sincere and devoted friend

Ro. Armstrong

90 General Matthew Arbuckle was in command of the United States troops stationed at Fort Gibson.

44

Mr. Price reports favorable of you & J. M. Lynch. As one of us your friend Mr. Miller sends his respects to you & Joe M. Lynch. We concur with Col Armstrong in what he has stated as we know the same to be correct.

JOHN A. WATIE
J. C. PRICE
J. R. MILLER
G. W. BELL
A. H. HUDSON

⇜ Sarah C. (Bell) Watie to Stand Watie

Benton C N   July 19 1846

MY DEAR HUSBAND

I received you kind letter of the 21 of June I was much disappointed when looked in it and found you would not be home soon. I have been looking for you some time, as you did not write to any of your friends I thought you would soon be home. I am so tired living this way. I don't believe I could live one year longer if I knew that we could not get settled, it has wore my spirits out just the thoughts of not haveing a good home. I would be very well satisfied if I was a way of in some other country or in a smaller cabin of my owne, one can't feel free at other peoples place at least that is my feelings about it. Saladin had a sever spell of sickness the fourth of July but he has got quite well now. I was fearful at first that it would prove fatal but god in his mercy has spared him to us a little longer, all the rest of the children are well. I wont trouble your mind with telling our wants to you. I have been trying very hard to get all of my work done before you get home so that I might have time to be with you a great deal when you get home. I am perfectly sick of the world. I really wish I was in the last corner of it if there is any corner to it. I have not heard a word from my fathers house since you left. I think C. among the rest had forgotten me but why should I grieve I haven't always to live, a few more days or years at least will tell that I am no mor and then I will not kneed the consolation of friends

45

in any of my troubles. many times have I retired to myself and wept in the bitterness of my heart over my troubles but it does not lessen them any. I don't only think that my best earthly friends have left me to self but I fear God himself has said let her alone she is joined to her idol. This has troubled me much with all the rest. in all of my troubles I have not showed the spirit I ought. We are both to blame for our negligence to God. Ther is no news at present worth relating to you. they had Elick Cockrel up for steeling horses. they sent him to little rock. they bound him hand and foot tight enough. there will be several more arrested soon. they have been steeling senica horses and I suppose there is a gang of them up in Missourie as well as in this country.

Sam Harlin and several others were engaged in it. I don't believe John is Clever at all he has not been to see us since you left nor has he acted at all like a friend. I do not know what I would have done had not Sam been in that great place. M— he is a brother worth having I dont know how to live with out him. Louis Rodger will soon make afortune of the tickets they sell awful high besides shaveing 33 and a third. I wish I had some thing to write that would interest you. Saladin will talk when you get here. tell Sally her mother is well. Now my ink is so bad that can't write at all with it. tell Mr Huss his people are well. I had like to forgotten to tell you they have Charles Reese in chaines about burning Harnages house him and John Melton [and] old Mac Daniels are both confined hard and fast. I have not heard what they have done with them. there trial had not come on the last we heard. it now time to get supper and I must quit. I hope we will soon be allowed the priviledge of [seeing] you. from your affectionate wife. S C B Watie

⤚§Mary H. Boudinot[91] to Stand Watie

Manchester July 31 1846

My Dear Uncle

Ever since we heard you were at Washington I have several times determined to write you but, hoping that we should soon see you here, I have as many times delayed. When William went I should have written, but for want of time.

We see from the papers and from other sources occasionally that the Cherokee question is being agitated with some degree of earnestness at Washington. It looks like it will receive all the attention. It seems something will be done to relieve the miseries of our poor oppressed party. Has not precious blood enough been shed to arouse [the] Government now to do justice to their *faithful friends.* I am sure *they* deserve it. I am sure *we* as a family need it, and many others with us.

We hear that the President in his Message to Congress relative to Cherokee difficulties recommends a division of the people, and it seems to be the prevailing opinion that this is necessary — in short the only thing that can procure peace or at least prevent further violence. If this should be done and we should receive even a portion of our just claim from the Government wherewith to complete our education, I intend to return to my country whenever it is best — for that is where I most wish to live but if not I must be still longer an exile from home.

Eleanor visited us with William. I have not seen her before for nearly three years. I think you would hardly know her. She is about as tall as our mother was, and she is very thin, her health has been quite poor for two or three years. I think she is predisposed to consumption. Ma and the boys are as well as usual.[92] Cornelius is working on a farm a few miles from here this vacation, and Ma, Frank, and I compose our little household. Cannot you come and see us this summer. I need not tell you how happy we shall be to see you. Do come, if physically possible. Give my love to Mr. and Mrs. Paschal and Uncle Wheeler[93] and any other friends that we may have there.

The rest of the family would send love if they were at home,

[91] Mary Harriett Boudinot, younger sister of Elinor Boudinot whose letter to Elizabeth Webber appears earlier in this chapter, was living with her stepmother and other members of her family in Vermont.

[92] "Our Mother" was Harriet Gold Boudinot; and "Ma" was the writer's stepmother, Delight Sargent Boudinot.

[93] "Uncle Wheeler" was the husband of Stand Watie's oldest sister, Nancy.

but they are all gone and I am alone. If you do not come soon please write and gratify us all and particularly

Your aff. niece
MARY H. BOUDINOT

J. B. Lynch[94] to Stand Watie

Maysville Benton Co.
Augt. 1, 1846

DEAR SIR,

Notwithstanding I have not heard from you agreeable to your promise, I know you have many correspondents who have greater claims on you than myself & can excuse you as many of our old friends have favored me with a persual of your letters & I am kept informed, as business progresses. I have a leisure half hour just previous to the closing of the mail & concluded to write you a few lines. As regards the news in this place I can furnish you none of interest, save the arrest of *"Jo Raper"* by a party of Cherokees headed by Cho-a-chuck, our sheriff he was taken two or three days since up on *"Cow Skin."*

Alex Cockrall has been arrested & sent to Fort Smith & yesterday the sheriff of Delaware left with 100 men to go up the line from this neighborhood supposed in pursuit of *Tom Starr, Rider* & *Mat Grasing.* The people on both sides of the line are very much excited. There are many *"Cloven feet"* sticking out —confessions upon confession are made and being made & many *secrets are out.* To day is the day for State Elections, and every body gone to vote. *"Yell"* is the popular man for next Senator in this county. We have a company of mounted malitia on the frontier composed of men belonging to this place & neighborhood & a company of malitia are expected every day to occupy Ft. Wayne in place of Dragoons. Louis Rogers is doing a very large business in *"Watie Tickets";* he has, so his clerk told me to day, taken about $6,000 & his most desirable goods yet behind & not open. He is building a large store House in the Senaca nation at Senaca Mills. If the Cherokee business

---

[94] J. B. Lynch, prominent Cherokee, was related to Stand Watie by marriage.

48

is settled & your Tickets are paid I believe it would be well for you to purchase a good stock of Goods in Phila or New York to sell in this country. You could make money & I know your credit is good. I am now doing business for Mr. Blackstone whose goods have arrived here safe & doing well. I feel as if a large business and large stock of goods done in the right way would do a *cash* business here & now is the time to strike & do it I advise you if the arrangements are made to suit you with the Government. I saw Mrs. Watie Saturday she was here buying some articles. Herself and family are well & to day she sent a letter to mail for you. In this country I find a great change in politics. You know the propensity of the *crowd* & *mass* to be with the majority — that great changes are daily taking place — nay very many. There is up in Missouri just over the line 360 people who are fed, called reffugees, many of whom are still afraid to go home & some who will shortly return. As I understand Gen Arbuckle says he cannot feed any after Green corn comes in. It is confidently expected, by the people generally, that there will be a compromise of difficulties and no division, but may be a separation. The whole Cherokee people are impatient to hear their final destiny and prospects & much dissatisfaction is manifested at the delay, the common people not knowing the cause. I Hope my dear Sir you and our friends will be able to accomplish all your visions & wishes. Danl. McCoy is still pursued by the police. He was followed to Ft. Gibson but not taken, he is now clerking for the Sutler at that place, as salesman & interpreter. This little town remains in *statu quo* no new Brick Buildings or stone Houses. The people generally are in good health & not much sickness generally. I wish you would send me some interesting documents & some late papers, send me this report of the commissioner of Patents. — for 1846, as I have 44 & 45 — please give my respects to Lynch Adair, Tom Taylor and all friends and accept assurances of Esteem from your friend,

J. B. Lynch

Genl. Mays has just stopped in from Flint & says no news from his neighborhood or Evansville.

✎§ Charles Watie,[95] Sarah C. Watie and Elizabeth Webber to Stand Watie

Benton County Ark.

DEAR STAND.
August 27th, 1846

Washington City

It is the desire of Sarah that I should write to you and indeed, when I conclude that this is the first time I have undertaken to address you since you have been at Washington, I am led to condemn myself for not writing to you before.

I arrived at Baties Prairie the evening before you left. I thought I would arrive in time to see you but could not. I immediately went to the Fort with the intention of joining your company; but John having no person to stay at his place & take charge of things, I concluded to do so.

Since the time you left I have been until lately living with him. All is at present quiet in the nation; but no one can tell how long it will remain so. We have not heard exactly the truth of the issue of our contest; but I suppose we will hear shortly.

I did hear that the Ross & Treaty partys had come to an agreement — had consented to forget all party difficulties & bury in oblivion all hatred and jellousies. In a word, to become "good friends" & come under the new government, as before. We have long borne the oppression of John Ross & his faction — our Delegation went to Washington & then at the tribunal of the United States has asked for that justice, which was denied their people at home, and what is the result? If we are to come under the laws of Ross & be placed in the same situation in which we have been placed, I cannot see that our case is altered for the better.

As for you I know you are as desirous to promote the happiness of your country as any person; & I have no doubt but that you did your utmost. The question, however, having been left to the decision of three Commissioners, you were obliged

[95] Charles Edwin Watie was the youngest brother of Stand Watie.

to abide by their decision. But as I said before we shall be able to hear more about the matter. I was at Osage Prairie not long ago & left Mrs. Ridge & her family well.[96] Mr. Candy's youngest child died not long since. He [Mr. Candy] is now working at Park Hill. No more news of any importance. I would write more but leave enough of this sheet for Sarah (& perhaps for Elizabeth), for I cannot tell how much a woman can write when she has been absent from her husband for some time & under takes to address him on paper. I received a letter from William a few days ago but he did not say anything about your affairs at Washington.

Excuse my bad writing and have written in haste.

Your affectionate brother,

CHARLES E. WATIE

MY *dear* STAND

it seames as if you had forgotten to write home but I will not complain of your silence perhaps it is my fault and not yours. Charlotte[97] has been to see me. she staid one week with us. she was sick part of the time. Jarratt came with her.[98] he had come to see some pretty girl but *he* got mistaken at how sick he was he left *sooner.* and Rollin[99] he come down and staid one day and a half and he *got* in the same row with Capt. he went home sick too poor fellow. I feel for them dont you. I should think you did. If I do not hear something from you by to morrows mail I shall go to flint and stay till you come home that is if you are not coming home soon. I am so tired of staying here by myself on this rocky hill. you need not trouble you mind about us, we will do very well a while longer. as to provisions we have meat yet. Sam is very good to me he gets anything we want. it is a little difficult to get bread. one thing I do not know how you will come out so I dont know how to

[96] The writer is referring to the widow of John Ridge.

[97] Charlotte Bell, sister of Mrs. Sarah C. Watie. Charlotte was married to Doctor W. J. Deupree, the father of Mr. W. E. Deupree of Vinita, Oklahoma, who has been of considerable assistance to the editors in determining the intricate family relationships.

[98] Jarrett Bell, brother of Mrs. Sarah C. Watie.

[99] John Rollin Ridge.

act. I dont want to go in debt more than I can help for bread or meat but Samuel will see that we do not suffer for any thing. I find he is the same old seven and six with me he has always been my best friend and he certainly has been very good since you left. Saladin is well and grows fast he cannot talk yet but he tries hard to learn he will soon begin to talk now. Charles dreams of you every night.

yours affectionately
SARAH WATIE

MY DEAR BROTHER,

I received your kind letter few days ago I was very happy to hear from you. We all want to see you bad enough. The children ask about you often and says why dont uncle Stand come home, he stays so long. Charles says if you dont come home he will go to Washington, he dreams every night that you whiped John Ross. I hope you will soon come home. We are all trying to get fat as we can, before our provisions gives out, but I do not think Sarah can live long on the fat of her — for she has no fat about her, she is as poor as a snake.

Charles sends his love to you and says he will kiss you. give my love to Mr. Huss.

Your sister
ELIZABETH

I told Charles he was not like Jarratt and Rollin that [he] did not know how to love he raised his hand above his head and brought it down with a *mity* force and said *I do know what it is to love*. [Charles was her little son.]

⚜R. M. McWilliams[100] to John A. Watie

Monerey Mexico October 12th 1846

MY DEAR FRIEND

I write you a line on this sheet accompanying my discharge from the service for which I was enlisted, my motive in so do-

---

[100] This letter has nothing to do with affairs and conditions in the Cherokee Nation but is included because of its interest as a Mexican War document and to show the wide-spread activities and interests of the Cherokee.

ing is I have again joined for twelve months longer and have no way to preserve it. I wish you to take good care of it. I would not have it destroyed for any amount for it tells that I am a soldier, and in saying so the fact has been proven in Eight different Battles all of which were hotly contested though we had the better of the whole Eight though not without the loss of many brave men, though the Regiment to which I belonged lost but few. The Great City of Montrey (and a great city it is) is ours. it is one of the richest cities that I ever have seen, the most wealth and pomp and silver and gold and fine things and fine fruits and &c; and this is a fine country there [is], the best water here that I ever have seen in the Southern [states], and if the American people were in the possession of it and cultivated it it would be the best on the face of the earth. But I think that it will not be long before it will be cultivated by the citizens of the United States.

I think that it is uncertain about peace being made as is surmised by a great many; there is a Truce until the 25th of November and by that time it will be known what will be the aim. there is an army of Twenty five Thousand strong and if there is not peace we will have more hard fighting and many men lost. I will let you hear from me and the seat of war. I have escaped so many tight places that it all most frightens me to think about it, the cannon balls & grape shots flew in showers about me an my hat was knocked off of my head by a cannon ball and the men fell in heaps all around and killed horses from under riders. Oh! it is indiscrible. I hope to see you and tell you all about it.

I am well and hearty and doing well though somewhat home sick I think often of you all that I left behind but I live in hope of seeing you again. I have lots of good friends out here and lots of things which drive dull cares aways.

Preserve my discharge until I return, you can read it to my friends Mrs. Fields and all my dear friends.

Write to me at all times convenient. my respects to all.

This letter will be mailed at New Orleans. I send it by a

friend. you direct to Head Quarters Army of occupation Mon-
itery Mexico. yours &c.

Very Respect
R. McWILLIAMS

✍§ D. B. Brinsmade[101] to Stand Watie

Washington Ct.
Oct. 15th 1846

DEAR SIR

With much pleasure I rcd. yours of the 23d of Sept. from
Washington City and was right glad to hear that you had a
pleasant journey and found all things going on as usual at a
snails pace. I suppose by this time you are welcomed to your
own home and are recounting to your family and friends all
the incidents that occurred during your absence. How good it
will seem to go back to your Nation with the prospect of Peace
among yourselves. It must be peculiarly so to you who have
been hunted and harrased for seven years, to now have an opportunity "to sit under your own vine and your own fig tree
and none to molest or make *afraid*." The last word I suppose,
not exactly applicable to yourself, I added it to complete the
quotation. One that has seen human-nature acting out its
worst form and passed through so many thrilling scenes cannot
justly be charged with fear. We are in usual health and while
I am writing *Abby, Nell* and *Mary* are in high glee sewing and
talking and the keeping room rings with their laughing. Nell
now has seated herself at the Piano and is giving some of her
best tunes. She has commenced teaching and gives lessons
daily to several schollars.

Mary has a school of 15 young ladies which keeps her busy
and with which she is very well pleased.[102] Mary Boudinot has
gone to Mount Holyoke school at South Hadley which we are

---

[101] General D. B. Brinsmade was the husband of the older sister of Harriet Gold Boudinot.

[102] This was the writer's daughter.

all happy to hear.[103] I think it will be a first rate place for her. I regret that her mother had not allowed her to go there last year while Mary was there.

I hope you will come to the North next winter. I regret that I did not go to Washington last winter. I should have had such a fine time to have become acquainted with your friends and seen some of Nells relatives. I think I may meet you in Washington next winter. If I can be of any service to you or the children I will certainly come. I hope you will write me all about your journey home and how the new treaty is recd. by your people and what are the prospects?[104] Has Jno. Ross returned to the Nation or is he still at the North? I shall always have an interest in every thing relating to the welfare of the Cherokees — and may we not hope to have seen the worst of their case and that here-after prosperity will be as triumphant as adversity has been. Remember me affectionately to your wife and all your relations and accept my best wishes for your prosperity and that of your Nation. I subscribe myself

Your very humble Svt.

All send abundance of love.   D. B. BRINSMADE

[103] The records of Mt. Holyoke College show Mary Boudinot to have been a student there from 1846 to 1848. She married L. W. Case in 1849 and died in Winchester, Connecticut, in 1853.

[104] Commissioners were appointed to hear the delegates of the two factions and, as a result, on August 6, 1846, a treaty was signed settling the difference between the two parties. The Cherokee Nation was not divided; but comparative peace and tranquillity prevailed until about the middle of the next decade.

ᴇᴥ CHAPTER II ᴥᴇ

THE GOLD RUSH AND INTERNAL STRIFE

A N era of comparative peace and prosperity in the Cherokee Nation followed the signing of the Treaty of 1846. Schools were established, including the Male and Female Seminaries begun in 1847 and opened to students in 1851, to provide higher education for Cherokee youth. An orphanage was created to care for orphan children of which there were a considerable number, due to the heavy loss of life in the murderous period that had so recently closed. With life and property once more comparatively safe new homes were built, additional farm lands cultivated, and orchards planted. Live stock increased greatly in number and new business houses were established.

The discovery of gold in California in 1848 sent a considerable number of Cherokee westward in search of fortune. These included several members of the Ridge-Watie-Boudinot family; among them John Rollin Ridge and John and Charles Watie, together with a number of their friends.

By the middle fifties, however, most of these had returned and dissension and strife began to appear once more among the Cherokee people. The close relations of Cherokee with the whites in nearby states made it inevitable that they should be affected by the growing hostility between the North and South, which was so soon to take the form of civil war. No doubt the disorders in Kansas, following the passage of the Kansas-Nebraska Act of 1854, were not without some influence upon the Cherokee people.

As the rift between North and South widened those Cherokee citizens, who held a considerable number of slaves or who were connected by ties of blood with some of the large slaveholding families of Georgia or Tennessee, naturally felt their sympathies drawn toward the South. On the other hand certain missionaries from New England were stationed in the Cherokee country and some of these were strongly anti-slavery and preached the doctrine of the abolitionists. Some of these New England missionaries had great influence and were quite active in voicing their opposition to slavery.

The slavery issue and the bitter hatreds engendered by the Ridge-Ross feud were, however, not the only reasons for the rapidly growing dissension and disorder. The Cherokee people, like most other people, tended to divide themselves into two groups, the conservatives and the progressives. The former included most of the full bloods and those mixed bloods who believed most strongly in the old Indian way of life and objected to taking up the customs and manners of the whites. The latter, composed largely of mixed bloods and yet containing a considerable full blood element, believed in borrowing from the whites anything that would serve to advance the civilization and prosperity of the people. They sought to provide education, as the whites understood the term, and evidently expected that sooner or later the Cherokee would largely follow the "white man's road." Nearly all of both groups, however, believed implicitly in the holding of lands in common and in the perpetuation of the Cherokee Nation as a political entity separate and apart from the government of the United States, except in so far as their little republic might be bound to the greater one by treaty relations.

The conservative element eventually became largely associated with the full blood organization known as the Kee-too-wah. This was a secret society, originally formed to conserve the purity of Indian customs and traditions. Its members were commonly called "Pins," since the insignia of the order consisted of two common pins worn in the form of a cross on the lapel of the coat or the front of the hunting shirt. This group was, largely speaking, anti-slavery.

The progressive mixed blood element, on the other hand, began to form chapters of the Copperhead society, so common in the old Northwest, known as "Knights of the Golden Circle." This pro-slavery group was quite aggressive and the "Pins" perhaps even more so. By 1860 the Cherokee Nation had swung back to the conditions that had existed in the law-

57

less days prior to 1846. Murders and depredations were of almost daily occurrence. Disorder was everywhere and the fires of hatred and jealousy, which blazed up on all sides, cast their evil glow over the entire Cherokee country. It required only the actual outbreak of hostilities between North and South to plunge the entire Cherokee Nation into strife and almost hopeless confusion.

Charles E. Watie[1] to Stand Watie

Honey Creek C. N. Sep. 7th, 1847

DEAR STAND:—

I suppose that about this time you have arrived at Washington.[2] We have not heard of you since you left, except through a letter which you wrote Maj Armstrong. We hope however it will not be long before you will favor us with an epistle.

Sarah[3] is at this time rather unwell; she has been very weak for a few days pass'd but is now recovering.

I have just recovered from an attack of the chills and fever; Major Bradley has been very low but now getting better; however, he is still very feeble. Saladin has however kept his health and is as lively as ever.

Elizabeth and her children are well.[4] Tom will commence gathering your fodder today. I am on the point of going after your Negroes. Pierce Miller has got back. I am sorry to inform you that a few evenings since, David Nightkiller was killed. He had just returned from Maysville to Tom Lungis where he was killed by Elis Benge who was with him. Elis has made his escape.[5] I have nothing more of importance to add. Write as soon as you can.

I remain your's truly,

Excuse my haste   CHARLES E. WATIE
All send their love.

---

[1] Stand Watie's youngest brother.

[2] Stand Watie was in Washington probably to secure settlement of claims of the Treaty Party under the treaty of 1846.

[3] Mrs. Sarah C. Watie.

[4] Elizabeth Webber, Stand Watie's sister.

❧ D. B. Brinsmade[6] to Stand Watie

Washington Ct.[Connecticut] Sept. 16th 1847

DEAR SIR

I was very agreably surprised in receiving a letter from you informing me that you was in Washington City. I should have been much pleased to have found you there in May. I had a fine journey and accomplished my business with the government to our mutual satisfaction. Mr. Medill told me that no one had done as much in the time since he had been in office, you know very well how they put off things and thus detain you from day to day so that the expenses eat up the profits. I should like right well to be in Washington during your stay, shall you be able to get through in the short time you mention? Shall you be in Washington next winter? I have conversed with our member of Congress Mr. Smith, he says that if I will draw up a petition he will get each of the children a section of land; he thinks Congress would vote that rather than money and I think I will try.[7] Eleanor & Mary have written you they are here and well.[8] William I have placed in Cornwall under a fine instructor hope he will do well, the little boys are at Manchester at the Brown Seminary doing well.[9] I hope you will write William and encourage him to persevere and get a good education. He will have to use economy in order to make his money hold out which I hope he will. There are few temptations in Cornwall. You say in your letter you shall have something more for them. I am glad of it, hope you will send it by

---

[5] Murder and lawlessness continued for a time to prevail among the Cherokee, in spite of the treaty of 1846.

[6] General D. B. Brinsmade, an uncle of the Boudinot children by his marriage to their mother's sister, acted as their guardian while they were in New England.

[7] The widow and children of the murdered Elias Boudinot forfeited their share in the tribal rights and annuities when they removed to the East. Brinsmade's efforts to secure land for them from Congress were apparently unsuccessful.

[8] These were Elinor and Mary Harriet Boudinot.

[9] These were the other children of Elias Boudinot, William Penn, and his younger brothers Elias Cornelius, and Frank Brinsmade.

draft or by a member of Congress. I have many things to say but not time this evening, please write me on receipt of this and let me know how you get along with your business; are there any Cherokees in Washington but yourself? there were several when I was there, Mr. Fields and others, Judge Paschel was expected so Mr. Medill informed me. I saw one of the Commissioners, a small man. I forgot his name. Mr. Fields introduced me to him. Is the $500 mentioned in your letter all that the children may expect? or will there be something more?

Should be happy to see you in New England at my house, hope you will make it convenient to come next time you visit Washington; with much love from my family I subscribe myself in haste

your friend,

Stand Watie Esqr.   D. B. Brinsmade

⇜ Elinor and Mary Boudinot to Stand Watie

Washington Sep. 20 1847

Dear Uncle,

I received your letter Saturday night. I thank you very much for writing to me so soon after you received mine. I should like to correspond with you all the time. I do like punctial correspondence although I am very deficient myself in that line. I think we and our Cherokee friends might keep up a more frequent correspondence, and know much more about each other, how we are and what we are doing. I am sure I should like to know everything about you all. I hardly know what is going on in the nation now, except that things are moving on more quietly than they did a year or two since.[10] How sad it is to look back upon the seven or eight years just past and think that it has been entirely lost with the Cherokee's; before then they seemed to be improving in every particular, but now even if they will look at their situation and be determined to improve their privileges, both political and religious, they will before

---

[10] This indicates that the treaty of 1846 was having its effect.

long be raised up to the proper standard of men. I know uncle Stand you will be happy when all things are restored back to the place they were eight years ago, although many of the most influential men have been taken away, and those too who were active all their life time in doing good for their people, and were ever ready to sacrifice themselves for their nation. How strange it does seem that so many of the Cherokees should have been so blinded and so easily led by John Ross; but now I presume it is all for the best. God saw fit to take Pa and others away at that time. He has a design in every thing he does and there is some good reason unknown to us why Pa was snatched from us, and the time too it seemed when he was most needed by his family; but we have found friends and very near ones too, yet how many times have I thought if I only had a father and mother I would be happier; but it is wrong to murmur and I will try and not indulge myself in such murmurings. You asked me if I did not intend to go to Arkansas, I have expected to visit you in about two years from now, but I cant tell exactly how it will be, it seems to me if I could see you all now I would be perfectly happy. Give a great deal of love to *all* every one, Charles[11] in particular and kiss litte Saladine for me, tell him Cousin Elly wants very much to see him. All uncle Brinsmade's family are well, cousin Mary is teaching school here and has 37 scholars. Abby is going to be married to Mr. Ginn, perhaps you saw him when you was here, he used to be my teacher; cousin William is still on the railroad at Norvelk about 30 miles from here and he too is going to be married to a lady in Mass. I am going to Hartford in two or three weeks to spend eight weeks and take music lessons, so I shall feel more competent to give lessons when I return. You asked about Grand Pa and Grand Ma, Grand Ma is well and seems as smart as ever, Grand Pa died last April.[12] William is boarding with Grand Ma. I have not heard from them very lately.

11 The children seem to have been particularly fond of Stand Watie's younger brother, probably because Charles was not many years their senior.

12 These were Colonel and Mrs. Benjamin Gold, the parents of Elinor's mother, Harriet Gold Boudinot.

I am writing more than I thought I should when I sat down. I am very busy now getting ready to go away. Please excuse the haste I have written this in and write again soon

To your affectionate niece
ELINOR

DEAR UNCLE,

I have time to write but a few lines in Eleanor's letter before the mail leaves. I am pursuing my studies here with cousin Mary,[13] and hope to make this winter as profitable to me as though I were at South Hadley.[14] In the spring, if nothing prevents and my health is good, I shall return there. I hope I may go to my old home at the West, before many years if it is best. I am glad they are building Seminaries,[15] and trust they will do a great deal of good to our people. We shall expect Charley here next Spring, and shall be very glad to see him. He must not disappoint us. Please write to us when you get home. Tell Charley to write. I am afraid he will not get the letter I sent him at Fort Smith. Give much love to all our friends.

From your affectionate neice
MARY H. BOUDINOT

❧William P. Boudinot to Stand Watie

Philad. April 26th 1848

MY DEAR UNCLE,

I have been so troubled of late and my hands have been so full every way that I have found it impossible to find time to answer your gratifying letter. For the last week I have been sick; neither the business nor the climate nor city agree with

---

[13] This was Mary Brinsmade whom Elinor previously mentioned as having "a school of thirty-seven scholars."

[14] Mary Boudinot had attended Mount Holyoke College at South Hadley the previous session. She returned the following year.

[15] Actual construction of the Cherokee Male and Female Seminaries began in 1847, but it was not until 1851 that the buildings were ready for use. The Male Seminary, located about a mile and a half southwest of Tahlequah was about three miles distant from the Female Seminary, located about a mile northeast of Park Hill. The buildings, of the same architectural style, were built of brick made near the sites of the buildings.

my constitution. I have decided to leave the city by next August or September for the West. I am tired of the North and equally averse to remaining any longer in this city.

Last fall I started from Washington Ct [Connecticut] with the determination to go till I saw you; I arrived here and got badly sick and lame which of course drew the cash from my pocket and the resolution from my head simultaneously. That is the reason why I have spent another winter in engraving. I am now in an excellent business, as good an one as any in my line in Philad. I suppose Uncle Brinsmade would advise me to continue in it till I got rich which would take about ten years, but my eyes are too weak and my health is too poor to allow me any such prospect.

I will visit my Yankee relations next summer and I hope by the middle of October or November to see those faces I have often thought of — my Indian friends.

I think I should enjoy myself among you first rate. Elinor is going to marry Frank Brinsmade's clerk Henry Church. Mary is getting Matrimonial also; who the unlucky man is I am unable to tell.[16] Frank and Cornelius are in Vt. as usual. Ma has issued a proclamation declaring herself unwilling to take farther charge of the boys.[17] It lies upon my Connecticut relations how to dispose of them. I beg you to pardon me for giving you so short an answer; I am somewhat unwell and as I have written you all the principal news then nothing remains but to subscribe myself

Your affectionate Nephew

WM. P. BOUDINOT

P.S. Love to all my friends you meet or see. Tell Charley I will write a long letter to him within a week.

[16] As earlier indicated, Mary Boudinot was married in 1849 to Lyman W. Case.

[17] "Ma," referred to here, was the stepmother of the Boudinot children, Delight Sargent Boudinot.

[18] John Rollin Ridge was 22 years old at this time. Returning to the Cherokee Nation after ten years of study in New England and in Arkansas, he had some time previous to the date of this letter killed David Kell, with whom he had become involved in a controversy. It has been asserted that enemies of

⌁John Rollin Ridge to Stand Watie

Springfield, Mo., July 2, 1849

DEAR COUSIN:

Your letter of June 25th I have just received. I was rejoiced to get it, as I had received letters from every other quarter and I was more particularly anxious to hear from *you* than from any one else. My mother and the family are very desirous that I should leave the nation forever, and have nothing more to do with it — so that information from them with regard to affairs in the Cherokee country wouldn't do me much good, because they would represent impossibilities to return, and dangers thickening every time I might happen to mention the name of the Cherokee Nation.[18] But from you I would expect (of course) the true state of the case. There is a deep-seated principle of revenge in me which will never be satisfied until it reaches its object.[19] It is my firm determination to do all that I can to bring it about. Whenever you say the word, I am there. Whatever advice I receive from you, therefore, will always presuppose that I have not left the nation forever, and be given in view of that object. I believe you understand me fully on that point.

I have talked with a great many persons out here on Cherokee matters, and carefully drawn the distinction between the two parties; the feeling here is that of indignation against the Ross party. They would be glad to have every one of them massacred. I have been out a few days in the country on a visit, by invitation, to an old fellow's named Weaver. Yesterday there was a "reaping" which took place in the neighborhood and I attended. While I was there a good many common Hoosiers gathered round me and wished me to enlighten them somewhat about the differences in the nation. I gave them a

---

the treaty party had sent Kell to provoke a quarrel with young Ridge for the purpose of killing him. If so the result was the opposite of what was intended. Ridge fled from the Cherokee Nation and sought refuge in Missouri, where he was living at this time on a farm.

[19] The reference here is to the murder of Ridge's father.

statement of what Ross had done; described the murders of '39 and with all the aggravations of the act (such as killing the best and truest friend of the Nation etc., etc.) described the events which took place previous to your collecting your men at Fort Wayne, etc. They all listened with intense interest and when I went into particulars, how young men were dragged out into the yard and murdered while their mothers were crying over them and begging the inhuman assassins to have mercy, and how husbands were taken out of their sick beds and butchered to death in the presence of their distracted wives, several of the rough old fellows spoke out.

"The whole Cherokee Nation can't take you out of here."

I *had* thought there was a feeling of apathy existing toward the Cherokees, but I find it is the very reverse. The whites out here, and I have seen a great many, say, if [the] Government would only hint to them to go in, they'd slaughter "that damned Ross set" like beeves.

This man Weaver, who is quite a rich old fellow, owning some fine blooded horses and young colts besides a good many breeding mares and who lives about twelve miles from town, is very anxious to induce me to raise a company of some twenty-five or thirty white men to go and kill John Ross.[20] He says it can be easily done and he will furnish the horses to escape on. I thought I would mention the fact to you as I wish, since I am out in the States, to keep you informed of whatever is said and thought with respect to matters which concern you and me. If you think it best to undertake such a thing, I will try it, and I have no doubt I can succeed. Other persons have urged me to undertake the same thing, that is, white persons out here. I have, however, held back my sentiments on the subject, not knowing but what you might have something better in view.

I'd like it well, if we could finish matters pretty shortly. But patience may be necessary. One thing you may rest assured of, the whites are with us.

[20] The Ridge or Treaty Party was decidedly in the minority and Stand Watie doubtless realized the folly of such a plan as Ridge outlined.

I was out at Osage (as you understand). I went for the purpose of getting some funds if I could raise them, but I could not. My mother is not able to do anything for me. My only dependence is my Grandmother.[21] I told Lizzie, [22] as I was starting back to this place, to go down and see her and get her to let me have my share of the property now, because now is the time that I need it more than I ever will again in my opinion. Lizzie writes me that Grandma says she must have a letter expressing what I intend to do. I must therefore write her a letter and get you to mail it to her, or cousin Elizabeth, one. It is not worth while to be so very particular about waiting for everything to go in due process of law, dividing the property and so on, just let Grandma say how many negroes she will give me, and send them on to me by Lizzie or someone else. You see I haven't time to wait so long. I need money or what can be converted into money right away. I might sell the negroes or I might hire them out as it suited. I would like very well to take the trip out to the East as you recommend, but I haven't the wherewith at the present.[23] I will board out in the country at Weaver's until I can get money. He is a man of great respectability out here. I have Simon hired here in town for only three dollars a week.

P.S. I suppose I need apprehend no danger from the U.S. Marshall. J. R. R.

John Rollin Ridge to Stand Watie

Osage Prairie, Arks.
DEAR COUSIN, Septr. 20th, 1849.

I was happy to receive the word which you sent me the other day respecting my prospects in the Nation. I was greatly in hopes that I would walk triumphantly out of my difficulty. With high expectations I showed your letter to my mother, to

[21] Susie Wickett Ridge, the widow of Major Ridge.
[22] Probably Elizabeth Wilson Ridge, the writer's wife.
[23] Ridge evidently failed to secure funds for his journey to the East, for he soon returned to Arkansas.

Susan, Herman, Enas, Andrew, and Flora![24] They hesitated about agreeing to your proposition because they had been looking to the money, which you have in your hands, for the payment of considerable debts which are hanging over the estate and threatening every day to crush it. If the estate was free, they would agree immediately. Finally, my mother approved of the arrangement, and Enas consented to it heartily, as well as Andrew and Flora, but Herman was unwilling and Susan very much opposed to it, because she has a great aversion to the Nation any how and besides must hear what Woodward says about it.[25] It would surprise me if he would agree to it on any consideration. To induce *all* to agree with me, I offered to pay back to each one what they had let me have, as soon as I could sell property sufficient. But this they wouldn't agree to. Now you have the state of the case and I must candidly confess I don't know what to do. I am afraid this is the only opportunity that presents itself under present circumstances. I know it is money that will take me out, and nothing but money, but it is impossible for me to raise it unless your proposition could succeed.[26] The heirs are willing to sacrifice *property* if you could dispose of it for that purpose, but they say that it is taking their very blood to spend $500.00 at this time of trouble and necessity. It is likely the Andersons will shortly have to be paid, Sutton will have to be paid to a certainty, and there are other smaller debts for which people are threatening to sue. They say they need money immediately. God only knows what I am to do, for I don't. Please write back by Jim.[27]

From your Cousin

JOHN R. RIDGE

[24] These were the younger brothers and sisters of John Rollin Ridge. Enas was Æneas; but the name was doubtless pronounced as Ridge wrote it and not in the traditional Latin manner.

[25] Susan was married to J. Woodward Washbourne, son of the Reverend Cephas Washburn who was a missionary to the Cherokee. The spelling of the name was changed by the son.

[26] It would seem that Ridge wanted money to finance his trial for his killing of David Kell.

[27] Jim was possibly a slave boy.

❦John Rollin Ridge to Stand Watie

Osage Prairie,
Septr. 21st 1849

DEAR COUSIN,

I wrote yesterday morning by Jim, stating how your proposition has been received and what the heirs were willing to do. If it had been merely my mother's consent and my own in the matter of the $500.00, we should have authorized you to spend it for the purpose specified. Matters stand here about the same. There is a reluctance about giving up the $500.00 from the fact that, although the money is not to be divided forthwith, yet it will reduce the Estate of Majr Ridge that much to lose it and will be a sacrifice at any rate. I wouldn't wish to *force* things upon the heirs. In my dilemma, therefore, I have concluded to make this proposal to you. If you could take $500.00 out of Watty's property, I would, as soon as I could reasonably do so, return the amount. Watty is better off than myself, or any of the family, and could afford to spare the amount of 500 dollars for a reasonable time. As for myself, if I bear at this time the weight of 500 dollars expense I am smashed tee-totally!

It is necessary to inform you of one-thing, which I very much regret — when Billy came home he knew that my trial was in contemplation, and by some means or another Jinny knew of it before Billy got back, notwithstanding the matter was carefully concealed in the family.[28] Woodward tells me that it was known at Old Peter's, when he was passing back to Osage. Now, how such things can get out it puzzles me to say. Perhaps the story will not go very far. But it is the *devil* that things of importance *will* get out.

It is not necessary to write long letters because they can not supply the place of conversation face to face, no how. I should like to see you, if practicable.

Aff. yr. Cousin
JNO. R. RIDGE

---

[28] Efforts to finance Ridge's trial, which was to have been held in 1849 or in the spring of 1850, failed. Early in 1850 Ridge joined a party of argonauts bound for California where he lived until his death nearly twenty years later.

◆§ J. W. Washbourne to Stand Watie

Osage Arks. Sept 21st 1849.

DEAR SIR:

Since I got home, I have talked with Rollin & his mother about the business we spoke of.[29] As I told you when I saw you, the Estate here is greatly embarrassed and unless Mrs. Ridge can get 400$ or 500$ to pay off certain debts and stop the issuing of executions against her, her property will be sacrificed and her credit greatly lessened thereby. Nearly a thousand dollars has to be paid, and Mrs. Ridge's hopes have been resting upon her ability to get at least one share of Maj. Ridge's Estate in money, if possible. This forms the only difficulty, in my mind, to the spending the $500. The amount Susan would lose is not much, but the chance of saving her mother's property is gone, and we do not act as we would if there was a certain and actual danger to Rollin. The heirs do not agree and unless they all agree it's no use in urging the matter. So far as I am concerned, I am willing to do what is right and reasonable but I cannot advise or agree to anything unless absolutely necessary that will prevent Mrs. Ridge adjusting her estate. But if you will come up I think we might agree upon something. If Mrs. Ridge is forced to sacrifice her property, why I am willing to let the five hundred dollars go upon terms to which *all* can agree.

The affair has got aired some how. I think they know it at Peter's. You will be cautious accordingly. I *do not* think we can possibly come to any agreement, with out you come up. I am afraid that Bell will hear it but hope he will not. I have kept it as still as I could but negroes can hear thro' stone walls.

Yours Respectfully

J. W. WASHBOURNE

[29] The matter in question seems to be the financing of Ridge's trial.

[30] James M. Bell, son of John A. Bell, was born in 1826 in the Old Cherokee Nation in Georgia. He was a younger brother of Stand Watie's wife.

[31] This was probably John Candy, Jr. whose father was Stand Watie's brother-in-law and formerly Elias Boudinot's assistant and printer.

James M. Bell[30] to John Candy[31]

At Home Nov 29th 1849

Dear John

Excuse the long delay which was impossible for me to prevent on account of the pressing business that I have had to attend to since my return which was on the 15th Inst. After a rather long but pleasant trip of 13 days in company with Mr. & Miss T's, Miss L. N., aunt Rachel and a few others. So you perceive that there was nothing requisite to the perfect enjoyment of my journey which I regreted very much had come to an end on Martha's account. She certainly is a rare specimen of the fair sex presenting as many different appearances as the changing moon — often clothed in smiles that seem to be caused by fancied odities, then again dark frowns gather over her countenance for awhile. She puts on the deepest apparent indignation, breaks forth in haughty strains pouring without discrimination her sarcasm on all who approach her. Yet after all her freaks she's great company. I could ride all day with her and at night she still seemed to have something new to communicate; but hold I said there was nothing wanting to make the trip a perfectly pleasant one. I mistake, many places where we stoped over night there was no more accomodation than there would be at Old Dumplings or Brushheaps. Americans may talk of heathan countries dark and benighted people but charity ought to begin at home. If the people of Washita Cove don't want missionaries, if they don't want the Gospel preached to them, then I will just "give up the *Skates*" and say that all are civilized, for to make this plain evident suppose yourself in the house of a Mr. Lewis of Washita Cove — a little house about twelve feet by fourteen two scaffolds, bedstead with sheets and quilts the scent of which would capsize a genuine African, three old chairs one without a bottom the two hind legs of one off the others broke and the last of the three with the rounds all broke out in front, a little table three feet by four with a piece of cloth thought by the company to be dark calico but was found on examination in the morning to be covered with dirt accumulated probably in the youth of their great grand parents; it certainly was out of the question I could not bear to put my bread on it. But words cannot in adequate terms explain to your mind what was harbored in that ancient soil then for me to tell you that the boy was ten years old and did'nt know what a towel was seems almost absurd, but all that is bearly enough and that was a place of public entertainment but I will weary your patience. When I got home I found the people all well and doing as well as they could in a prosperous country, your Grand-papa had a great many questions to ask about you. Charlotte also had many things to inquire about you. I gave them a very favorable account of your improvement &c &c. I hated very much to leave the Nation but I could not do otherwise. When I shall return to that Country is more than I can say. You must learn fast. Take up some proffession. I think you would do well to study Law. Write soon, tell me what you intend doing; give my love to all the girls, my best respects to *Clem* and also to the other boys; tell Clem to write when I write to him; don't let any person see this scribbled letter and believe that I remain

Your affectionate
JAMES M. BELL

P.S. Direct to Mt Enterprise   Rusk Co Texas

◄§John Rollin Ridge to Stand Watie

Osage Prairie,
December 18th 1849

DEAR COUSIN,

I am making arrangements at the present time to pay you the amount of the mortgage which you hold on Grigg, and receive him again into my possession. It is in relation to this matter that I now write to you. The woman Peggy, whom I received as my share of old Mrs. Ridge's estate, is very unhappy on this side of the line and is anxious to get back to her husband Tom. Tom, himself, when up here expressed great dissatisfaction at being separated from his wife. On these accounts I have concluded to make the proposition to you that you take Peggy in satisfaction of the mortgage. I have just now forgotten the amount, but if she be worth any more we can easily adjust that part of the business. I am confident that she is worth with her child Ellen, at least as much as the mortgage money. I have made this proposal because I preferred to redeem Grigg in that way, but if you prefer the money I can raise it for you I think in a short time.

Please write me an answer at your earliest convenience.[32]

Your cousin and sincere friend
JOHN R. RIDGE

William P. Boudinot to Stand Watie

Fort Smith March 13th 1850

DEAR UNCLE,

It is impossible to get my money before a month or two, so I believe I shall wait and not go to California this spring.[33] When my money does come, which I suppose will be about the first of May, I will hand over to you about $200 to help you out of your difficulties. I owe you nearly a hundred anyhow. I offered Uncle Wheeler[34] a first rate bargain if he would raise $175 for me and he would have done so if he could but he could'nt. Besides I could'nt choose him Guardian till the next session of the County Court which will not come on till next month.[35] So I wrote a very respectful letter to Uncle Brinsmade and got Uncle Wheeler to add a very saucy note and between us both I believe the old fellow will succumb. Meanwhile I have concluded I have health sufficient to do something for myself

[32] This letter has been included because it shows the interest that the Ridges took in their slaves.

[33] As far as is known, William P. Boudinot did not make the trip to California, though several members of the Watie-Ridge-Boudinot family became California gold seekers.

[34] John F. Wheeler, Stand Watie's brother-in-law through his marriage to Watie's older sister Nancy.

[35] Upon his return to Arkansas from the East, young Boudinot evidently wanted his guardianship transferred from his uncle D. B. Brinsmade to another uncle John F. Wheeler.

now[36] and Wheeler promises to give me enough for that purpose to earn my salt. I called on old Carter for a little cash and he very politely said he could nothing for me, using excruciating English all the while.

He hinted that I might call on him in two months time, expecting of course that I would be half way to California by that time. I shall keep the note in my hands and if the fellow dont fork over I shall be constrained to dun him Jack Gill fashion. The other note I send you. I had not opportunity to surprise Taylor. I called at his house Monday morning and was told he had gone to Tahlequah, and I forthwith followed his illustrious footsteps to that everlasting city. But he had just absconded to Flint and I gave up the pursuit. He probably smelt a rat.

I am

Affectionately Your Nephew

W. P. Boudinot

◦§John A. Watie to Stand Watie

10th Nov. 1850
Sonora diggins California.

Dear Brother

I arrived here yesterday at this place after being on the road six months and ten days the rout that I come is about 3000 miles.[37] I could not have got here until this winter if I had not sold my waggon & mules and took water which I did at Los angelos. I took sick at that place been sick ever since. But I am a good deal better only I have a cough which I am in hopes will leave in a few days so I can go to work.

This is Sunday morning tomorrow we will go to work. Every body is waiting for rain in these dry diggins they say the

---

[36] In 1851 William P. Boudinot was elected clerk of the National council which was the beginning of an interesting career of public service.

[37] Of the many overland routes to the California gold fields, John Watie must have taken one of the southern trails.

wet-season is the time for mining.[38] I think we will be able to make from $4 to $6 a day until the wett season sets in then a man can expect more, a great many is mining here in the streets some are making a great deal.

I understand all the company that came the Northern rout has got in at the Northern mines. I have not heard from your folks or Bro. Charles But I suppose they are up there. If I had come the Northern rout I could have Brought in my team & waggon which would have Brought $1000.

Thier was six of us that come together & we are the only ones of all our company that has got to the diggins.

The five men that came out with me are all here and good hands to work — Bob Bunyan, Timothy, James Berryhill, William Triplett & Sam Sopley. There is two persons in this place that I know, Jerry Bo & Mr. Harris from Marysville.

I think we will be able to make money this winter at any thing we go at, we will stay in this place, gold is plenty every where in this neighborhood.

I left Holt on the Rio grand in August, he must be a long ways behind. Henry Hickey Borrowed 250 lbs flour from me & I missed a robbing party at Collorado — the people say they are robers, & a good many Emigrants Found them not knowing any thing about it.

I sold one of my horses at the Rio grand & Bought flour enough to last me to this place but Hickey & Judge Brown Borrowed me out so and that was one thing which compeld me to sell out. Brown boged about 70 miles from San diego he Broke down 2 teams. Hickey's team looked very well for he never had anything in the wagon as long as he could sponge about the other waggons, I will write to you again in a few days when I have something to write or when we get in a good way of mining, this is what is called the Southern diggins about 65 miles from Stockton.

You can tell my folks I am here, you must write to me & tell me how my folks is gettng a long, you must tell them

[38] Sonora, a settlement of about 500 inhabitants in 1850, was located about sixty-five miles east of Stockton and was known as the "dry diggings."

to kill all the hogs I got from Judge Brown this winter as they might run wild, their was 25 or 30 spade sows & Barrows — 2 sows I got from Drew, Some shotes But their is 25 or 30 head besides which is 2 and 2½ years-old

Direct your letters to So-No-ra. Callifornia

Give my best respects to your family & my folks from Your Brother

JOHN A. WATIE

ᘿ§ John B. Ogden to Stand Watie

Stand Watie Esq.   Van Buren July 19 1852
D. SIR

Mrs. Paschal[39] desires me to write you about her negroes. She appears to be getting impatient to have them, she says she can hire the boys at one dollar per day here during harvest, and they would pay the board of herself and children while here. She says she wants you to start Stephen & William home as soon as you receive this and Tom & his wife she says you will send down if you cannot sell Tom for $800 to Elijah Mose who has been to see her. He tells her he has a negro woman *Stephens wife* I think and she says if he will give 800 for *Tom* and if he will make the exchange of Stephens wife for *Peggy Toms wife* so as to accomodate the negroes you can *do so* and if you think Mose's negro *woman* worth more than *Toms wife* You can arrange it with Peggy's child. If in your opinion Peggy is worth as much as Moses negro woman make him pay for the child. If no chance for this trade she says send *Tom & wife & child* down at once as she can sell them here to some one in the nation herselfe.[40]

Yours respectfully
JOHN B. OGDEN
for Sarah Paschal

[39] Mrs. George Washington Paschal, daughter of Major Ridge.

[40] In this letter are further evidences of the consideration of Cherokee families for their slaves. Most of the wealthier Cherokee owned a considerable number at the outbreak of the Civil War, so it is natural that they should be Southern in their sympathies.

⛌John Rollin Ridge to Stand Watie

Marysville, California
September 23, 1853.

DEAR COUSIN STAND:

Several years have elapsed since I left my beautiful home in the Cherokee Nation and since I bid you amongst my other friends and relatives adieu — and during all this time a line has not passed between you and me. We, who were once such warm friends, bound closer even by the ties of friendship than by the ties of blood, we have been as silent and as cold as if we were strangers! I think it is wrong and I am going now to break the silence which has existed unnecessarily and too long between us.

I suppose you know pretty well from different sources what my history has been in California. It has been a series of bad luck. I have worked harder than any slave I ever owned or my father either. All to no purpose. I have tried the mines, I have tried trading, I have tried everything but with no avail, always making a living but nothing more.[41] If I could have contented myself to remain permanently in the country I could have succeeded in making a fortune, but I have been struggling all the time to make one in a hurry so that I might return to Arkansas, and (I will say it to *you*) to the Cherokee Nation also. I am engaged at present as a Deputy Clerk, Auditor and Recorder in the county of Yuba, California, at a remuneration of $135 a month, which gives me a pretty decent living and some surplus money. I am about to settle a place in this vicinity, a fine patch (160 acres) of government land, which happens to be free from Spanish grants and all other encumbrances, with a view of locating my family upon it. I will proceed to have a house built upon it in a short time hence. I am tormented so by the folks at home whenever I talk of going back to the Nation, and they urge me in their letters so much not to venture to stay even in Arkansas with my family that I am resolved to

[41] Ridge wrote for the San Francisco *Golden Era,* in 1852, under his Cherokee name which, translated, means "Yellow Bird."

quiet their fears by providing for my family in this country so as to place them above all want; and then I will be at liberty to follow the bent of my mind which leads me back to my own people and to my own country. It is only on my mother's account that I have stayed away so long. It was only on her account that I did not go back in '49 or the spring of '50 and risk my trial.[42] I am not afraid to do it at any time, provided my friends will only agree to back me. But let that be as it may, I intend some day sooner or later to plant my foot in the Cherokee Nation and stay there too, or die. I had rather die than to surrender my rights. You recollect there is one gap in Cherokee history which needs filling up. Boudinot is dead, John Ridge and Major Ridge are dead, and they are but partially avenged. I don't know how you feel now Stand, but there was a time when that brave heart of yours grew dark over the memory of our wrongs. But we'll not talk about it because I believe you feel right yet and I admire your prudence in keeping so quiet. I want you to write me freely and frankly. Tell me exactly how things stand, what are the prospects of coming safely out of a trial, etc., etc. I never mention the subject to my folks at home because they only answer me that there is "danger, danger, danger," as though a man had to be governed by his *fears* in place of his reason and his judgment. The Lord deliver me from the advice of women. They never think of anything but the danger — the profits and advantages all go for nothing with them, if there is any risk to run at all!

I send this to the care of Woodward Washbourne, who will see that it is delivered to your hands. I will write more fully on the reception of your answer. Love to all. Has Charley got back?[43] I haven't heard from him in a long time.

Affectionately Yours,

JOHN R. RIDGE

[42] Ridge apparently entertained little fear of conviction for his killing of David Kell, had members of his family consented to his return to the Nation.

[43] Charles Watie had made the trip to California in 1850. He was still in the gold fields in October, 1857.

✑ Barbara Longknife[44] to Stand Watie

Coloma June 8th 1854

DEAR SIR,

I gladly embrace the present opertunity of addressing .you by the way of this letter. we are in moderate health at the present time and hope these lines may find you and your family emjoying the same blessing. we have made nothing in this country as yet more than barely supported the family. William has been trying his luck in the mines, did not make it pay over board, we have had a great deal of sickness in our family since we came to this Country and our doctor bills has cost us a great many dollars together with other expenses connected with Dr. Bills. we are still living in Coloma and I think it is very probable we will remain here as long as we stay in this Country. I would like very much to see all my old friends in the nation. California is not what it was represented to be, if I was back again I would let California be the last place that I would go to.[45] I am engage in washing at present and have been for a considerable length of time it pays better than anything else that I can do. give my best respects to Mr. Huss and all enquiring friends & receive for your self and family the same. You will please write when this comes to hand and give me all the news of importance. William & myself are the only ones of the mess that I know anything about. R. Tuff died on the plains. Welch died after we got here, the last I heard of your Brother Charles he was going north in 52, have'nt heard from him since. John Candy is in this country somewhere, was in this place a few days since, he has not made his pile yet.[46] when you

[44] Barbara Longknife and her husband William Longknife were old friends and former neighbors of the Watie family. This letter was evidently dictated by Mrs. Longknife, whose spelling was very bad, to someone else who did the actual writing.

[45] In this letter is evidence of the disappointment and disillusion that were the lot of most of the Cherokee gold seekers.

[46] John Candy's letter from James M. Bell appears earlier in this chapter.

[47] Nancy (Bell) Starr, wife of George Starr, was a sister of Mrs. Sarah C. Watie. She was one of a group of Cherokees that had migrated to Rusk County, Texas.

78

write you will direct your letter to Coloma Eldorado Co California

Very Respectfully your friend

BARBARY LONGKNIFE

you will please forward this to Brother when it comes to hand

B L

⊷§ Nancy Starr[47] to Sarah C. Watie

At Home Rusk County, Texas

July 24, 1854

MY DEAR SISTER,

This will inform you that we are all well, one of my children has been very sick but is well at present.

The health in general is good at the present time.

Mayfields people, Thompson's, aunt Rachel, Miller's, Jack Bell's &c are all in good health. We have plenty of good Peaches to eate and some flour to put with them and of course we all living well at present. Mary is a good big *Girl* and is or has been going to school, they say she learns well.

My boy Joe is a great big fellow & *they* say he is awful *pretty* I cant say what you will say to his beauty; but I think him one of us.

We have our house finished, except the chimmies they are yet on hand, I think by the 1st. of Oct'r. we will have it completed. Well from what Jack & Sabra tells me I may look for you about the 10th. of Oct'r. I want you to come prepared to spend the winter here. You can make my or our house your head quarters, then you can branch round to Charlotts, Jack Mayfields, Mrs. Pitners and Col Thompsons as You think proper, they are all well fixed and will [be] glad to see you. I think Sabra is well pleased with Texas no notion of living any at *Baties Prairie*.[48] We will all prepare for chicken, Pie &c when you come.

The weather is extreamly warm at present and no rain and

---

[48] The old Ridge-Watie-Boudinot homes were located in the northeastern part of the Cherokee Nation on Beatties Prairie.

have not had any for the last six weeks, but the raising of chickens does not depen on the wet weather as cotton, corn &c.

If you should see Martha[49] Say to her that we are all well and would be glad to see her once in this Country. As for me, I am a fraid to think of travling North, my health is such that I could hardly trust myself that far in a cold region, and Then you are aware of the number of The *Litle* responsibilities on my hand. There is *Jack,* Mary, Cole, Ezekiel, now sick. *Joseph* & the babies. Is this not a hand full in fact they [are] all *babes*.

Well E. Ridge[50] can tell you all about us all better than I can write.

My respects to Mr. Watie and a World of Love to yourself and your Sweet *Little Children.*

Good by Sister
NANCY STARR

J. A. Bell[51] to Stand Watie

So here it is:
Mrs. S. Watie,
DEAR SIR:

I call my place Mount Taber
Mount Taber, Texas
July 24th, '54

We are all well. I am yet Staying with G. Starr. My house is not yet completed, though I intend to move up in the course of this week. I am making a fine crop of corn and counting every thing I am doing well and ought to be Satisfied but I have been *drove* off, that is what *hurts.* Is Dave Vann to master me, even to Clem is ploting against me.

Why do I never hear from none of you are you too Lazy to *scratch* a few lines. I would be glad to hear any thing from you.

Well we had a big horse race the Nicholson Mare *Jinney* Lind or Sin won a big race a few days since. She is a race *horse sure.* The principle bet was 300$.[52]

---

[49] Martha (Bell), another sister of Mrs. Watie, was the wife of the Reverend W. A. Duncan.

[50] Æneas Ridge.

[51] J. A. Bell, whose note to Stand Watie forms a part of Nancy Starr's letter, at the time of this letter was living with the Starrs.

[52] Stand Watie was interested in horse racing. The shoes from one of his race horses are in the Frank Phillips Collection at the University of Oklahoma.

Well now for Sally and her trip to this Country.[53] In the first place She must not think of bringing more than *Two* of her children with her and let *Seladin* and the baby be the ones. Then you must have the carriage well fixed before you start, the Harness in good repare, the Horses well Shod and fat and if you will let Seladin ride a fat pony or horse out I will Sell it, for you. [you] must not load the carriage heavey it is the worst road gracious goodness, you no that I have lately come over the road. If you bring a trunk let it be a small one you can put the clothing in a Sack it will be so much lighter start with a few horse shoe nails & a hamer. Come to Lany port, from There to Decalbs, from there to Stephensons Ferry on the Sulpher, 12 miles from the Sulpher, Enquior for Mr. Terrel Son in law to old Robert Hughs, 4 to Terrel, 1 mile to *old uncle* Robert Hughs, then it is 14 miles to Skinr's. in this Settlement Sally can rest, come at Leasure in 2 days to Starrs or my house. It is best by Lany port — a good tavern at decalb. From Fort Smith to Waldon 2 days 4 miles further on is a good house kept by one of Temp Ross' sons then come to Mr. Whites on the left of the road 28 mils. Then cissely 27 mils, Then Bell on 25 mils, Then Mill Wells, Then Cooper. Coopper here you are in 18 mils of Lanes port. Cooppers a good house.

J. A. BELL

ᥱᅌJohn Rollin Ridge to Stand Watie

Marysville Cal October 9th[54]

DEAR COUSIN STAND:

Notwithstanding I have written you several letters without receiving an answer, I will make another venture and write to you again. This time I have good news for you; and that is

[53] Mrs. Watie was planning a visit to these relatives in Texas. Later letters show that during the latter part of the Civil War she left the Cherokee Nation and lived among them for some time. The remainder of this letter shows that an overland trip from the Cherokee Nation to Texas was a serious undertaking.

[54] The year is missing in this date, but it would seem that the letter was written in 1854.

81

that our long missing Charley is found again.[55] After advertising for him in the papers and enquiring for him in every quarter for a long time, I had the happiness to get a letter from him a few weeks ago, and a short time after, he came down here to my house in town and staid with me several days. He is now at Rough & Ready, has a claim which is paying him 3 or 4 dollars a day and is in good health. He is anxious to go home and will start as soon as he is able pecuniarily to leave. I presume he has already written to you since he saw me and told you all the news relating to himself.

For my own part, I am struggling along with adversity as well as I may. I expected to have made a great deal of money off of my book, my life of Joaquin Murieta (a copy of which I have sent you) and my publishers, after selling 7,000 copies and putting the money in their pockets, fled, bursted up, *tee totally* smashed, and left me, with a hundred others, to whistle for our money![56] Undaunted by this streak of bad luck, I have sent the work on to the Atlantic States for a new edition, and when that is sold out I will have a few thousand dollars at my command. There is not so much danger of one of those heavy eastern houses failing as these mushroom California concerns at San Francisco.

Now the main object I have in writing to you at present is to make you a proposition. Dont you believe it would be a good plan to establish a paper somewhere in Arkansas, or some place where it will be safe from the commotion of Cherokee affairs, and devote it to the interest of the Indian race? It is my opinion that it would pay well and it would certainly do a great deal of good. The Indians certainly need friends and a newspaper properly wielded would be the most powerful friend that they could possibly have. It would be a medium not only of defending Indian rights and of making their oppressors tremble but of preserving the memories of the distinguished men of the race, illustrating their characters and keeping green and fresh

55 Charles Watie.

56 Ridge's book, *The Life and Adventures of Joaquin Murieta*, was the story of the famous California-Mexican bandit.

many of the most important events of Indian history which should not be allowed to perish.[57]

Now, Stand, if you will furnish the money to buy a press, I will engage to edit it with all the ability that I possess and with as much true devotion and patriotism as any other man in the Cherokee Nation. I want to place myself in a position to do some good. I want to preserve the dignity of our family name; I want the memory of my distinguished relatives to live long after we have all rotted in our graves. I want to write the history of the Cherokee Nation as it *Should* be written and not as white men will write it and as they will tell the tale, to screen and justify themselves. All this I can never do unless I get into the proper position to wield influence and to make money. Dont you see how much precious time I am wasting in California? Instead of writing for my living here I should be using my pen in behalf of my own people and in rescuing from oblivion the proud names of our race. Stand, I assure you this is no idle talk. If there ever was a man upon earth that loved his people and his kindred, I am that man. Now $2000, yes $1500, would buy a competent press, with all the apparatus, at New York, would transport it to Arkansas and there set up the paper. Any merchant, by your order, going on to N.Y., could purchase it for you and see that it was duly shipped for Arkansas. That the paper would succeed is just as certain as that the sun shines. What is to hinder it? The subject, the cause to which it would be devoted, everything would conspire to make it interesting.

I made you the proposition in all sincerity, and I await your answer in the same spirit. What is the use of our lying down like common men to be forgotten, when we can just as well blow a trumpet of our own that will waken the world to listen to what we say?

If you will write me that you have sent on for a press and that you want me to come home to Arkansas to edit it, you will

[57] An exile in a strange land, Ridge could not forget his beloved Cherokee Nation.

see me on hand, right away, as fast as steam and paddlewheels can take me.

I dont care whether I can get back into the nation right away or not. The paper will do just as well, and better, in the State. However, write to me anyhow what the prospect is of getting safely back into the Nation. Love to all friends.

Affectionately,

Direct to Maryville, Yuba County, Cal.   JOHN R. RIDGE

✑ Elias Cornelius Boudinot[58] to Stand Watie

DEAR UNCLE,   Fayetteville Sept. 11 1855

AEneas told you why I was not at your place the day of the election so I need tell you nothing about my being sick &c. I am now so far recovered as to be able to study regularly though I do not feel well by any means, my head is still dizzy.

Everybody is very much pressed for money. AEneas in particular declaimed loudly against the scarcity of money in the country generally, but more especially the emptiness of his own pockets. He wishes me to tell you that he gives you full authority to sell anything on his farm except a nigger. I intend to visit you about the last of this month, and AEneas tells me if you do not effect a sale of his property by that time and dont have any money yourself that I must make a sacrifice of his black pony, for, he says, "I *must have money.*"

Everybody and everything is awful dull and stupid, there is no news of any interest about here. Mr. Wilson[59] told me the

---

[58] Elias Cornelius Boudinot, son of Elias Boudinot, was born in 1835 in the Old Cherokee Nation near Rome, Georgia. After the murder of his father, his stepmother removed with the children to New England. At Manchester, Vermont, young Boudinot studied to be a civil engineer. His first job in his profession was with a railroad company in Ohio. An injured knee caused him to give up this work and return to Arkansas, where he took up the study of law. In 1856, a year after writing this letter, Boudinot was admitted to the bar, which was the beginning of an interesting career in the service of his people.

[59] This was A. M. Wilson, prominent lawyer of Fayetteville, Arkansas, and a friend of Stand Watie and the Treaty Party.

other day that several white men had been evicted from their improvements on the Neutral land, and were grumbling about it considerably.[60] I get letters from Nell pretty frequently.

Mrs. D. B. B. has paid no attention to my letter demanding a full and thorough account of her guardianship, if she dont write soon I shall write her another letter no less authoritative than the last.[61] I went to a Camp Meeting at Cane Hill last week it was the first I ever was at. Saw a good many people and heard a good deal of whooping and shouting by both sexes and more singing than ever before at one time. I lost a spur and a bran new shirt and spent a dollar, and on the whole, it was a losing speculation for me.

I shall be with you the last week of this month if well enough to ride. My pony is doing very well. I wish to sell him at the earliest opportunity. Give my love to Aunt Sarah[62] and all the rest. I am your very affectionate Nephew

ELIAS C. BOUDINOT

❧ John Rollin Ridge to Mrs. S. B. N. Ridge

At home in Marysville,
Oct. 5, 1855.

POST SCRIPT:[63]

Lizzie has explained to you the prospects before us. I have only to add to what she has said that I will not practice the law unless I am driven to it. The general science of the law I admire — its every day practice I dislike. But for the sake of having something upon which to rely in case of necessity, I have

[60] The Cherokee frequently complained of intruders in the 800,000 acre tract known as the Neutral Lands. Agitation became so strong that Captain Sturgis with United States troops drove out the settlers in 1857.

[61] The writer was referring to Mrs. D. B. Brinsmade who with her husband had acted as guardians for the Boudinot children while they were living in New England after their father's death.

[62] "Aunt Sarah," to whom Elias Cornelius Boudinot wrote many interesting letters in the decade after Stand Watie's death, was Mrs. Sarah C. Watie.

[63] This post script, found among the Stand Watie papers, seems to have been added to a letter written by John Rollin Ridge's wife to his mother, Sarah Bird Northrup Ridge.

patiently burned the midnight oil since I have been in Marysville. I was determined that if untoward circumstances gathered around me and I was thrown out of employment I would have some sure thing to depend upon, so that I might stand boldly up and say to the world, "I ask you no favors." I prefer a literary career but if I cannot place myself in a position as a writer I will even go into the drudgery of the law. I have been promised, by the State Printer elect, a lucrative situation as a writer for his paper. If I get that, of which there is every probability, I will locate at Sacramento and go to making money.[64] If I do not, my knowledge of the law is sufficient to enable me to obtain a license and I am therefore independent and fearless of consequences. In either case whether I get the expected position under the State printer or whether I begin the more slow and tedious task of building up a legal reputation in California (as I have already established a respectable literary one), [65] in either case, I will act with a view to carrying out the project which I proposed to Stand Watie, namely — the establishment on the white side of the line (where it will be safe from the commotions in the nation!) of a newspaper devoted to the advocacy of Indian rights and interests. If I can establish such a paper I can bring into its columns not only the fire of my own pen, such as it may be, but the contribution of the leading minds in the different Indian nations. I can bring to its aid and support the Philanthropists of the world. I can so wield its power as to make it feared and respected. Men, governments, will be *afraid* to trample upon the rights of the defenceless Indian tribes when there is a power to hold up their deeds to the execration of mankind. What prouder object could a man propose to himself than the great idea of civilizing and improving these mighty remnants of the Indian race — bringing all these

[64] It is not known whether or not Ridge received this position. He did, however, become a candidate for the position of state printer of California in 1861.

[65] During the two decades Ridge resided in California he was editor or manager of the Sacramento *Bee*, *The California Express, Daily National Democrat*, the Marysville *Democrat*, the San Francisco *Herald*, *The Trinity National*, and the Grass Valley *National*.

scattered tribes one by one into the fold of the American Union
— saving those at least who can be saved and perpetuating the
memories of those who cannot — handing down to posterity
the great names of Indian history and doing justice to a deeply
wronged and injured people by impressing upon the records of
the country a true and impartial account of the treatment which
they have received at the hands of a civilized and Christian
race! If I can once see the Cherokees admitted into the Union
as a state, then I am satisfied.[66] Until then, whether I win lau-
rels as a writer in a distant land or whether I toil in the ob-
scurity of some mountain village over the dull routine of a
small practice, winning my way by slow and painful steps to
wealth and influence in this far-off state, I will bear that holy
purpose in my heart of hearts. And if I fail in all I undertake
and lie down to die, with this great purpose unfulfilled, my last
prayer shall be for its consummation and the consequent happiness of the Cherokee People! Stand has written to me that
he is in favor of going into an arrangement with me for starting a newspaper such as I have spoken of, as soon as he is pecuniarily able. I shall wait anxiously for him to get ready for
the enterprise and as soon as he is I want him to let me know,
the sooner the better.[67]

Jim Rogers is in the mountains above here, at least I have
been told there is a Rogers up there in the mines somewhere
and I take it to be him. I hope, dear mother, to be able sometime before many months are over to send you something more
than letters.

I wish you would send this half-sheet to Stand, that he may
know what I still think of our plan.

Your affectionate and ever devoted son,

ROLLIN

[66] In marked opposition to the views of an overwhelming majority of the
Cherokee people, Ridge and Elias Cornelius Boudinot felt that the admission of
their Nation to the Union might be the best solution of their tribal problems.

[67] Ridge did not realize his dream of establishing a newspaper in Arkansas devoted to the advocacy of Indian rights and interests. Apparently, Stand
Watie could not see his way clear to furnish funds for such an enterprise and,

✎ D. Jarrett Bell[68] to James M. Bell

Drytown California
Oct. 16th 1855

DEAR BROTHER

I take this opportunity of writing you a few lines. I still enjoy good health and have a moderate share of the good of Earth as it passes. I think health is tolerably good and is improving. We have been doing nothing but living privately and quietly as possible for almost four months. I rented out my house and I am taking things easy. I keep a hand employed at my Livery Stable which I have in town. I try and keep my expenses below my income and as long as I do that I hope to proffit a little bye and bye. I can't sell my property for near its worth and as I have it I want to keep it and live easy and *independent.*

Once and a while I see a friend and I enjoy a day or so in a very pleasant way. Clement McNair passes occasionally and we have a pleasant confab on persons and the subjects that affords me grand relief. Bug Eye Smith was to see me about the 15th of September the old fellow was amazingly glad to see me, he looks rather despairingly, he regrets his trip to this country and says he will return as soon as he can.

I have heard of the arrival at home of my old friend Sinacowee — the old man became very anxious to go back home. George Downing[69] is here he is very anxious to go home. James Hardin is about 15 miles from here. He has married and keeps house — not boarding house — he does very well I think. Mrs. Jane Langdon sister of Jef Parks was here about a week ago and passed a week with us. She is in fine health and is excellent company — being old acquaintances in our youthful days it affords me a pleasing recreation to converse of olden times. Chap England was around town for a week past, his

---

in the meantime, the clouds of the Civil War soon overshadowed any ideas of progress.

68 D. Jarrett Bell was a brother of Mrs. Sarah C. Watie and James M. Bell.

69 George Downing was a relative of Lewis Downing, afterwards principal chief of the Cherokee Nation.

Mrs. Sarah C. Watie

characteristic is the trial of good liquor — however he had nothing to purchase with. I use no personalities about any of my countrymen to their prejudice, but many might do better if they would. Clem McNair will start home this fall and you may expect him at fartherest by Christmas. I had a letter from Jack from Texas he said he was going back to the Nation — well if he can live there in peace I think it the best place for any and all of the Cherokees. The laws, the customs, the pleasures and every convenience for easy and pleasant living is as uniform in the Nation as anywhere, also leave this Nation and you come in contact with every variety of taxation, road working corporations, charters, property tax, licenses of every description and variety that keeps a man always out of sorts to paye — all to support a set of officials universally unprincipalled in feelings of humanity.

Well did you settle that French note, if so let me know. Sam Mayes[70] borrowed twenty-five dollars from me when here you call on him for it and use it — if you get it. If I return I can have it off you — but I would rather you have it. I want you to write to me often, if you have nothing else to write about [write] just as much as you can in praise of my babies. I would like to see Mrs. Caroline Bell;[71] be sure and give her my love, and also my respects to Jo Lynch and family — tell me who is Chief, assistant Chief and officers generally.[72] Juliet is talking Indian as hard as she can to George Downing.[73] Indian talk is a great rarity. She sends love to you and Caroline.

Your Affectionate Brother

James M. Bell   D. Jarrett Bell

P.S. I mail this at Sacramento as the mail here is closed — direct your letters to Drytown.

[70] Samuel Mayes, father of Samuel Houston and Joel B. Mayes, both of whom later held the office of principal chief, headed a party to California in 1849. In this party was another future principal chief, Dennis W. Bushyhead.

[71] This was Caroline (Lynch) Bell, the wife of James M. Bell.

[72] John Ross was principal chief and George Lowrey was assistant chief.

[73] Juliet (Vann) Bell, wife of D. Jarrett Bell.

ᎤᏍ Charles E. Watie to Stand Watie

Sacramento City, Cal.
August 18th 1856.

Mʀ Dᴇᴀʀ Bʀᴏᴛʜᴇʀ,

I have only time to write you a short letter, as the mail will leave here in a hour.

I came down to this place from the mountains, about a month ago, and with the intention of going home in the fall,[74] but if I can get into any business that will pay me I do not know but that I will stay till next spring. Rollin and Lizzie are in tollerable health. Rollin is still employed as one of the editors of the Cal. American. My chief object in writing to you at this time is to make enquiries about the press which you have thought of establishing somewhere in Arkansas and which is to be the advocate of the Indians. Rollin and I have spoken a good deal upon the subject and are both of the opinion that the establishment of a "News paper" devoted to the rights of the Indians is the best thing that can possibly be done for them, and we hope that it *will* be done.

We will expect to hear from you immediately on the subject. The sooner the press is procured, the better.

Rollin may not be able to go home to take charge of the paper just yet, but others *might* be found who *could do so* till he could return to the nation.[75] I am not doing anything although I write occasionaly for the "American." I have not seen Bill Longknife and his wife[76] for some time. I intend however to see them in a few days. You know I suppose how Jack played the rascal and ran off to Canada.

I do not think that I will follow Mining any more and (as I have just said) if I can't get into any other business shortly you may look for me in the latter part of next fall.

I will write you again before long and more at length.

[74] Charles Watie did not return to the Cherokee Nation until the following year.

[75] As explained in an earlier footnote, the plan to establish an Indian newspaper in Arkansas did not materialize.

[76] William and Barbara Longknife.

Meanwhile, you must be certain and write as soon as you get this and let us know what you can do towards getting that press. Direct all your letters for me to Rollin.

Give my love to all. Lizzie and Rollin send love.

I am my dear brother,
Yours affectionately

I am in good health.
CHARLES E. WATIE

⊰ Barbara Longknife to Stand Watie

Mr. Standwatie　　　　　　　　Coloma Cal October 11th 1857
DEAR CIR

I take this oppertunity of wrighting you a few lines to let you no we are yet in the land of the living.[77] Charles E. Watie was hear to day, he is working at 3 dolars per day, that is good wages for this time. we are all well except my little girl, she has had the billious fevor and it has left her all most blind of boath eays. I live in hopes that her site will come back a gain. if I had money I would take her to some other Doctor but as it is I have the best Doctor thir is in this place. we have made a living in this Country and that is all. to rase money enough to take us home we could not if it was to save us all. we could not do that mush and we have not had that mush at one time cince we have bin in the country and Charles says he dont no wether he ever will make that mush or not; that he feels old now that he has worked so hard. not only him that has worked I have worked hard as the next one in the Country and all I have is a living. if I did not work as I do we would be so mush behind that we never would get strate again and if I had never come to this Country I would have now what I have not and that is good health. we have dun the best we could cience hire we have been. every thing has been hy and is yet. baken is 28c per pound pork 25c per pound and beef 25c per pound muton 25c perpound and flower 7c per pound corn the same, wrice one bit pound, potatoes 6c pound, eggs $1.00 dosson. Chickens. one

---

[77] This letter further pictures the bad conditions among the Cherokee gold seekers in California.

dollar pieces and take one thing with another times is hard and no hopes of getting better. no the times is gon when Labor was from 5 to 8 a day for some people. it was good for some but not all. we thire would suspose that if one person could make that mush another could but it is some Lucky one that Strikes a good claim and makes his pile an goes home with plenty money. thire is ten men out of 15 that doe not make thire Board. them that are call rich are the cloucest ones now. we have lived clouce in order to get home some time but as soon as we get a little head something turns up that all has to go. now Mary Jane is sick not confine to her bed but blind in boath eays tha are not inflamed but thire is some thing wrong a bout her head that we no nothing a bout. I live in hops that it will come write a gain as she is young thow no telling what can be dun untill tryed. three monthes a go she was going to school and was learing as fast as a child could learn any where. She could read as fast as she could talk in the third reader. her eyes looks jest as tha did when well to other people but to us tha looks different if thire is is any one who now what to do please to write and tell us what to do. I would like to see you all one time more in this world and injoy the plasure of siting and talking with you all one time more. It is hard that we have bin in the Country 7 years the 6th day of October in 1857. it brings me now to think wether I ever will or not see you all again. have seen the teem with rig mueles all Belled but you nor tom Sure Watey neether was with them. it was a bout 4 weeks a go William come in and said I saw the bell[78] teem but did not see no Stan nor tom. when we was leaving home for this country you and tom said that you would be hear in two years.[79] you are not hear yet and now I say to Mr. Longknife if we doe not have moeny enought in two years to take us home I will then Baige mine and my childs way home. to stay hear and work as I do any longer then that time I will not put up with it if I can help it. I am willing to help all I can but I

---

[78] The writer was referring to the Bell family.

[79] This indicates that Stand Watie had planned going to California soon after 1850.

an tyeard of this Country. nothing more at present I give my respects to you all please to write as soon as get this I remain yours A Friend and well wisher[80]

Mrs. Barbra Longknife

To Mr. Stan Watie

⌐₰W. A. Duncan to Sarah C. Watie

Mrs. Sallie Watie   [January] 27th, 1858

Dear Sister,

After I came home I spoke to Mr. Torry about our having a two days meeting at Honey Creek. He is so situated that he could not go till sometime in March. I have agreed with Bob Bassham to go this round on his Circuit and let him go round mine, but I found I have to go after Annie which would throw me two days too late to meet his appointment. I will try and go up anyhow when I get round [the] Circuit again.[81] I will now tell the news. Margaret Garvin was buried a few days ago. Cook Still is on trial for the murder of John Chambers. Old Aunt Nancy had a *"grand social party"* a short time ago. Martin Bell is ma[rri]ed to John Harnages daughter. I am not married [ye]t. I am so fraid all the gals will marry off before I get a chance.

Cham[berlin got] a letter from Nancy at her uncle Same's. He said she spoke of staying there. Nothing more at present.

No more at present.

W. A. Duncan

P.S. We are all well. My sweet little boys are as pretty and cheerful as birds. This brings up a serious thought. What am I to do? who will make a suitable mother? That's the question. There are ladies whom I could love, but I do not *know*

---

[80] It has been necessary for the editors to insert periods in this letter to make it intelligible except by great effort on the part of the reader. The original is entirely devoid of punctuation marks.

[81] The writer was a circuit preacher in the Cherokee Nation.

they would be good to my little orphans. Sallie I wish you would advise me.[82]

W. A. D.

Sallie, be sure and write to me by brother Bassham. I have requested him to bring the news.

D.

⌁ P. D. Clarke[83] to Sarah C. Watie

Amherstburg Canada West
Jan. 7th, 1859.

DEAR MADAM:

It is enough to make you believe that I have entirely forgotten you for neglecting to write you any more. But I have thought of you often and have never forgotten the many kind favours you have done me. When I look back in times past and reflect upon your hospitality and kindness towards me, it comes home to me that it would be ungrateful in me to never write to you and let you know that I am living and how I am getting along. A little over two years ago I came back to this Country with Sabra and she has been here ever since. Next April will be two years since I was at Kansas last. We are living on the old homestead which my Mother has given me. She is getting old and nearly helpless, otherwise I would be now living in Kansas. I try to content myself by carrying on some Kind of business. Our place fronts on the delightful River Detroit and I like to live here on account of its being so very healthy. Since we came back here I have built a Dock and a store house on it. It is a grand landing place for Steam boats and vessels. I sell wood to some of the steamers when they are running and sell groceries.

We have plenty of snows, good sleighing and the weather is just Cold enough to make one feel good. Tomorrow we go

---

[82] The Reverend Duncan's wife, Martha (Bell) Duncan and a sister of Mrs. Sarah C. Watie, had died shortly before this letter was written leaving three small children.

[83] This letter was written by a Wyandotte Indian friend of the Watie's.

up to the City of Detroit, sixteen miles from here, in a sleigh. I have a pair of Canadian horses that can trot off at a brisk rate.

We have a comfortable home and enough to live on here, yet after all I'd like to be in the West about Kansas or down some where in your Country, buying Coon Skins. And another thing the Pikes Peak and Arizona Mines are Causing a great stir these days, in the West.[84] I'd like to be out in those Regions. I have a nephew in Kansas who writes me that he is going to the new discovered gold mines next Spring, a son of my brother George that died at Wyandott nearly a year ago now, he died of Irycipilas, this fatal disease was raging there then. I was Sorry and I feel sorry for him yet. His wife and one of his daughters, died in times when the irycipilas was in the neighborhood. Only one son and daughter are living now out of the family.

Since the last Treaty the Wyandott Nation are pretty much broke up. Some have emigrated to the Senecas. Some to Ohio and some remains in Kansas.

Give my best Respects to Mr. Watie. It would give me the most heartfelt pleasure to hear from you.

I hope you are all well.

Sabra is in good health

Nothing more at present from your friend,

To Mrs. Sarah C. Watie   P. D. Clarke
Cherokee Nation.

◄§ Stand Watie to Sarah C. Watie

Millwood, September 22nd, 1859.

MY DEAR WIFE:

It is now four weeks since you left.[85] No tidings but once and that was a letter you wrote from Fort Smith but mailed at Waldron. We are all well. Miskey is here with me.[86] There is

---

84 The discovery of gold in 1858, in the Rocky Mountain area of Colorado and in Arizona, was followed by a large immigration into that section.

85 Mrs. Watie was visiting her relatives in Texas.

a good deal of sickness through the country, several deaths, among those you will be sorry to hear of the death of the great cancer doctor, Standing Deer. He died about two weeks ago. You see there is one great secret lost. Mrs. Sam Hildebrand is dead, left two young babes, twins. Jacob Alberty's wife is also dead, so is old Mike Hildebrand, the great mill wright.

There was a sad accident happened a few days after you left, in our neighborhood. Little Jim Conner had his hand ground up and the flesh stripped from the bone up to his elbow. They were crushing Chinese sugar corn, when his hand got caught in it. He lay over twenty-four hours before they could get a doctor to do anything with it. Doctor Hoyt was afraid to undertake it. Doctor Thompson was not at home. Booth was not found, James would not come. Sloan came the next day. For the want of proper instruments, he went to work with Hoyt's big Bowie knife. The little fellow bore the mangling butchery like a *hero*. His arm was taken off between the elbow and shoulder. Poor boy, I feel sorry for him. After his arm was taken off I took our little boys to see him. He told them how it happened. He said he could hear the bones of his hand crack. He is doing well. Tom Monroe was shot a few days ago through both thighs by some person unknown. He will get well.

Bob Parks shot John Ramsey, broke his arm and shattered his shoulder which may kill him. I am told that Bob was justified in shooting him.[87] Saladin started to Fayetteville on Friday before the first Monday of this month and took sick at Bill Buffington's and stayed there until Thursday following. Tom went with him. He says he was well when he left him. I thought when I commenced this letter that I had a great deal of news to tell you, but now I don't know what it is. I have forgotten it. It is useless for me to say that I very much wish you back for you know well that I do. How do you find the

[86] Cumiskey, or Miskey as he was commonly called, was Stand Watie's third son.

[87] This letter indicates how far disorder again prevailed in the Cherokee Nation.

folks in Texas? Are they friendly kind of people or do they all go in for the Almighty Dollar? How do the children like their kin? Do they ever speak of their Daddy? Tell them that I shake hands with them, and you too. Kiss the children for me. We are making a great deal of lumber at the mill now. Miskey sends love to you, and the little sisters.

Affectionately yours,
STAND WATIE

Much respect to every body. Tell me something about my friend Kitt. I had almost forgotten. Julia Candy is married. John is the happy man. Mrs. Morris and three of her children have been convicted. They are to be executed Saturday, the 24th. Shame to our country. I did not attend the trial Miskey was sick at the time when I was to go. George McPherson broke custody.

✑§ CHAPTER III ᠍᠍ᵇᵉ

A NATION IN ARMS

AT the outbreak of the War between the States the Indians of the Five Civilized Tribes were included in what was known as the Southern Superintendency which was administered from Fort Smith. The Superintendent was Elias Rector of Arkansas. Under his direction and control were the various Indian agents, usually one for each tribe except that the Chickasaw and Choctaw had a single agent for both tribes in the person of Douglas H. Cooper. These agents were charged with the details of transacting all business between the United States and the tribe to which they were accredited. All of them, as well as Elias Rector, were Southern men and, when war actually broke out all resigned their positions and were provisionally retained by the Confederate government for service among the Indians.

The Confederacy was eager to form an alliance with the Indians of the Five Civilized Tribes. It was felt that they could not only furnish a considerable number of soldiers for service along the border or as home guards, but Southern officials also reported that their great numbers of cattle would be sufficient to supply meat for the entire Confederate army. Accordingly in the spring of 1861 Albert Pike was made Commissioner to the Five Civilized Tribes by President Jefferson Davis, with instructions to proceed to the Indian Territory and attempt to secure treaties allying these Indian nations with the South.

Pike journeyed from Little Rock to Fort Smith and from there to Tahlequah and Park Hill. Everything seemed to favor his mission. Before the actual outbreak of war the federal troops in the Indian Territory had been withdrawn, leaving the Indians with no protection against the forces of the Confederacy. Also, the annuities due these various tribes from the sale of their lands in the East had not been sent to them in 1861, since officials of the United States feared that the money might fall into the hands of the South.

Before Pike reached Tahlequah, however, Chief Ross had called a convention or mass meeting of the Cherokee people. Here he made a speech in which he declared that the Cherokee were friendly to both North and South and, in his opinion, should maintain a policy of strict neutrality in the impending conflict. The convention accordingly expressed its confidence in its leaders and voted that the entire matter should be left in the hands of the regularly constituted authorities of the Cherokee Nation.

In the interview between Pike and Chief Ross, held at the latter's home near Park Hill, Ross reaffirmed his opinion that the Cherokee should take no part in the struggle between North and South but should remain entirely neutral. This position he steadfastly maintained in spite of Pike's pleadings. Grievously disappointed, the Confederate Commissioner accordingly left the Cherokee Nation for the Choctaw-Chickasaw country where he was warmly received, since these Indians had already voted to join the South.

Having signed a treaty with the Chickasaw-Choctaw by which they were allied with the Confederacy, Pike proceeded to the Creek and Seminole. These also signed treaties of alliance in spite of the bitter opposition of a considerable element in each tribe that declared it would not be bound by the action of the majority. From the Creek and Seminole countries Pike journeyed to Shirley's trading house on the Washita near the site of the present town of Anadarko. Here he met representatives of a number of bands of the wild tribes of the plains residing in that region and secured treaties with them. It was not until early autumn that he was able to return to the Cherokee country and, in the meantime, conditions there had changed. A number of adventurous young men of the tribe had hurried across the Arkansas line to join the army of General McCulloch. Companies of home guards had been formed and most of the anti-Ross faction was earnestly urging an alliance with the South. The fact that the other Indian nations had joined with the Confederacy also had its effect. Chief Ross became convinced that the Cherokee could not stand alone in its position of neutrality and decided that they must follow the example of the neighboring tribes and sign with Pike a treaty of alliance.

This was done early in October. By this treaty the Confederate States of America agreed to assume all obligations due the Cherokee from the government of the United States. This included a guarantee of title to their lands and the payment of annuities. It was further stipulated that the Confederate States should protect the Cherokee against invasion and furnish them with arms and ammunition to protect themselves. They were to be allowed a delegate to the Confederate Congress and might enlist soldiers for service with the Confederate army but were not to be called upon to fight outside the Indian Territory.

Much pleased with the complete success of his mission, Pike returned to the Confederate capital but was soon sent back and placed in command of the troops in the Indian Territory. In the meantime, strife had broken out between the Northern and Southern factions of the Creeks. The former under the leadership of Opoth-le-yo-hola were at first successful but, late in December, 1861, were defeated by the southern Creeks at the battle of Chus-te-nah-lah. The demoralized loyal Creeks fled from the field back to their camp, where they hastily assembled their women and children and continued their flight toward the north. The weather was bitterly cold and the fugitives suffered terrible hardships. At last they reached the military camp of General Hunter in Kansas where their most immediate needs were in part supplied from his army stores.

Here they were joined by many other loyal refugee Indians including a considerable number of Cherokee. They spent the remainder of the winter in refugee camps near General Hunter's encampment enduring untold misery from hunger, cold, and disease.

After the treaty with Pike had been signed, the Cherokee troops that had been enlisted as home guards definitely entered the Confederate service. Additional troops were quickly enlisted and Stand Watie was chosen colonel of the second Cherokee regiment of mounted rifles. He immediately demonstrated those qualities of military genius which were eventually to make him the most distinguished Indian leader in the service of the Confederacy. His ability was clearly shown very early in March, 1862, at the Battle of Pea Ridge.

When spring came the refugee Indians were eager to return to their homes. It was decided, therefore, to form two regiments of Indian soldiers and place them with two regiments of white troops for an invasion of the Indian Territory.

The expedition was organized and moved south under the command of Colonel William Weer. Stand Watie and Colonel John Drew fell back before this overwhelming force. Weer advanced to Tahlequah and Park Hill, where Chief John Ross was made prisoner. He was immediately released on parole, however, and soon after went to Philadelphia where he remained until the close of the war. It seemed that the entire Indian Territory might be occupied and the Southern Indians driven out, but difficulties arose between Colonel Weer and his second in command Colonel Frederick Salomon. The latter asserted that his superior was either insane or plotting treason, and placed Weer under arrest and himself took command of the expedition. Salomon ordered a retreat and the entire force returned to Kansas where the Indians spent another miserable winter in refugee camps.

In the spring of 1863 a second invasion of Indian Territory was made by a force under the command of Colonel William A. Phillips. This expedition advanced south, seized Tahlequah and occupied Fort Gibson from which point raiding expeditions were sent out from time to time. In the wake of Phillips' army came the non-combatant refugees from their camps in Kansas to reoccupy their homes, and drive out the Southern sympathizers. The latter fled from their homes to refugee camps along the Red River in the Choctaw country or, in some cases, to Texas.

In the meantime, a large part of the Cherokee bitterly complained that the South had not kept its promises to them as

101

laid down in the treaty of October, 1861. Very early in the spring of 1862 Indian troops had been taken to Arkansas where they fought in the battle of Pea Ridge. After this defeat Pike fell back to Fort McCulloch in the southwestern part of the Choctaw country and it seemed to many Cherokee that he had abandoned them. With the fall of Vicksburg and Lee's retreat from Gettysburg it seemed, moreover, that the fortunes of the Confederacy were on the wane.

At a meeting held on Cowskin Prairie early in 1863 the Cherokee repudiated their alliance with the South. Stand Watie and the Southern wing, however, refused to consider this action as that of the tribe and during the latter part of the war there were in reality two Cherokee Nations. One was the Northern wing, claiming John Ross as principal chief and asserting loyalty to the North. The other still clung firmly to the South and had chosen Stand Watie as chief. Each group insisted that it was the real Cherokee Nation and the other only a faction.

The year 1863 closed with the Cherokee Nation in this chaotic condition. The North was largely in control of the country. Stand Watie and other Southern leaders were with their troops in the field, while their wives and children and men too old or infirm to fight were, for the most part, huddled in refugee camps in the southern part of the Choctaw country along Red River.

⋙ Elias Cornelius Boudinot to Stand Watie

Fayetteville Feb. 12, 1861

DEAR UNCLE,

Saladin handed me your letter requesting me to meet you as soon as possible and come to some definite understanding concerning the matter of which Aunt Sarah has spoken. Tomorrow I must go to Evansville to attend to a law suit, or I would go back with "Uncle Tom." Next Monday is the election and the day after I shall go down to see you, unless detained by pressing business. But lest something might prevent I will here apprise you of my plans in the speculating line.

I wish you to assist me in purchasing improvements on Grand River where large farms may be hereafter made. And I also intend to purchase on the Arkansas river. A few hundred dollars together with stock may be expended in this way, which will in a short time return an immense percentage. My own means will go but little ways, but a gentleman — whose name I will tell you when we meet — who has made a fortune already in land speculation stands ready to back me, however extensively I *go in*.[1] In cooperating with me you may turn your stock to great advantage. The Vann place at Webbers falls was offered me a year ago for $2500. One half payable in stock. I will give that sum for the place now. The John Buffington place above your farm on Grand River, Aunt Sally tells me, may be bought and from accounts I would like to get it. Any trade you will make I will ratify.

This gentleman of whom I speak says you have a foundation for an immense fortune, land only considered.

I must be at Little Rock by the 2nd of March and consequently cannot be with you but two or three days, if I go down next week. I wrote you a letter two or three days ago on our business matters.

I am firmly of your opinion that *"now is the time to strike"* and that quickly. There is money in it and we can make it.

I hope to see you in a few days when we can talk the matter over more thoroughly when we see each other.

The State authorities at Little Rock have taken possession of the Arsenal there. The Southern Confederacy in Convention assembled at Montgomery Alabama unanimously elected Jeff Davis of Miss. and Alexander Stevens of Georgia President & Vice P. of the seceded states.[2] Active preparations are being made to commence an attack on Ft. Sumpter and the

[1] Only improvements could be bought, since all Cherokee lands were held in common. The purchase of improvements, however, entitled the buyer to possession of the land as long as he used or cultivated it.

[2] On February 4, 1861, a week before the date of this letter, representatives of the seven Southern states that had passed ordinances of secession met in convention at Montgomery, Alabama, and bound themselves together under the title of the *Confederate States of America*.

attack and capture are considered a foregone conclusion.[3] John Ross has published a letter in the Van Buren [paper] in which he says the Cherokees will go with Arkansas and Missouri.[4]

Love to all   As ever
CORNELIUS

◄§ L. P. Walker[5] to Douglas H. Cooper[6]

Confederate States of America
War Department

Maj. Douglas H. Cooper   Montgomery May 13th 1861
Choctaw Nation

SIR — the desire of this Government is to cultivate the most friendly relations & the closest alliance with the Choctaw Nation and all the Indian tribes West of Arkansas and South of Kansas. Appreciating your sympathies with these tribes and the reciprocal regard for you, we have thought it advisable to enlist your services in the line of this desire. From information in possession of the Government it is deemed expedient to take measures to secure the protection of these tribes in their present Country from the aggressive rapacity of the North that unless opposed, must soon drive them from their homes and supplant them in their possessions, as indeed, would have been the case with the entire south but for present efforts at resistence.

It is well known that with these unjust designs against the Indian country the Northern Movement for several years has

---

[3] A state of war existed from the formation of the Confederacy and the seizure by the states of the arsenals and other federal property. The actual hostilities did not begin, however, until the bombardment of Fort Sumter on April 12, 1861.

[4] John Ross was a large slave owner. Whether he actually favored the South or not is a disputed question. Perhaps at this time he was merely attempting to win the favor of the people of these states, since their hostility in this troubled period would be fraught with grim consequences to the Cherokees.

[5] Leroy Pope Walker, a native of Alabama, was the first secretary of war in the newly formed Confederate government. He was appointed to President Davis' cabinet in February, 1861.

[6] Douglas H. Cooper had been United States agent for the Chickasaws and Choctaws for a number of years before the outbreak of the war.

104

had its emisaries among the tribes for their ultimate distruction. Their destiny has thus become our own and common with that of all the Southern states entering this confederation.

Entertaining these Views & feelings and with these objects before us, we have commissioned Genl. Ben McCulloch,[7] with three Regiments under his command, from the States of Ark, Texas & Louisiana, to take charge of the Military District embracing the Indian Country. And I now empower you to raise among the Choctaw & Chickasaw a mounted regiment to be commanded by yourself in cooperation with Genl McCulloch.[8] It is designed also to raise two other similar Regiments among the Creeks, Cherokees, Seminoles and other friendly tribes, for the same purposes.

This combined force of six Regiments will be ample to secure the frontiers upon Kansas & the interest of the Indians while to the South of the Red River three Regiments from Texas under a different command have already [been] assigned to the Rio Grande & Western border.

It will thus appear I trust that the resources of this Government are adequate to its ends and assured to the friendly Indians.

We have our agents actively engaged in the manufacture of amunition and in the purchase of arms, and when your Regiment has been recruited organized in ten Companies ranging from sixty four to one hundred men each and enrolled for twelve months if possible, it will be received in the confederate service and supplied with arms and amunition.

Such will be the course pursued also in relation to the two other Regiments I have indicated. The arms we are purchasing for the Indians are Rifles & they will be forwarded to Fort Smith.

> Respectfully
> L. P. WALKER
> Secretary of War

[7] Major Ben McCulloch of Texas, was appointed brigadier general in the Confederate army in May, 1861.

[8] In obedience to this order Douglas H. Cooper raised the first Choctaw and Chickasaw Rifles of which he became colonel.

⤳A. M. Wilson and J. W. Washbourne to Stand Watie

Fayetteville Ark

Capt. Stand Watie,   May 18th, 1861

Dr. Sir:

Several of our citizens addressed lately a letter to you on behalf of a meeting of the County held in this place, on the 6th of May last, and on behalf of the County and State, urging you, as a private and public citizen of the Cherokee Nation, to join us in our efforts for mutual defence.

Every day strengthens the probability that the soil of the Cherokee People will be wrested from them unless they bow down to Abolitionism and every day convinces us that it is very important that the Cherokee be up and doing to defend their soil, their homes, their firesides, aye their very existence. To this end the State of Arkansas and the Confederate Government will also strive, and bloodless will not be any victory over us. The integrity of the soil of the Southern Indians must and shall be maintained. We shall do all that men can do to so maintain them.

We are happy to inform you in accordance with our promise of said letter that we would afford you all the aid we could that a certain number of guns, good guns, have been granted to the State of Arkansas, for the use of the Cherokees in the defence of their and our frontier. So, push on the good work and train your men and apply for these guns. Under your management they will certainly do effective service for the Cherokee soil and so serve Arkansas as effectually. We earnestly exhort you to take this matter immediately in hand and advise that you should hasten to the organization of your companies.

It is reported that Jim Lane, the notorious Abolitionist, robber, murderer and rascal now disgracing a seat in the old U.S. Senate from Kansas has been recently appointed Cherokee Agent.[9] If this be true, you will know what it portends. The

---

[9] James H. Lane, United States senator from Kansas, was busy raising troops in that state to be used against Missouri and Arkansas.

subjugation of the Cherokee to the rule of Abolition, and the overwhelming of the race before the hordes of greedy Republicans. Of course you will all be prepared to repel so distasteful an appointment, and resist all efforts to enslave the Cherokees.

We should be pleased to hear from you, your success in organizing your people and concerning their feelings and intentions in the present state of war. The interest of the Cherokees are identical with ours, we feel them to be so and we will do all in our power to aid and protect them.

Respectfully,
Your Obt. Servt.
J. W. Washbourne
A. M. Wilson

P.S. Since writing to you I have learned that it is not Lane appointed Cherokee Agent, but that a man, by name of Griffin a Black Republican is appointed Superintendent and Lane is to protect him with an army. It amounts to the same thing, As to the guns, 2500, with large amount of ammunition, have recently been sent up for this region in which I hear the Cherokees are to share. How many guns they may get I do not know. But raise a company and send on the request, that they be furnished with the guns and ammunition. We shall strive to have at least 200 guns sent you.

J. W. Washbourne
A. M. Wilson

P.S. Again, Since the above I hear that President Davis is determined to arm the Cherokees, Creeks and Choctaws. Probably in the course of six or eight weeks there will be many guns for the Cherokees. Two regiments of Arkansas troops will soon be concentrated somewhere near Maysville. Communications from the South part of the State are already arriving here, and the two Regiments will be ready, fully equipped.

We will do our part towards keeping back the Kansas rascals. The Cherokees ought to be silent in their preparations for Lane does not anticipate any opposition from them, so they can the more easily ambush and surprise him & take *booty*. I have written to the Creeks. They have six companies of warriors ready at call.

J. W. W.

107

ᎦᎤ William P. Adair[10] and James M. Bell to Stand Watie

Col. Stand Watie,   Grand River, Aug. 29th 1861

DEAR FRIEND,

You have doubtless heard all about Ross's Convention, which in reality tied up our hands & shut our mouths & put the destiny & everything connected with the Nation & our lives &c in the hands of the Executive.[11] You no doubt have seen A. Pike's letter as published to the Chief etc.[12] Pike is disposed to favor us and to disregard the course our executive has taken. The Pins already have more power in their hands than we can bear & if in addition to this they acquire more power by being the Treaty making power, you know our destiny will be inalterably sealed.[13] It seems we should guard against this. Now is the time for us to strike, or we will be completely frustrated. Wm. Ross has already sent a runner to see Pike to win him over and every means by Ross is now being used to draw the Agent [Crawford] on his side. Ross's Resolution adopted at the Convention, endorses. Ist. his neutral policy, 2nd. his correspondence with Gen. McCulloch & Mr. Hubbard Commissioner, & 3rd. they recommend continual friendship as well with the Northern as Southern States hereafter, 4th. they give the Executive the sole right in his wisdom to transact all matters of interest that may pend with the U.S. or Confederate States, 5th. they dont say a word about a Treaty with the South-

10 William Penn Adair was a member of a prominent Cherokee family. He was an active leader of the Treaty Party and a close friend to Stand Watie.

11 The convention here referred to was the mass meeting in which it was agreed to leave everything to Chief Ross and the regularly constituted authorities of the Cherokee Nation.

12 Albert Pike was of New England birth, but had lived for many years in Arkansas. He had been a soldier in the war with Mexico and had risen to the rank of captain. He had been appointed commissioner to the Five Civilized Tribes by President Davis and, at the time this letter was written, had already made treaties of alliance with all of the Five Civilized Tribes except the Cherokee.

13 The Kee-too-wah, or Pins, the full-blood organization referred to in the preceding chapter, were unanimous in their support of the North.

ern Confederacy, which is the most essential thing. Every thing is yet left open at the discreation and "wisdom" of the Executive whether to continue neutral or prolong a Treaty indefinitely or make a Treaty at all or to renew even our covenants with the *old North*.[14] Under these circumstances our Party, [the Southern Rights Party] want you and Dr. J. L. Thompson to go in person and have an interview with Mr. Pike to the end that we may have justice done us, have this pin party broken up, and our rights, provided for and place us if possible at least on an honorable equity with this old Dominant party that has for years had its foot upon our necks. We have selected you for reasons that we will not name on account of modesty, but which will appear obvious to you, from the well known fact that you have had an honorable reputation abroad in the South for years and are well known by A. Pike and many other prominent Statesmen of the South. If you will go, please come right away & see Dr. Thompson as you will see we have no time to spare. I am at this time quite unwell and have not been well for 4 weeks. I just got home yesterday from Tahlequah and am completely worn out, If you can't go please to send us a note and let us know but if possible you must go.

Yours fraternally,

W. P. ADAIR

P.S. If you see J. S. Night please to tell him for me that if I do not get to Delaware Circuit Court next month to have his case put off as in all probability I will not be able to be present.

Yours.

Col. Stand. Watie   W. P. ADAIR
DR. SIR

There is one thing to which Wm. P. Adair has not adverted and that is Ross has ordered the raising of twelve hundred men, John Drew Col. Tom Pegg Lieut. Col. Wm. P. Ross Major.[15]

---

[14] This indicates that the growing sentiment for a treaty with the Confederacy was soon to influence Chief Ross to make a treaty with Pike.

[15] Apparently these were home guards to defend the Cherokee country. John Drew was later a colonel in the Confederate service; Tom Pegg served as acting chief in 1863 during the absence of Chief Ross; and William P. Ross,

now I have been under the impression that these were commissioned by the Confederate States. It will require a rapid and prompt movement on our part or else we are done up. All of our work will have been in vain, our prospects destroyed, our rights disregarded, and we will be slaves to Ross's tyranny. write back immediately what we must do, it dont do for you to hold back, declare yourself ready to serve your country in what ever capacity we may want you.

Yours truly

Stand Watie Esqr. JAMES M. BELL

Blue Springs D. D. C. N.

◄§ Elias Cornelius Boudinot to Stand Watie

Honey Creek, Oct. 5, 1861

DEAR UNCLE,

I went down to see you to-day but could not get across the river. I can say by note, however, what I wished to say in person. Just as I left Tahlequah Tom Taylor came to me and told me to tell you that he would start for your headquarters Monday next and then told me that you had promised to have him appointed Lt. Col. I hope there is some mistake about this for of all men I think him least deserving and least fitted for that post; he is as you know a timid flexible wavering unstable speculating politician always ready to profit by the labors of others and selfish to the last degree. You told me in Tahlequah if I would go with you you would do a good part by me. *I am willing and anxious to go with you* and as you have it in your power to do a good part by me, and thinking without vanity, that I deserve something from your hands I venture to ask from you either the Lt. Col. or the Major's place. I do not wish the post of Adjutant or any other than one of the two I have named. If any accident, which God forbid, should happen to you so that another would have to take your place, you will see

---

nephew of John Ross, was twice chosen to fill vacancies in the office of principal chief.

the importance of having some one in responsible position to keep the power you now have from passing into unreliable hands.

John Ross and you are rivals, he has appointed his nephew Lt. Col. intent on keeping a foothold in the military organization; perhaps my appointment would give dissatisfaction to some, a great many no doubt want and some expect it, but you can't please all and I hope you will judge as your own feelings dictate. I have been a dray horse for Tom Taylor and others like him ever since I figured in the Nation. I have made sacrifices for them continually while they got all the pay. You have it in your power now to put me in a position where I can do honor to myself and to you. Will you not give it to me? Send your answer by the boy. I will go to Fayetteville and if your answer is favorable I will purchase some things you will need, and return next week.[16]

As ever
Your Nephew
CORNELIUS

P.S. Destroy this as soon as you have read it.

B.

◄§ Stand Watie to Douglas H. Cooper

Steam Mill Deleware Dist.
Cherokee Nation Feb. 19 1862.

COLONEL—

I came to this place day before yesterday for the purpose of investigating certain matters of which Col. Drew has complained and reporting the *facts,* as near as I could obtain them.[17]

---

[16] Apparently Boudinot was successful in his plea, as he soon became a major in Stand Watie's regiment. It seems that political life was more to his liking than military service, however, as he later was elected as delegate to the Confederate Congress at Richmond. His chief service to the Cherokee during this period was in his work at the Confederate capital.

[17] Shortly before the Battle of Bird Creek four companies of Colonel John Drew's regiment deserted and went over to the side of Opothleyoholo, leader of the Northern Creeks. Stand Watie may have been referring to this incident and the possible effect this Cherokee desertion might have on the remaining forces.

As I said in my letter written to you a few days ago, No one can regret the killing of "Chunestootie" by my *"Nephew"* more than myself, for aside from the circumstance itself, I am well aware that the personal relations of myself with the unfortunate faction is seized upon with avidity by those whose only ambition seems to be to misrepresent and injure me.[18] Great stress seems to be laid in Col. Drews letter — upon the facts that Chunestootie was a member of Capt. John Ross' Company and accompanied you in your late expedition against Yopothleyoholo and that Charles Webber, who it is charged killed him, is the "Nephew of Stand Watie." I regret exceedingly to see this, as it does not tend to reconcile the factions already too bitter for the good of the country. Chunestootie has been for years past hostile to southern people and their institutions; he was active last summer in repressing southern movements with a strong hand, with the advise and assistance, as I am assured, of Capt John Ross, "who accompanied you in your recent expedition"; he went at the head of many others of like opinions, to Tahlequah, last summer, for the avowed purpose of butchering any and all who should attempt to raise a southern flag — the flag was not *raised* as you perhaps remember[19] as to his accompanying you in your late expedition, it is well known to Col Drew that 400 or 500 others also accompanyed you in a similar expedition and did themselves but little honor. So I cannot see the significance of the fact that Chunestootie was along on your recent expedition. I would not tread roughly upon the ashes of the dead and will not mention other things in connection with this unfortunate person, which would detract from such sympathy as may be bestowed upon him; and indeed I should have said nothing concerning him had I not perceived an effort to prejudice the matter. The Killing was done by one beside himself with liquor; he was alone and the asser-

[18] Chunestootie was killed and scalped by Charles Webber, nephew of Stand Watie.

[19] As previously indicated the Cherokees were by no means unanimous in their support of the South and it was not until October, 1861 that they became formally allied with the Confederacy.

tion that there were others who participated in the scalping is wilfully false. No one assisted at the killing or had a hand in that scalping, but all regretted the deed and none more than I. It is futile at this time to think of settling the affair according to the usual course of law—you are aware that such an attempt would end in "unaccountable confusion" and the breach between parties becoming wider than ever.

It is better to advise quiet and peace until such time as the matter can be calmly and dispassionately considered.

The report of the killing of Arch Snail is also, as I believe, purposely misrepresented. He also is claimed as a member of Capt. Hildebrands company[20] and, Col. Drew might have added, "accompanied you in your *former Expedition* against Hopotheyohola."[21] He *did* accompany you, deserted with hundreds of others to the enemy, fought against us, and did not even accept the poor excuse invented by Mr. Ross, that "he did'nt know what he was doing"; he was traveling in company with two of my regiments, when he suddenly darted into the thicket, firing the first shot which was succeeded by shots from the thicket from persons unknown to my men; the admission of Col. Drew that there were two others of his regiment along explains the Extra shots, and convinces me that my men were waylaid. Snail was killed with his own pistol. As to the other two assassins I know nothing of them, but presume that they are safe in Col. Drew's camps.

This is called a barbarous crime and shocks the sensitive nerves of Col. Drew, Mr. Ross and others, who of course have never participated in the shedding of innocent blood.

I have written Col. more an answer to Col. Drew's letter

[20] Captain Isaac N. Hildebrand was in command of Company D. of the 1st Regiment of Cherokee Mounted Rifles under Colonel John Drew.

[21] Sentiment in the Creek Nation was also much divided on the question of an alliance with the Confederacy. The Southern wing signed a treaty with Albert Pike, but a large group under the leadership of Opothleyoholo remained loyal to the North. On December 26, 1861 Opothleyoholo and his troops were defeated by the Southern Creeks and driven north to Kansas, where they were later joined by a number of loyal Cherokee and Seminole.

than to yours. I have given the facts of the affair, mentioned by you as truthfully as my means of information would allow.

I have the honor to remain
Very respectfully
Yr. Frd. and obt. serv.

To   STAND WATIE
D. H. Cooper   Col. Comdg. 1st Chero. Regt.
Col. Comdr. Indian Brigade

✒️ Stand Watie[22] to Albert Pike[23]

Flint District C. N.
BRIGADIER GENEL. PIKE;   Feb. 27th 1862

According to your order of the 17th in. I reported in advance of the arrival of my command, to Genl. McCulloch;[24] on my return to the camp found the Regt. had marched on to Fort Davis.[25] The information upon which your order of the 25th is founded of the advance of Hopotheyohola is altogether an error.[26] Men have come in whom I had previously placed high up on the Neosho. They report nothing of the kind. I have therefore recalled my command to this vicinity. I enclose a letter from Genl. McCulloch to yourself in pencil marks it was written on the road.

Respectively your Obt Servant
STAND WATIE
Vol. C. S. A.   Col. 1st Regt Cherokee.

[22] In 1861, Stand Watie and the men who had served with him earlier in Delaware district and in the Neutral Lands formed the First Regiment of Cherokee Mounted Volunteers. Stand Watie was elected colonel of the regiment.

[23] Albert Pike had been given the commission of brigadier general. On March 7, 1862, only a few days after the date of this letter, Pike commanded a regiment of Indians at the Battle of Pea Ridge.

[24] Benjamin McCulloch, appointed brigadier general in May 1861 was killed in the Battle of Pea Ridge.

[25] Fort Davis, a fortified position on the south side of the Arkansas River opposite the mouth of Grand River, was later destroyed by the Union forces under Colonel Phillips.

[26] The report that Opothleyoholo was returning to the Indian Territory was obviously incorrect, for the old Creek chief was to die in exile before many months had passed.

⊷§ Albert Pike to Stand Watie

North Fork Village
1st April 1862.

COLONEL:

I think it due to you, in view of your loyalty to the cause in which we are engaged and in which all we have or are is at stake, that I should acquaint you with my intentions in regard to the defence of the Indian Country.

If the forces of Generals Van Dorn and Price had held the western part of Arkansas and controlled the roads running westward from Fort Smith, I would have placed myself on the south side of the Canadian River and invited an attack there, because I would then have had in front of me all the roads by which the enemy could safely advance. Fort Gibson and Fort Davis became equally intenable, when our forces abandoned the position north of Boston Mountain; both, because an enemy marching from the North can turn either position, by crossing the Arkansas above or below, and Gibson, because in addition receiving an attack there, we should fight with a river on our left and one behind us, defeat would be ruin and retreat impossible.

As long as our forces held the position North of Boston Mountain no enemy could safely march from Kansas or Missouri to Fort Gibson without first defeating those forces, because if he pass southward they could cut his line of communication and leave him without a base of operations, the result of which would be his utter destruction.

When those positions were abandoned, the positions at Gibson and Davis became worthless. The Canadian became the next line, behind which to with draw our supplies. I meant then to fortify and hold the position at Scalesville south of the Canadian.

Unexpectedly, all western Arkansas is abandoned, Fort Smith invites its occupation by the enemy, and the roads in [the] rear of the line of the Canadian are proffered to him. It is certain that he will accept the offer, occupy Fort Smith,

115

and have it in his power to cut off from Red River and all supplies, any force on the Canadian. Hunter and Opothla Yahola
may also be expected to cross the Arkansas and Canadian higher up, reach Fort Cobb or Arbuckle, and then marching east-
ward to interpose between us and the Red River. That or a
movement from Fort Smith westward toward Boggy Depot,
would involve the destruction or surrender of any force on or
near the Canadian. At Starr's Settlement we should be like a
rat in a trap.

I will therefore, placing my supplies in my rear, take position beyond the point of junction of the roads from this place
and Fort Smith to Boggy Depot.[27] There I will concentrate
all the troops coming to me from Texas and Arkansas, throw
up field works in front and rear and invite attack from the
East, North or West. In front I will control the two only
roads. In the rear I will have three lines of defence, the three
Boggy's. Texas will be my base of operations and I will have
an uninterrupted line of communication Southward and easy
access to supplies.

I will keep your Regiment and Colonel Drew's in your own
Country.[28] You will give information of the approach of the
enemy, harrass his flanks and rear, stampede his animals, destroy his small foraging parties, and at last if he still advances,
gaining his front join me within my lines and aid in utterly
defeating him there. I beg your men to bury all old animosities
and remember only that all are now fighting for the honour,
independence and safety of the Confederate States and the
Cherokee People.

The Creek and Seminole troops I will keep in their own
country, to render similar service. The Choctaw and Chickasaw troops I will have near me to aid or as occasion may offer.

[27] General Pike had been censured by the Cherokee for establishing his
headquarters in the Choctaw country and not farther north where he would
have been on hand to prevent invasions from Kansas.

[28] Pike may be commended for insisting that the Indians should fight in
their own country and in their own manner.

116

I will not abandon your country.[29] You will be my advanced Guard. I shall have four Regiments of well mounted Texas Cavalry. I will send them alternately into your country, to aid in harassing any invading force. Listen to no report that I mean to abandon your country. If our forces had remained at Boston Mountain, as McCulloch always advised, the Northern Armies would have been compelled to make an inglorious retreat or incurred certain defeat by an attack on our position. I will not let the enemy gain my rear and compel our destruction or surrender. I go to that point where calling to me the Indian troops from all quarters, I urgently hope and plan destruction to any force that may dare to attack our works.

This communication is entirely confidential I am, Colonel,
very truly and respectfully
Your friend and Servant.
ALBERT PIKE
Brig. Genl. Comndg Dept. of Ind. Div.

William P. Adair[30] to Stand Watie

COL WATIE,

As we have all our papers to fix up, it is impossible for me to send any of our Clerks up to attend to our business. I have employed J. W. Clayton[31] to act for me. He can give receipts with instructions that we will duplicate or pay for the stuff bought as the case may be when presented at our office. You will see that our Regiment is nearly out of Caps.[32] And I think it would be a good plan for you to send an express to Fort Smith after Caps. We have about Sixteen Kegs of powder & several Boxes Cartridges & several pigs lead. We are needing

[29] It must have seemed to many Southern Cherokees that Pike had already abandoned their country since he was now entrenched far south of the Cherokee southern boundary, not many miles north of Red River.

[30] William P. Adair enlisted in the 1st Cherokee Mounted Volunteers under Stand Watie and served as assistant quartermaster.

[31] J. W. Clayton was a private in Company J of the 1st Regiment of Cherokee Mounted Volunteers.

[32] Brass caps used for firing percussion lock guns and pistols.

caps worse than anything. We will keep you advised about what is going on down here if there is any danger. There is great Deal of sickness in our Regiment. Mr McNair died the other day.

Your friend

April 29th 1862   WM. P. ADAIR

❧ William P. Adair to Stand Watie

4th, May 1862
Grand Saline C. N.

COL WATIE,

Mr. Anderson can give you what little news we have[33] &c. Brother John this morning is some better but in a very feeble condition. I am fast improving tho not yet fit for business. I wish to have your advice as to whether our Q. Ms Bond will have to be renewed since father's death; if so shall I renew it?[34] To do so a trip will be necessary to Ft. Smith. Also, our Caps and some of our amunition brother Brice says are getting scarce. Shall I order more and how much and what kind? *Your* Duplicates will be duly attended to by me as I know more about the business Than any other. I had a thought of sending to Genl Pikes head Quarters for Stationery. Our paper is almost out. Any business that can be attended to in that quarter by my Expressman at your order will be attended to for you. Should I be under the necessity of sending, I would like to keep about two volunteers for expressmen if you are willing. You will please excuse our Clerks, as our business has so much accumulations in our hands.

We want to have our papers well posted by the expiration of our present Term of Service. I turned over two vacant waggons to Capt Livingston and took his receipt. He says he has a commission from Genl Pike to raise a Company to report to you and also to draw on your Regt if necessary for supplies &c

[33] This must have been Thomas F. Anderson, later Stand Watie's adjutant.
[34] The writer's father, George Washington Adair, had been quartermaster of this regiment.

118

&c. This brother Brice told me. Capt Livingston I learn will leave Grand River for your Camps tomorrow (Tuesday).

I remain as ever   Your friend

W. P. ADAIR

✑§ B. M. Adair[35] to Stand Watie

COL STAND WATIE,   At Home May 10th 1862

I send up to you to ask of you a great favor. It is to let Brother Wat[36] come down and see my wife. She is in a very critical condition & been so for several days but seems to be worse at this time. If there were any other doctors that had medicine & whom I had confidence about here I would not ask this of you. If you cannot possible spare him from the regiment, as a matter of course I will not complain for I know we all have our dutys to perform. But I am very anxious for Brother Wat to come and see my wife. You know the Anxiety which one feels for those who are dear to them when they are very sick. I am doubtful about her recovery if she does not get relief in 30 hours.   Truly yours Fraternally

B. M. ADAIR

P.S. We are getting [along] with our papers very well.

B. M. A.

✑§ Elias Cornelius Boudinot to Stand Watie

DEAR UNCLE,   Little Rock, Jan. 23, 1863.

I delayed proceeding to Richmond until I could know something definite concerning the fate of our army here, upon which rested the only hope of *our* country. I wished to carry such intelligence of the State of Affairs as would enable me to do more at Richmond than I could otherwise.[37] Marmaduke's

---

[35] Brice Martin Adair, brother of William P. Adair, became quartermaster upon the death of their father which had occurred a few weeks earlier.

[36] Dr. Walter Thompson Adair was one of the surgeons of the regiment.

[37] Boudinot had been chosen delegate to the Confederate Congress at Richmond.

success in Missouri [the taking of Springfield and Rolla],[38] VanDorn's splendid raids on Holly Springs and Memphis, the attitude of Kentucky in regard to the emancipation proclamation and many other matters that I might mention relieves my anxiety for the nation and the fate of the Confederate States. An early peace I think beyond doubt is inevitable.[39] The Post of Arkansas was carried by the Feds & Churchill and his army, 3,500 men taken prisoners. But *their* reverses elsewhere caused them to abandon in haste both the Arkansas and White rivers; if they should come to Little Rock, and with the present stage of water they could do so, they would be compelled to abandon it as soon as the river fell. In prospect of early peace it is all important that we should maintain *our* civil and military organization. I have procured a copy of the Late Treaty and find that such sums of money as may be due the Cherokees will be paid to *any person* authorized to receive it by the *"Constituted Authorities* of the Cherokee Nation." A good deal of money is due us and I suggest that the convention assemble and adopt the accompanying resolution authorizing me to receive such moneys, if they will pass this ordinance I am satisfied I can get the money, and with a full treasury you know what new life will be infused into our infant government.

Your buggy was taken from Fort Smith and run down to Judge Wheelers to keep it from falling into the hands of the enemy, in the general confusion, panic and stealage going on at Fort Smith I think it well it was taken off, though it doubtless has put you to much inconvenience. Wheeler lives 30 miles from Fort Smith nearly on the Waldron road. If John has got back you might send him home leading a horse and he could get it for you. I will keep you posted.

As ever Yours

CORNELIUS

P.S. If the convention adopts the ordinance send me an official

[38] Major General John S. Marmaduke had led an expedition into Missouri, capturing Springfield and Rolla.

[39] Boudinot's optimism is refreshing, but many others held the same opinion about this time.

letter as chief, enclosing the ordinance. Genl. Cooper will send it if you have no other way.[40]

BOUDINOT

⋙W. D. Polson[41] to Sarah C. Watie

Camp Near Scully...[42]
April 10th 1863

DEAR AUNT SARAH,

The Col. has just arrived in cam[p] looking quite well. I am Sorry indeed to hear [of] poor little Meska's death.[43] I can truly sympathize with you in this deep affliction. My youngest child died on the 18th of February. She took cold traveling from Fayetteville to Fort Smith and when I got to Fort Smith She had just died. O My feelings were indiscribable. I never can become reconciled to it and poor Flora She had not yet got over Henry's death & thought little Kates death would kill [her]. Well undoubtedly it is all for the best if we could look at it in the right way and [no] doubt they are far better off than those they left behind to grieve for them yet kno[wing] all this if I could bring my child back I *would*. Flora and Susan got over from Fayetteville and are living about three miles below Dardenelle. Susan is living with one of the Woodards Sisters and Flora boards about half a mile from her they had an awful time amongst the Federals they would take the bread out of the childrens hands and them [cryi]ng for it. The Pins have killed a great many good men. Some of them have

[40] When John Ross withdrew to Philadelphia following his capture and parole by Colonel William Weer, the Southern Cherokee claiming that he had abandoned the Nation elected Stand Watie principal chief. This position he held until the close of the war, though his right to the office was disputed by the Northern Cherokees who asserted that Ross was still chief.

[41] W. D. Polson married Flora Chamberlin Ridge, daughter of John Ridge. Descendants of this branch of the Ridge family live in Oklahoma today. Miss Frances Polson, granddaughter of the writer of this letter, has supplied the editors with information regarding the family.

[42] The original of this letter is in a fragmentary condition. The writer was doubtless writing from Camp Scullyville in the extreme northeastern corner of the Choctaw Nation, near Fort Smith.

[43] Cumiskey, Stand Watie's third son.

121

been Served the Same way. [I] think we will make a forward movement soon. [The] Pin families I understand have all moved back to the nation. Hinman Hoyt is dead and aunt Carrol has Elizabeth's child. Old Juda McGhee is dead. I told Judge Wheeler he could have that Carriage you got from Boudinot for what you gave for it and he took it though he did not pay the money for it but I Suppose he will soon. I thought as you did not get the Carriage when you most needed it you would not likely want it and another thing I did [not] know at what moment the enemy might come into Fort Smith and then it would be [lo]st. Wilson Wood's Wife is at Colemans near Fort Smith. She has a fine Son. Sela can tell [you] all the camp news. My love to all the children.

Truly Your Friend
W. D. Polson

◄§ James M. Bell[44] to Mrs. Caroline Bell

Skullyville C. N. May 16 1863

My own dear Carrie

I left camp three days ago near Ft. Gibson on detached duty to Ft. Smith to see Genl Steele in regard to army and to carry an order to Capt John Miller who was in the State of Arkansas getting recruits for our Regt and whom Genl Steele wrote about interfering with other commands and asked his removal to his command immediately. I was fortunate enough to meet the Capt on the road and went on to Ft Smith where I met Maj Boudinot & Woodard Washburn direct from Richmond. The Maj informed me that as soon as another Regiment could be raised we would be entitled to a Brigadier General and that Col Watie would receive the appointment certain,[45] we have two companies towards the Regt and will soon have the other eight as we are authorized to go into the States to raise them. You can tell Dr Dupree that I shall have him appointed Sur-

---

[44] Bell was at this time a captain in Stand Watie's regiment.

[45] It was not until the following year, on May 10, 1864, that Stand Watie received from President Davis the appointment of brigadier general.

geon of that Regiment if things don't take some *mighty* changes. I have already told him that Col Watie was desirous of securing him a situation and wanted him in his command.[46] Col. W. P. Adair is also in favor of it. Some of our Surgeons have undergone an examination at Little Rock and were rejected, so that there might be a chance even now. if we knew that there was no ra[s]cality about it. Little Rock is full of applicants who are it is thought bribing the board of examiners to reject some and fill there places with a more hungry set. I shall do my utmost to get him a good situation.

Times are hard no one starved yet though, plenty of beef milk and butter, bread is rather scarce, have ate some good meals in the last two or three days, had "Sure enough coughphy" three times this week "in luck" aint I?

There is some prospect of a fight soon I think if the Feds and Pins stand their ground.[47] it is reported that they have fallen back we will know soon, everything is quiet now, but I dont think it can last long. I would like the best in the world if it could continue and we had our Country. How I would like to settle down again and hear the cows lowing the hogs squealing and see the nice garden and the yard with roses in it the waving wheat and stately corn growing, and be conscious that there was no one in want and be blessed with the society of those I love most on earth you and our children. Sometimes I fear we will not be permited to be situated so again but you know that I have faith in a power that can always keep us out of trouble and can restore anything that we ask if he choses. I would not be without this infatuation as many please to call it and laugh at me for, for nothing in the world. I could not think of going into a battle without it. So let us hope that what ever may come we may be restored at last to each other. I have just seen a man from camp — says the Feds & Pins are in Ft

[46] The appointment of Dr. W. J. Deupree as surgeon of Stand Watie's regiment was made on July 24, 1863.

[47] It is interesting that the writer divides the enemy into two groups; the Feds or white soldiers, and the Pins, or Cherokees in the Northern service, most of whom were members of the Kee-too-wah.

Gibson, our forces are just a cross the River, the prospect is good for a fight. I will be with the Regt in two days — how I wish I had my horse, I feel lost without him, be sure and send him by a good chance.

You must send me some reciepts and orders to Capt Alberty for tobacco given some boys belonging to my company as I want to collect them and a blank book with some accts against W. P. Adair, Hooley[48] & R. F. Martin. Your Uncle Dick is quite unwell at Skullyville seems to be on the decline — but lively as usual. Your uncle Jo has just returned from Texas. I havnt seen him. Granvill Rogers died. Bony Edmondson married in Ft Smith to a Miss Edmondson formerly — she was a widow with three children. Wm W Buff has the juandice.

Your friends the Campbells send you respects Old-man Campbell is badly crippled. *Can't* walk. Kiss all the children and make them walk with you every evening and tell them they must learn very fast. *Jose* must learn to answer a great many questions.

Yours as ever
JIM

let Jarratt take George Starr's note and take it in your own name. I paid Juliette the balance on it. JIM

◄§ Sarah C. Watie to Stand Watie

May 20th 1863
Rusk Texas[49]

MY DEAR HUSBAND

I do not know what to say first there is many things to say. I never could begin to tell you half as every thing seames to go wrong. I have been here at sister N one week.[50] I find her very low yet she gaines very slow I do not find her as well as I thought she would be. I heard from her before I left home.

---

[48] Lucien Burr Bell, a nephew of Mrs. Watie. He was known familiarly as "Hooley," which is the Cherokee word for "bell."

[49] Life in the Cherokee Nation eventually became so perilous that Mrs. Watie and her younger children sought refuge among relatives in Texas.

[50] Mrs. Watie was referring to her sister Nancy, the wife of George Starr.

I thought she would be able to walk when I got here but now I dont believe she will ever get well. I find much discord here. there is hardly two of them friendly. poor Joe she finds but poor consolation here. if I could not get along with folks better I would leave and go to my self but instead of helping herself she wants other people to help her my self. I do not feel disappointed at all for I did not come here with the expectation of people laying down there work and doing mine it is every man for himself here. I shall go back in a few days so as to get some clothes for you but there is no chance to get only to spin them but C.[51] and I can do it in two or three weeks. we are as good hands as there is in the state. I cant begin to give you the faintest idia of all the little troubles they have. I do not want to be in any of it so I just keep as close as I can. I will send you some things as soon as I get back. you black horse is not in good order so I will send you the bay so that I can get the black in good order.

We have no news here about the army. we hear of several fights in tennessee but I do not know as to the truth of them. this state is just like all the rest one half for the north.[52] I want you to write to me and tell me what I must do if they get in here must I sell the boys[53] or not I do not want to be so near the Choctaw line as am now. Nancy wants to buy a place here or near here, there is one here for sale at three thousand in confederate money. Lucian Bell knows the place. I want to get near the school so the children can go all the time but you can guess better than I can how long we will have to stay. there is a good school near here and I would like to get a place and send [the children] to it. the new session begins in September I will try and get paper so as to write you a good long letter.[54]

[51] This was another of Mrs. Watie's sisters, Charlotte. She was the wife of Dr. W. J. Deupree.

[52] This is an interesting statement but it must be taken only as an expression of Mrs. Watie's views with regard to this particular part of Texas.

[53] Mrs. Watie took two or three slaves with her to Texas.

[54] Many evidences exist as to the scarcity of paper among the Cherokee refugees. Several of Mrs. Watie's letters were written on sheets torn from old ledgers.

I wish I could just see you an hour or two. I know you would laugh at some of the experiences of these white folks. I saw Carlott Ivy you know that she knows all. I will go to see you as soon as I can get the children to school and some clothes for you. I cant live through the year and not go, you can write and tell me whether there will be danger or not. I will not go till I know that there will be no danger, you know too that, I cant stay away so long from you. it greaves me to think that we are so far from each other if any thing should happen we are too far of for to help each other. be a good man as you always have been. at the end a clear conscience before God and man is the advise of your Wife

S Watie

burn this for it is nonsense. all the children send love. all well.[55]

⇜§James M. Bell to Caroline Bell

Camp Coody's Creek, May 29th/63

Dearest Carrie

I will write you a short note per Mr. Seely, Col Watie's friend who stays with sister Sally. I was not aware of his going back so soon but even then I could not have written much as my time is all taken up in daytime and we can get no candles half the time to do anything at night. Our Convention[56] has been in session for several days, there are a good many important questions up for the consideration of its members. One to offer inducements [to citizens of the Confederate States to enlist in the 1st Cherokee Regiment] of One Hundred & Sixty Acres of land is meeting with considerable opposition — there is a Committee of seven of us to report and draft a bill — have

[55] The editors have found it necessary to insert a few periods in all of Mrs. Watie's letters to make them more intelligible.

[56] The meetings of the Confederate Cherokee government were held in the field, while the soldiers were in camps. As a consequence, they were not held with regularity and were subject to interruption. According to the best information, the convention mentioned in this letter was in progress from May 22 to June 1, 1863.

had five days and are not ready to report yet all from contrary-ness as much as anything else. Hooly, Joab Scales, Skaggs, Brown, Dr. Adair, D. R. Narr, M. C. Frye & I are the committee. There seems to be some indication of an opposition party arising in our Legislative body.

An Ordinance was read twice yesterday in the convention to feed the people.[57] I think it will pass without opposition after the third reading.

One to establish schools near the depots of the Refugees will also pass I think.

It looks singular Thus to be legislating in Camps. Our Council House is a large Sybley tent or was until we were run out of it by the lice. They seem to be as numerous as ever. On the 20th we had a skirmish with the Feds & Pins they are in Ft Gibson and are fortified our 1st & 2nd Cher Regt and some Creeks went over and completely surprised them killed between sixty & one hundred men and Captured at least fifteen hundred head of stock if they could have got them away but they could not get them all off and fight *them* too.

George West was killed — died in about an hour after he was shot; a man by the name of Bean was also killed, he lived near Gibson and did not belong to the army. they were all that were killed. We have any amount of mules some of the finest kind, a good many belonging to our citizens. Our boys have had a great deal of fun out of the enemy since The Arkansas River only separates our soldiers from theirs and they talk across the River all the time. Our boys proposed swapping ox yokes for their harness the Pins would tell our boys to come over and get their negroes. They would tell the Pins to come over and get their mules and then they would open a fire for a few minutes. Fighting has been going on since the 20th Inst across the river they have wound some of our soldiers and we have killed and wounded some of them as they can be seen carrying them off. Geo West was shot about six or seven hundred

[57] This refers to the providing of food for refugee Cherokees driven from their homes by the war.

127

yards, one of our men killed a Fed. officer [at] a thousand yards.

Jack, Saladin, and Jo Lynch are all well. A young man deserted and came over to us but I could hear nothing from Lon, Billy or Brack, though I think they are in the Nation. I am going to try to get them out; if they are there. You must be cheerful and happy, encourage the children. Make them get up soon and study their books. They must send me some word when you write. I have only received one letter from you yet I have written you a dozen. You must write. You *don't* know how bad I want to see you all and particularly you. I will have a poor chance to go. Col Adair wants to go the first chance & he ought to. love to all and believe that as ever I am

Yours affectionately

Kiss all the children for me. JIM

◄§ Sarah C. Watie to Stand Watie

June 8th, 1863

MY DEAR HALF

I have just got home from Rusk and found Grady here and a letter from you dated the 27th of April.[58] it gave me a great deal of pleasure to know that you still have time to write and cast a thought on home and home folks. Mr. Kelly and W. Fields will start as soon as I finish my letter. I have not had a chance to write you a long letter since you left. Grady tells me that Charles and Saladin have killed a prisiner.[59] write and tell me who it was and how it was. tell my boys to always show mercy as they expect to find God merciful to them. I do hate to hear such things it almost runs me crazy to hear such things. I find myself almost dead some times thinking about it. I am afraid that Saladin never will value human life as he ought.[60]

[58] Mrs. Watie was still in Texas.

[59] Charles Webber, Stand Watie's nephew (previously mentioned) and Saladin Watie.

[60] Saladin was hardly more than fifteen when he became a captain in his father's regiment. He was generous but young and impetuous, so it is not surprising that his mother was often concerned about him.

if you should ever catch William Ross dont have him killed. I know how bad his mother would feel but keep him till the war is over. I know they all deserve death but I do feel for his old mother and then I want them to know that you do not want to kill them just to get them out of your way. I want them to know you are not afraid of their influence. always do as near right as you can. I feel sorry that you have such a bad chance and so much to do be careful of your self. we have not a bit of water here we almost starve for water.

Old man Hardin is sick. I have not seen him since you left. he started the next day after you left and went to some house some fourteen miles of. I expect he will die as he has the consumption & sister Nancy I do not think will live through the summer. she wants me to go and stay with her while she lives. She cant walk across the house.[61] tell Major Bradley to hunt me up and I will take care of him if I go to Rusk for the summer. I will get me a house in Bellview so the children can go to school, it [is] impossible for me to stay here. I will get some one to stay and take care of our corn it will do to fatten our horses. you must write every chance and direct it to Lanagin and let him mail it to Rusk, Bellaview. it looks like I cant live and not hear from you.[62] you must write and tell me when it will be safe to come. I send the bay horse the black was too poor to go I will bring him. you can either send that back or keep him till I come I can sell him for six hundred here. I have not time to say good by. yours

Write soon   S. C. WATIE

ᴥᴐ Elias Cornelius Boudinot to Stand Watie

DEAR UNCLE,   Fort Smith, June 27, 1863.

I had decided to start to-day for your hdqtrs. but Genl. Steele tells me you are again on the scout across the river and

---

[61] Mrs. Watie's sister Nancy suffered from tuberculosis from which she died after a lingering illness of more than a year.

[62] The deep affection of Mrs. Watie for her husband is apparent in her letters, and his letters to her show an equally strong devotion.

there would be no chance for me to see you soon if I went. I therefore conclude I had better go to Fayetteville and see if anything can be done speedily about the cartridge boxes I partially engaged. I have received authority from Genl. Holmes to purchase any articles necessary for your command or to make contracts that I may deem necessary. I shall therefore have it in my power, I hope, to do something substantial.

William[63] has sent me a copy of the ordinances adopted by the Convention — to make the provision law work the Commissioner in place of money should either be furnished with warrants or bonds of the Cherokee Nation, or an arrangement should at once be made with Genl. Smith to allow him to draw on the army rations and transportation, until such time as other arrangements can be made with the Confederate Govt. If this be thought the better plan, the Commissioner should at once receive his appt. from you and be directed to go and see Genl. Smith personally. I will accompany him if the Convention should desire it.[64]

The Conscript law in the shape they have passed it amounts to *nothing* — they chose to strike out the only clause that made the law of any force; they substitute "arrest" and "imprisonment" for a deprivation of all rights as a citizen and the confiscation of property, as I had the penalty for not enrolling. What does a skulker care for *arrest,* while here at Fort Smith or in Texas or anywhere out of the Cherokee Nation? Suppose a man resists arrest and killed the man who arrests him, where's your redress? You can't treat him as a deserter; the fact is the law is of no binding force. I have said this to no one else, but you look at the law and see if I'm not right.[65]

As ever, Yours,
CORNELIUS

[63] William P. Boudinot, the writer's brother.

[64] Many of the Southern Cherokee were virtually destitute and it was necessary to make some provision to care for them.

[65] The conscript law adopted by the government of the Southern Cherokee provided for the arrest and imprisonment of Cherokees of draft age who did not enlist when called upon. Boudinot was urging the original provisions of the bill which provided for forfeiture of their rights as Cherokee.

P.S. Cally Thompson visits your camp; you might make him serviceable in some way. If you write to me, direct to care of Genl. Steele.   C.

≼ Stand Watie to Sarah C. Watie

MY DEAR WIFE,   Ft. Gibson[66]

I returned yesterday [from] my trip up the country, found Sealey [had been] here, and gone back, was sorry that I did not see him — I had a hard trip of it, while I was gone had one of the severiest fights that has been fought in this country on the bank of the Cabbin Creek fought two days, the Feds forced and drove our men away from the ford, the second day by a severe canonade, had 2 pieces the first day the 2nd had four, I lost but few men.[67] I am safe you must not be uneasy about me I will take care of myself. I received your letter. It makes me feel good to hear you talk. I shall write to you every opportunity I would be glad to see you — I can't tell you all, no time, I will write again. I shake hands with the children. Accept for yourself my love.

Your loving husband.

STAND WATIE

When I have time I will write a long letter

P.S. July 12th I sent this off to be carried by Mr. Thompson but has just been brot back — as I had just finished my last letter I will send them both. I thought I had mentioned in this that Joe Landrum, Procter Landrum, Fite, Henry Shaw, Major Lype and Calvin Miller were taken prisoners, day before the fight, but I find I had not in this letter.

WATIE

[66] July 12, 1863.

[67] News that a federal commissary train bound from Fort Scott to Fort Gibson reached General Cooper late in June. Stand Watie and his regiment were at once dispatched to command the crossing at Cabin Creek, which flows into Grand River about ten miles south of Vinita. The plan of attack, which was complicated and elaborate, was made inoperative by the flooded streams. After a sporadic engagement, which lasted from July 1 to 3, Stand Watie retired and the train proceeded to Fort Gibson.

◄§ Sarah C. Watie to Stand Watie

Rusk County Texas[68]
July 28th 1863

My dear S—

I have been here with sister Nancy nearly all summer but I have no hope that she will get better for her life seems to hang on a thread some time better and then worse but I do not think she can last but a short time. I did hope once she would get better but now I do not think she can I am in a thousand troubles for I have just heard that you are falling back; that is bad. I do not know where you will find a place to hide here. you have heard this time that Vixburg has fallen. that seams to distress the people more than any thing else.[69] we cant get a strait *tail* hear. some seams to think it is mear rummer but I do not know how such report could go the rounds so and not be counterdicted. it is thought there is some thing wrong about it by its being given up on the fourth of july. I saw a letter from Mr Ivey he said that he had talk to a great many of the paroled soldiers. they all seamed to think there was something straight about it they said while one part of the men was eating mule meat the others had bacon. I wish I could see you just a little while. I want to give you a short account of Rusk and its present inhabitants. poor Joe she will talk and go so it keeps her in a pickle all the time. she laid her complaining to me so often that I did not recollect half she told me not did she but she unfortunately told some else the same thing so it came right back to her aunt Nancey. she told several things her aunt says is not so but you know we never minded it but she will have to hold in here where she is not knowne. but the fun of it is she had forgotten that she had told anny body else so when she found that her aunt knew it she was angry enough about it. she could think of no one else that could have told it so she sits down and writes me one of the most insulting letters she could think of. I do not intend to write to her but I will make

[68] Mrs. Watie was away from her refugee home visiting her sister Nancy.
[69] Vicksburg had fallen nearly a month before, in what was pronounced by General Sherman one of the greatest campaigns in history.

her feel ashamed of her self for wanting to quarrel with me. you know that they have no respect for nobody. I wish they had sense, that is her and her sisters for they cant help from telling lies. I do hope that it will give her one lesson. She has no friends among her owne people. I have been hard at work all the time I have tried to get each of my folks a pair of boots. I think I will get them. tell them to have the money ready and save it. I will try and see you all soon. it depends in circumstances when I will be there but as soon as I can. I would not have staid so long here if the water had been good. I will not move [here] this neighborhood does not suit me to live in as there is too many of our kin here. Nancey will not last long and when she is gone I have no desire to be here, though all are good to me, but joe and charlotte will keep all in hot water. I forgot to tell you that Gen. Lee had washington and Baltimore.[70] I hope they will make peace. I see in the papers that the people of New York are tired of the war and are crying for peace. I wish it was over with. all well but I never saw so much sickness in my life at one time. F Thompsons wife is not expected to live. I will go home in few days. good by. love from the children.

S. C. WATIE

I will write next week by Matlock

◄§ W. J. Deupree to James M. Bell

Quitman, Texas.
August 4, 1863

Col. J. M. Bell

DEAR SIR:

I wrote to you several days ago, informing you that I accepted the appointment of Princepal Surgeon in Col. Waties Regiment. I re-enrolled as Militia previous to the reception of my appointment through your kind letter. I have laid my case before the enrolling officer requesting him to errace my name from the roll, he said that he would have to apply to a Superior

---

[70] Rumors of the capture of Washington and various other northern cities constantly reached the West during the war.

Officer before he could let me know whether the state Authorities would let me off from state services. The presumption is that I will be struck from the Militia List, if done, I shall be at Col. Waties Head Quarters as soon as I possibly can get an outfit which is very difficult to do. A pall of gloom seems to over hang our land since the fall of Vicksburg the general aspect of things all is danger and uncertainty. God save our country, we are gone under forever.[71] Our land is lost refugees from every state. It does not require a philosopher to fore tell what a deplorable future is in store for us, our wives & children. Woes, arrests, wretchedness & misery of every hue. Rapes, Rapine by the Feds & our negroes & every insult & disgrace that ever was offered a people we will have to bear. God help. God save us or we perish. Every negro in the Confederacy that is able bodied ought to be conscripted & be made to serve & to help our armies, or the condition of things at home will be intolerable. All the horrors of negro insurrection, murder & every crime that ever was perpretrated on earth will soon be the fate of the Lone Star State. These reflections are the products of all the bad news recently come [to hand.] Our wives, our children: O God have mercy on them. As soon as I can recrute my horses I will be off to your Head Quarters if I get off from the militia. *Our* kindest regards to Col. Waitie, Dr. Wat,[72] Maj Thompson & others. All better. Minnie is Convalescing. With the best of wishes for your health Safety & prosperity I remain

Yours
W. J. Deupree

Corn was never better. Made a fine grain crop.

(Read & Burn)

[71] This letter gives further evidence of the wretched condition of the South during the war.

[72] Dr. Walter Thompson Adair.

[73] Watica was Stand Watie's second son.

[74] Evidently to visit her husband in camp.

[75] Jacqueline, sometimes referred to as Jackie or Jack, was the younger of Stand Watie's two daughters.

[76] This was probably Charles Webber, who had just recovered from smallpox.

✑ Sarah C. Watie to Stand Watie

August 21 1863

MY DEAR HUSBAND

I thought I would write you a long letter but I find I have no pen. then the children pester me so. one want me to write for them and then the other want me to write. I am at home and I feel ten thousand times better satisfied then to be at other peoples. the only objection any one can have to this place is water we do live miserable as far as water and I don't know where we will get the next meat. we have got all along at the Commissary house but you do know I can get some where as long as I have money. I was at Quitman when I wrote last. I had your horse. I did not think you would want him so sorry he was, in no order to go at all. I was sorry about it but that fool would have him. I want to see you and then I can tell better what to do. I can't help depending on you judgment for I don't know what is best under the present circumstances. Grady would be a great help but he is sick. We will send the children to school soon as I can get them ready. I left Wataca[73] at Rusk as he wanted to stay. There was a very good school there and I thought he might stay as long as Nancey lived. I will send you plenty of clothes to do you through the winter; I have worked hard all summer as to have plenty. Mr. Bouden has been very sick for several weeks I would go soon if I had any one to go with me but I would not go with just any body.[74] I hope the old man Bouden will be well enough in a short time to go. Jacquline[75] says tell Charley she wants to see him bad since he is marked and made so ugly.[76] Ninny says tell her papa he always forgets me when he writes he don't write to me like he does to sister.

Jack says tell Saladin to send her a pencil so she can write to him. I can't get to write for them, I wish you could come and see what we are doing. I have a great many things to tell you that will make you laugh and some that would not. I never knew so much of this world as I do since I came to this country. I use to think that every one had some sort of a soul but one half of them has only gizards and some only craws but enoug of my foolishness for this time. every one says tell uncle Charlie we want to see him and they will send him some clothes.

S C WATIE

P.S. Forget not thy friend in time of need. I will have Boots as soon as I can. tell the boy[s] to have the money Ready. Ninny[77] say tell Saladin howdy and Charles too...

⁓§ James M. Bell to Caroline Bell

Boggy Depot Sept 2nd 1863

DEAREST CARRIE,

You will be surprised to get a letter from me Written from this place. I am satisfied though [that] you have already heard if the news has gone as fast as it does for Common that we are ruined beyond remidy. how does it happen that you always hear everything from this department in its worst aspect? it is bad enough to tell the truth or well enough to do so but to go beyond that is criminal it can do no good but a great deal of harm to exaggerate things as many of our people do. We have never been cut all to pieces yet, have lost none of our train; have never all been captured. Still you have heard this repeatedly. We were defeated at Honey Springs[78] and could have been ruined and you would say I was trying to allay any fears of yours if I was to tell you that we got the best of that fight but it is so. We had to retreat in the last instance for several reasons. Gen'l Cabal reinforced us soon after the Honey Springs fight, his Brigade becoming dissatisfied Commenced deserting and

---

[77] "Ninny," the older of Stand Watie's two daughters, was named Minnehaha but she was usually called "Ninnie," probably due to her younger sister's inability to pronounce "Minnie."

[78] After the Cabin Creek engagement, the Confederates at once laid plans for the capture of Fort Gibson. General Cooper established his position on Elk Creek, near Honey Springs and not far from Muskogee, and was to be joined by General William Lewis Cabell and his troops. The Federal forces got wind of the idea and General James G. Blunt forced an engagement with Cooper before Cabell could arrive. The two armies met on July 17, and, with odds against him, General Cooper was forced to retire.

all left him but about three hundred, he of course had to follow them back to Ft Smith & elsewhere to reorganize.[79] This got up a general Spirit of dissatisfaction and desertion became contagious, our men commenced leaving; we were consequently left with not more than fifteen hundred men, that is effective men, but what could we do against an enemy three times our number better armed and equiped than we were? I suppose we could have made a sacrifice of ourselves, if it was necessary, but I *don't* Think the occasion required it. There is so much expected of us. people in Texas think we have an army standing in line well equiped for fighting. The Regt's, two Choctaws, two Creek two Cherokees & three Osages, each had a thousand men. of course we have nine thousand men besides two Batts which will make ten thousand. now if I was to tell you that five thousand men is the most that I have known in Camps at any one time you would be surprised but people that are ignorant of how we have been treated here before would be more so but it is true. of that five thousand one thousand are without arms and many have not Clothing to change, without shoes and what any one in their right senses would say was in a deplorable condition looking more like *Siberian exiles* than Soldiers. Still I am constrained to say that they are never called on to make a Stand against the enemy but they do so cheerfully and with a determination that no one would expect. We are neglected. The Confederacy certainly does not know our condition.[80] Good Soldiers but without the means of resistance, but we are neither discouraged or Whipped and God forbid we ever shall be. I have been in an almost nude condition. I have still got an old grey shirt and pair pants on they are thread bear. My pants I wrote you about were spoiled in cutting. Mr. King a tailor cut them. I got a pr of pants from

[79] General Cabell, with a force of over 3000 men, advanced from Fort Smith into the Indian Territory to aid General Cooper. The deserted and forsaken land had a demoralizing effect upon his soldiers, great numbers of whom were conscripted Unionists, and many of them deserted.

[80] The Confederate government was in sore straits and, with the Mississippi patrolled by Union gunboats, was unable to supply the trans-Mississippi soldiers with proper equipment.

Benj. Goss. Mary Stedman is making them and an overshirt. Mary is well. Martha is sick with Chills. There is a great deal of sickness here, four deaths since I came here. Three yesterday, others very low not expected to live. James Landomen's daughter died yesterday, the last child he had living. Jo was killed at Cabin Creek. I wrote you he was a prisoner.

Col Watie is still back on Arkansas River. I *don't* believe our Regts will leave our Country. We are preparing to go back. Col Watie has promised as soon as we Whip The Feds we can go home. I hope it *won't* be long now until that is done. Col Adair is anxious to go home and would be off by this time were he not under Arrest. Genl Steele arrested him for disrespect, his trial will be removed to Little Rock. Col Adair has or will prefer charges against Gen Steele.[81] It would take a month to write you everything. Jo is well, Jack also, looks bad though. Tell *Ira* I received her cake and that her uncle Jo Martin & her Cousins Wm. R., Wm. P. Adair and several others pronounced it excellent to. Send me something else when she can. love to all, kiss all Children, tell them to be good, learn fast & be industrious. Your Uncle Dick sends love to you and says you must have a chicken for him when he comes. Mary sends love to you. I am as ever   Your Affect.

JIM

I want to see you you don't know how bad.

JIM

I expected to meet Jarrett & Dr. here but they have not come yet — make the Boys pull grass, feed and take good care of my bay horse. I am a foot

J

❧ J. L. Martin to Stand Watie

Boggy, Sept. 22nd, 1863.

DEAR COL.

I have just returned to this place. I have been looking out a place to move our people.[82] I have found a exelent place for

---

[81] It was difficult for white officers to maintain rigid discipline in the Cherokee regiments, since the Indian officers seldom exacted it.

them down on the Blue Creek about twenty miles from Nales
Mill. And about ten miles above the mouth of Said Creek,
there are plenty of water with good Cane, and to all appearances a healthy location. I shall commence moving our people
about thursday. Genl. Steele promised me he would Furlough
all the Soldiers who had families and friends to take care of to
build houses.[83] I was going up to the Regt. but am unwell. and
Genl. Steele I learn is at Bonham and will pass this way So I
have concluded to wait here till he comes along. I shall use
every endeavor to carry out the Bill or Ordinance and make
our people as comfortable as possible. This business is perplexing indeed owing to the way I have to draw my supply. I have
to keep the people reconsiled by a great many promises we only draw half Rations. I do hope that when we get settled down
on the Blue Creek we will be Permitted to draw our Rations
from Texas then we can give the people full Rations etc etc. I
have understood that J. M. Bryan has got permission to Rase
100 [hundred men] as partisan rangers and he expects to get a
good many men from the first and second Cherokee Regts this
I believe to be true. Col. Adair and I talked about it and he
and I concluded it would be a good policy to grant no Trans-
fers. Bryan also said that this family party would have to be
put down and that as for Jack Spears he was not fit to be Chief
over a gang of Prairie Woolves all this came from men who
wont lie, men who heard him say it. Johnson Foreman is also
cutting up so I learn but all this cutting up of Bryan's and
Foremans will amount to nothing If we stick all together
please tell Capt. Spears that I say that I am willing to serve under him as Chief, Altho Bryan says he aint fit to Rule over a
gang of woolves. I had hoped that all partyism had ceased and

82 The return of the Union forces to the Cherokee country and, particularly, their increasing numbers at Fort Gibson made life in the Nation unten-
able for the Confederate Cherokee. The tide of war had turned, and now it
was the Southern Cherokee's homes that were robbed and burned. It was for
some of these noncombatants that Martin was seeking a place of refuge, where
they would be safe from the North.

83 The Indian Territory had been made a separate military district by the
Confederacy late in 1862. General William Steele was in command.

still hope that it will be the case.[84] I have a letter for Capt. Spears it is from Nevarro Co. Texas. I expect it is from his wife I will send it up by hand. don't you think it would be a good Idea to have an act passed in Council autherising a Committy to sit upon Clames to have all our losses Regestered, the time is growing long and a great many people are dying and getting killed so that we will not be able after while to get at the losses of the people correctly. If such should be the case that a Committy is appointed I would Suggest that Col. Adair be one of the Committy and if it would suit I should like to be one also I will talk to Col. Bell and give him my views more particular on the subject.

I have not heard one word from Boudenot and Bell I am looking for them every day.

I am anxious to go home to visit my family I had a letter from them all well at the time they wrote. Lucy has lost her little Boy he died 30 July— the health of the Refugees is improving.

Yours most Respectfully

J. L. MARTIN

✑Douglas H. Cooper to James M. Bell

Hd. Qrs. 1st Brigade I. T.

Camp on Five Mile Creek

September 24, 1863.

[copy]

COL.

In your introduction to the publication of the official report of the affair at Elk Creek,[85] on 17th July, it is stated that the 1st & 2nd Cherokee Regts. were commanded respectively by Col's Watie & Adair, & in justification to these officers it is prop-

---

[84] This was John Spear, assistant chief of the Cherokee "South." "Partyism" never ceased in the Cherokee Nation. During the entire war period and long afterwards the members of the old Treaty Party were constantly quarrelling and bickering among themselves.

[85] General Douglas H. Cooper's report of the engagement at Elk Creek may be found in the *Official Records: War of the Rebellion*, Series I, Vol. 22, Pt. II, 457-61.

er to say that the 1st Cherokee Regt. was commanded by Major Thompson, Col Watie being at that time on detached service at Webbers Falls and the 2d Cherokee Regiment by Lt. Col. Bell, Col Adair being absent sick. It was regretted exceedingly that it so happened that Col Watie was not present on that occasion, as his service & well known gallantry would have given great encouragement to the Officers and men of his command.

Please make this explanation public.

[Seal]

Respectfully,
D. H. Cooper
Brig...

✍§ James M. Bell to Stand Watie

Head Quarters 2nd Cher. Regt.
Camp Ward C. N. Sept 24th 1863

Col,

Circumstances preclude the idea of me reporting myself for duty to this Brigade longer.[86] You are aware of the reasons that actuate me in this matter and unless things can be changed I must and will insist on at least a transfer from this department, we get neither justice or our rights and I am not inclined to be an idle observer of the wrongs of my people any longer. If to be a Southern man, to be alive to all the interests of the South & the Struggle they are engaged in &c would entitle them to any consideration whatever or to a just proportion of notice in the different reports of Engagements with the Enemy, our people are justly deserving. What have they ever received but sleights and neglect. We have borne it until now with patience. Shall we bear it any longer or will you command us to bear it longer, if so you are knowing to the wrong and encouraging it and we must regard you in the light of an Enemy.

---

[86] Bell, a fiery young Hotspur, had evidently lost patience with what he felt to be the neglect of the Confederate government and the failure of the Cherokee troops to receive proper recognition for their services. Apparently Stand Watie was able to soothe his ruffled feelings for Bell continued in service and eventually was promoted to the rank of colonel.

141

And until we know that you feel as we do in regard to this matter, We can supply neither Piquits or Scouts. We ask for justice. We are going to have it or I for one will wear a ball and chain during the continuation of the war.

Yours Respectfully & fraternally

JAMES M. BELL, Lt. Col.

If you see proper [you] can forward this to Genl. D. H. Cooper.   J. M. BELL

⤚§ Thomas F. Anderson[87] to Sarah C. Watie

Camp near North Fork, Oct. 27th 1863.

Mrs. S. Watie.

DEAR AUNT SALLIE.[88]

The Colonel started on a Scout Yesterday with a crowd of Cherokee, Creeks, Chickasaws and white vagabonds and Border Ruffians and with reasonable luck will return after having burnt up Gibson. Genl. Cooper had started sometime ago to Fort Smith to give the Feds a fight there and now, since Genl. Steele has got up with him, they will probably leave nothing of the enemy but a greasy spot. The Cherokees were sent up here to keep the dogs off and since we came here, a few straggling Chickasaws and Creeks have got into our camp to get something to eat and the Colonel no doubt having in mind the Scripture injunction that man should eat his bread in the sweat of his face concluded that the best thing he could do with them was to take them along with him and make them sweat. We are looking for news from Cooper every hour.

You will receive by Mr. Matlock, a Bedstead, Table, some Chairs, I sack of Coffee, some soap, candles, pepper, Rice and

[87] The writer of this letter was Stand Watie's adjutant and close friend. He apparently had no Indian blood, yet he served with the Cherokee during the entire war. Anderson was a gallant soldier, of good education with an unlimited fund of wit and good humor.

[88] Anderson was not related in any way to Mrs. Watie. The "Aunt Sallie" was merely a friendly use of the name by which she was often called by friends and neighbors.

Desiciated Mixed Vegetables.[89] This latter article is intended to season soup with though I believe that the article itself will make very good soup as the Boys say that they find it composed of hindlegs of bullfrogs, Snails, Screwworms, etc.

There is also an ammunition Box full of such delicasies & 1 Bot. Vinegar sent by Major Thompson to his wife to be left in your care until you have an opportunity of sending this to her.

The Col. & Saladin are both in good health.[90] Not so with me. I have been in bad health for sometime. The Doctor lays it to eating spoilt victuals which is very probable as we have now at our mess Four (4) Female Cooks and you know what they say too many of them will do. I would send names but as they have no doubt been duly reported before now, I forebear.

Capt. Mayes sends his respects, and I beg you to believe me, when I say it in all sincerity that nothing would give me more sincere pleasure, than the assurance of being held in esteem by you, not so much according to reports as according to my true deserts.

Please send my Sabre belt which I left at your house.

Should anything important occur, during the Colonel's absence I will send you intelligence forthwith.

Your Obdt. Servt.
THOS. F. ANDERSON

⋞ Elias Cornelius Boudinot to Stand Watie

Monroe, La., Nov. 4, 1863

DEAR UNCLE,

I managed to borrow on my own responsibility $10,000 for the use of our refugees.[91] It seemed that neither Smith nor Scott could advance a dollar without assuming a responsibility outside of their official characters, and while each were ready

---

[89] These items were no doubt a part of the spoil of one of Stand Watie's lucky captures.

[90] Stand Watie and his son Saladin.

[91] Boudinot, while delegate to the Confederate Congress, worked hard and unceasingly to bring relief to the Southern Cherokees who were in refuge along the Red River and in Texas.

to advance if the other would be responsible, neither would do it on his own responsibility, so the matter stands. You can say to the Commissioner, — Martin and the others — that in 8 weeks at the fartherest I will have at Shreveport subject to the order of the Treasurer, or of the Court, if I can so arrange it — at least $40,000. In this time if I can do anything I can accomplish it.

I have news to-night that Bragg has again whipped Rosecrans — tho the report of his having surrendered needs confirmation.[92] I dont believe it. Lee is also reported to have whipped Meade near Manassas.[93]

I will write you just what the news is, when I get across the Miss. which will be in three days, without an accident.

Affly Yours,

CORNELIUS

✑ Stand Watie to Sarah C. Watie

Camp near North Fork

Nov. 12th, 1863

MY DEAR SALLY:

I have not heard from you since your letter brought in by Anderson. When Medlock went away I was out on a scout. I went to Tahlequah and Park Hill. Took Dannie Hicks and John Ross. Would not allow them killed because you said Wm. Ross must not be killed on old Mrs. Jack Ross's account.[94] Killed a few Pins in Tahlequah. They had been holding council. I had the old council house set on fire and burnt down, also John Ross's house.[95] Poor Andy Nave was killed. He refused to surrender and was shot by Dick Fields. I felt sorry as he used to be quite friendly towards me before the war, but

---

[92] Groundless rumors of Confederate victories were common throughout the South during the entire war.

[93] George G. Meade had been placed in command of the Army of the Potomac in June 1863.

[94] It is interesting to note here that Watie complied with the request of his wife as expressed in her letter of June 8.

[95] This was Rose Cottage, the beautiful home of John Ross near Park Hill.

it could not be helped. I would great deal rather have taken him prisoner. Since my return I have been sick but now good deal better. Another scout has since been made to Tahlequah under Battles. He returned today. They found some negro soldiers at Park Hill, killed two and two white men. They brought in some of Ross's negroes.

There is a grand council of the different [tribes] to be held at Armstrong Academy on the 16th.[96] Would like to attend but cant leave the command. Since Steele's and Cooper's retreat from Fort Smith I have been placed in command of the Indian Troops [all] but Choctaws.[97]

When I first sat down to write I thought I would send you a long letter but I am annoyed almost to death by people calling on me on business of various kinds, this and that.

I will send you pork enough to do you in a few days. I have concluded to have the hogs killed here and the meat hauled to you. You need not try to buy any. I can get it here.

A few days ago I received a letter from Sally Paschal. She said she had written to us and received no answer. Thinks perhaps we are displeased with her about something. I am sorry we did not write, it seemed to me you did. I will write her soon. Let me hear from you often and let me know how you are doing. Whenever the troops go into winter quarters I will go home to you. I have not been as well this fall as I used to. I cant get rid of this bad cough. Saladin is well. He is going to start in the morning with a party under Mose Fry on a scout to Fort Smith. Fry is not dead but is now a Major. He commands a battalion. I will write soon again.

Love to the little ones and everybody else.

Your husband
STAND WATIE

96 The fall of Vicksburg and the Union victory at Gettysburg had released a number of Northern troops for use west of the Mississippi. From this time on the fortunes of the Confederacy were on the wane. Conditions became so bad in the Indian Territory that this council of all the tribes had been called to meet at Armstrong Academy to devise ways and means of defence.

97 General William Steele was the Confederate general in command of the Indian Territory at this time, with General Douglas H. Cooper as one of his

✌§Sarah C. Watie to Stand Watie

Near or at the same place[98]
Dec 12th 1863

MY DEAR STAND

I have not been in a right good [spirit since][99] you left for several [reasons] none [of which] I shall name here. We are getting along as well as we can under the circumstances. We always [go] about under more disadvantages than any one else. we always feed more folks than any body else and get less thanks. we have our troubles here as well as other places. I did not write by William Adair because I had no time nor room. let me tell you how we were caught when they got here we had not a scrap of meat or grease only some that I had thought not fit to use but I went to getting supper and made it do... I look for you home soon on account of having no place. I do not know whether to get this place or not, it will be let out the 19th of this month and I cant hear from you in that time they may not sell it or rent it till you come if Mr Bouden has any thing to do with it. Send us all that you can in the way of work tools, ploughs and other things. we have no such things — send me a loom if you can without to much trouble — dont risk to much for it if I had one I could do better.

I have been buisy ever since you left but it looks like we cant keep a head or even. I have spun every day since you left and still all are bare for clothing except Jack and Ninny but all are well now and we can do better. Charlotte has a bad cough I fear she will not last long — that is many years. I am sorry you are not so well as you were at the beginning [of the] war so many of our friends have died ... we have had such bad luck with our children that it keeps me always uneasy a about

---

chief officers. Cooper was later appointed to the command of the Indian Territory.

[98] Mrs. Watie was still in Texas.

[99] Large holes in the original have made it necessary to omit several passages and to insert a few words, to make the letter intelligible.

them.[100] bring Charles Watie with you and Saladin for I do not like for him to be there when you are not there. Charles Webber is not well yet. send all you can and come soon. Jack says come soon you know she always has the last word. Yours

S C WATIE

[100] The third son Cumiskey had recently died and Saladin had been quite ill.

⌐§ CHAPTER IV §⌐

THE FLOOD TIDE OF WAR

THE year 1864 was, in many respects, a gloomy period for the Southern Cherokee. Fort Gibson and Fort Smith were both in possession of Northern troops and furnished centers from which minor expeditions and raiding parties were sent out. The loyalist Cherokees, with memories of the two miserable winters spent in Kansas fresh in their minds, were bitterly hostile toward the Southern group. Irregular troops, and bands of white outlaws rode about robbing and plundering at every opportunity. Stand Watie was forced back into the Choctaw country where he spent the latter part of the winter of 1863-64, in headquarters at a place called "Camp Starvation." He was seldom inactive, however, for any considerable length of time, even in winter, but continued to make raids or "scouts," as he sometimes called them, against the enemy.

Late in the spring of 1864 Stand Watie was advanced to the rank of brigadier general. During the following summer he showed amazing activity and fought numerous engagements. Some of his exploits were almost startling. In June he captured with his cavalry a steamboat on the Arkansas River, loaded with uniforms and other equipment for the soldiers at Fort Gibson. In September, 1864, occurred Stand Watie's most notable exploit. This was the capture at Cabin Creek of a great wagon train on its way from Fort Scott to Fort Gibson. Accompanying the train were a number of sutlers' wagons loaded with supplies. With the spoils of this victory Stand Watie was able to clothe and equip his ragged and nearly barefoot army.

While the military forces were waging this active warfare the Southern refugees were living in temporary camps far down in the Choctaw country, where they endured all the horrors of cold and hunger that had been suffered by the loyal Cherokee refugees during the two preceding winters. Every effort was made to relieve their condition but without much

148

success. Elias Cornelius Boudinot, as previously noted, had been chosen as delegate from the Cherokee Nation to the Confederate Congress at Richmond. He eventually secured an appropriation for the relief of the refugees, but the money was not made available for a long time and Confederate currency had by this time depreciated so much that it is doubtful if the sum provided was of much help.

The women in these camps wished to spin and weave cotton in order to provide clothing for themselves and their children and also for the soldiers in the field. The necessary equipment, however, was often lacking, especially the "cotton cards" with which the fiber was made ready for spinning.

Sickness was also common in these camps, particularly malaria, and quinine and other drugs and medicines were hard to obtain. This was especially true since the Mississippi was controlled by the North, and Federal gun boats were quite active in patrolling that stream to prevent the bringing of goods across it from the East.

Late in 1864 Stand Watie sent his adjutant Thomas F. Anderson across the Mississippi to assist in securing medicine, cotton cards, and various other supplies and articles, but the amount secured must have been pitifully inadequate to supply even the most pressing needs of the people.

Stand Watie's wife and younger children lived among friends and relatives near Rusk, Texas during most of the latter part of the war. His oldest son Saladin, though only about fifteen years of age when the war broke out, served as a soldier throughout the conflict and attained the rank of captain.

By the late autumn of 1864 the Southern Cherokee faced conditions that seemed, indeed, desperate. They were vastly outnumbered in the field, their families were living in camps far from home and enduring every hardship and privation. They were cut off from manufactured goods from the East by the Northern control of the Mississippi. Efforts to secure goods by exporting cotton through Mexico had met with scant success. Worst of all, the Confederacy with which they had allied themselves seemed tottering to its fall. Its currency was almost worthless and while its capital city was not to fall for many months it was, even at this time, hemmed in by overwhelming Union forces. Under such circumstances the note of optimism and faith in the future, which appears in many of these letters, is surprising. It indicates a courage and strength of purpose among these Cherokee allies of the South not exceeded in any place where the flag of the Confederacy still floated.

✑ Elias Cornelius Boudinot to Stand Watie

House of Representatives
Richmond, Va., Jany. 24, 1864.

DEAR UNCLE

I regret exceedingly that I have not been able to forward money sooner. Mr. Scott did not make the arrangement that I expected, and he promised, when we left Shreveport, so I was compelled to introduce a bill to that especial end.[1] It passed with but one dissenting vote and has but just received the approval of the President. No one unacquainted with legislative delays will appreciate the embarrassment under which I have labored. I have procured the money at last without assistance and hope our Commissioners will make it go as far as possible, for it must be borne in mind that this money will have to be returned after the war, or else the C. S. will retain the amount out of moneys that may then be collectable, and that this $100,-000 Confederate is the representation of $100,000 gold.[2] Our claims for indemnity under the treaty are not affected by this loan.

Congress is making slow preparation to meet the enemy in the Spring; from the tone of Northern papers the Yankees be-

[1] The money here referred to was in the nature of a loan or an advance of future annuities, and was for the purpose of relieving suffering among the Southern Cherokee refugees. Colonel S. S. Scott was the Confederate Commissioner of Indian Affairs.

[2] In the treaty of alliance made by Pike with the Cherokee, the Confederate States agreed to assume and pay to the Cherokee people all obligations due them from the government of the United States. This $100,000 advance would, of course, when the war ended, be deducted from the amount due to the Cherokee from the Confederate government.

lieve they have us subjugated already, and are quarreling among themselves about what shall be done with us. Lee & Johnson will undeceive them in the Spring. 150000 men completely investing Charleston might starve it out, and I think that is the only way it can be taken.

I insisted on Genl. Steele's removal as soon as I arrived here last November; a few weeks since Rev. Robinson from the Chickasaw Nation came on with sundry petitions, praying that Cooper be promoted and placed in command of the Indian Territory.³ He said he represented the wishes and sentiment of all the Indians, Cherokees as well as Choctaws, and that it was the opinion of your best friends that you were incompetent to command a brigade and hardly able to command a regiment.⁴ These friends of yours I ascertained to be Judge Keys, Judge Taylor, Mackey, Drew, Parks, Bob and other *warm* friends: Robinson I found to be a simple fellow he goes home under the impression that he accomplished much, when in reality he did nothing. I told the President that while I did not think Cooper the best General we could select for the command of our Dept. we infinitely preferred him to Steele. And I was assured Steele should be removed long before Robinson arrived. My plan which I have submitted to the President is to place Price in command of the Dept. of Mo. *and* the Indian Country, give him all the Mo. Infantry skeleton regts., let Cooper command the brigade of white troops and organize the Indians into three small brigades to be commanded by citizens of the several Nations. The President told me he was much pleased with my scheme, and has written to Kirby Smith about it; if Price will accept, I think there is little doubt but he will

³ General William Steele quite early became unpopular with the Indians, while Douglas H. Cooper who had for eight years been agent for the Chickasaws and Choctaws had the confidence and affection of most of these people. Steele's place was filled by the appointment of General S. B. Maxey who was, in turn, replaced by Cooper just before the close of the war.

⁴ Stand Watie was commissioned brigadier general the following May. There was no braver man in the Confederate service but he always wished to lead his troops in person and hated the office routine and detail that must accompany high command. In consequence he was perhaps better fitted for the work of captain or colonel than that of brigadier general.

be assigned to that command, in spite of Robinson's threats that if Cooper is not made the commander in chief all the Indians will desert the cause. Judge Dick Fields is here he has not told me his business, perhaps he has a delicacy in telling me he is the bearer of dispatches from a secret caucus which affected to represent the Cherokee people, recommending Cooper for Major Genl. and declaring that I had lost the confidence of the Cherokee people, which they would testify to by electing another delegate, Bah! I can laugh at all such plots. I will be with you in May or June by that time I shall have done all for our country that I am able to do here. I shall succeed in collecting from the State of Va. $13500 which I will carry with me to our commissioners. Everything is extravagantly high here. My board costs me $300 per month, while I get $230 pay, so you see I am not making a pile being congressman, board at the principal hotels $20 per day. The Sec. of War has decided that Crawford and Vore must elect which position they will hold, Q. M. or Agent, and that they cannot hold both.[5]

The Yankees will summon all their energies in the Spring to take Richmond and Atlanta. McClellan is likely to be their conservative candidate for President, and either Lincoln or Grant the radical, the electoral votes of La. Arks. Kentucky, Tenn, & Maryland will be thrown for Lincoln or Grant. McClellan stands no chance in these States, although he alone is in favor of giving the South her Constitutional rights.[6] One tenth of the populations of these states is allowed to represent the whole.

I wish you would forward as soon as possible a statement of condition of your forces, whether you have a battalion organized toward your third regiment etc.

Give your letter to Scott and he will forward it.

My regards to all the boys.

As ever, Affly,
Yr. Nephew
CORNELIUS

[5] John Crawford and Israel G. Vore were Indian Agents of the Confederate States who had also been appointed quartermasters.

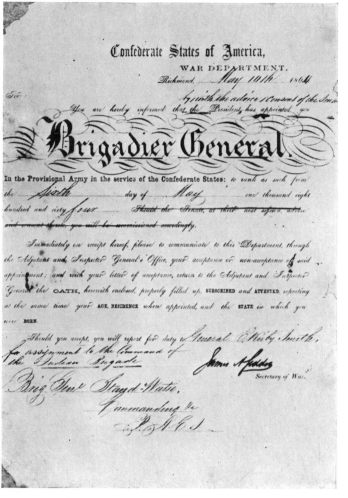

Commission of General Stand Watie

P.S. I have introduced two bills to provide for the payment of all Q. M. Commissary and Ordinance accts, in the Ind. country whether regular or otherwise, also a bill to pay the dead soldiers accts. in a more summary manner than now provided for. I will send a copy of the bill introduced by me and adopted, providing for elections to fill vacancies etc.   C.

✒§ Elias Cornelius Boudinot to Stand Watie

Richmond April 20, 1864

DEAR UNCLE,

Commr Scott started for the Nation last Febry. with $100,-000 which I got appropriated for the use of our Commissioners, he tells me he wrote to you from Miss. the reason of his return to this place. I regret that he turned back. I have done all I could to send money to you and the delay is not my fault. I think I shall be with you in June.

The morning papers here contain accounts of a brilliant exploit of yours 30 miles above Boggy Depot.[7] The most important battle of the war is impending in this state. I have recd. no word from the Nation except from Hooly dated in Dec. I hope to return with important authority for us Cherokees, and I trust such men as Hicks, Taylor & Co will not feel like putting me to death for it. I hope to get through congress bills providing for the settlement of dead soldiers claims and Q. M. & com. accts; a bill on the latter subject passed this House last session, but was not acted upon in the Senate.

Your Aff. nephew

CORNELIUS

P.S. I pay $350. pr month for board and received $230. per month salary — So see I am making money.   C.

[6] Lincoln's overwhelming victory in the election of 1864 is a matter of record; Boudinot's predictions of the trend of those events is interesting.

[7] This was a minor engagement the importance of which was probably magnified by the newspapers.

❧ William Steele[8] to Stand Watie

Army in Louisiana,
Near Grand Ecore,
April 21st, 1864.

COL.,

My attention has been called to an address by yourself to your people which contains statements reflecting upon myself and utterly at variance with the facts. As I have not supposed you to be a man who would wilfully make these false statements I suppose your information to have been derived from some one else. I will state the facts for your information deeming their publication improper. You state that the Commander (evidently referring to myself) abandoned the country with 5000 white troops, retiring at a time when a battle was imminent with the prospect of success in our favor. This evidently refers to the time when I withdrew the Brigade, commanded by General Gano, from the vicinity of Fort Smith (November 2 d).

The report made by Col. Lee from actual muster, given me, Novr. 1st, was as follows:

"Enlisted men present & on other duty."

Seminoles	106
Chickasaws	208
1st Creek	158
2d Creek	147
1st Choctaw	598
2d "	426
	1643
Choc. Militia	200
	1843

Demorse   291

Col. Hardiman, Comdg.
Gano's Brigade, officially

---

[8] Brigadier General William Steele (not to be confused with the union general of the same name), was assigned to the command of the Indian Territory in January, 1863. Steele was not generally liked by the Indians. In this letter he sought to justify some of his actions. An official report of Steele's operations may be found in the *Official Records, War of the Rebellion*, Series I, Vol. XXII, Pt. I, 28-36.

Wells	108		reported his Brigade at
	409	409	590 for duty.
		2252	
Infantry		125	
		2377	
Hardiman		590	
		2967	

to which must be added Howell's Battery and a small escort that arrived with General Gano on the 1st Novr., thus making my whole force 3000 men of *all kinds,* some without arms and many badly armed, instead of the 5000 *white troops* with which you say I abandoned your Country. The enemy's force was nearly the same that had whipped General Cooper at Elk Creek (when he reported over 4000 present) and some additional forces brought by General McNeill. Doctor Hart, at that time in charge of our hospital at Fort Smith, has since informed me that the Federal force on the 1st November was about 5000. General Cooper also, in a letter to General Maxey, placed them at about the same figures. How we could have engaged the enemy with the chances of success in our favor is beyond my comprehension. I have always thought you earnest in endeavoring to promote the welfare of the Country and had hoped that you would not have been misled by the false statements of a class of men whose whole aim is to sway the councils of the Nations for their own selfish ends.

For all the facts set forth above I have sufficient testimony.

Very Respectfully,

Col. Stand Watie   Wm. Steele

Comdg. Brigade   Brig. General

⮤ Stand Watie to Sarah C. Watie

Camp Watie on Middle Boggy
My Dear Sallie,   April 24th 1864.

Captain Alberty is going to Rusk and he will take this letter. News from all quarters is very cheering but you have

155

heard all so I will only relate what is going on here. The wild Indians from Kansas are getting to be very troublesome on the western border. Col. Adair crossed Arkansas river below Gibson but I have not heard from him since; a few men left off from him and returned; they fell in with some pins one of their number young Bent is supposed to be killed. Adair has stirred up the Pins no doubt before now. None but Creeks are at Gibson part of the pin Regts have gone to Scullyville.

Two men and two women came out from Fort Smith a few days since they reported the Feds there about 800 a few days after two young boys came out they report the same story. All agree that the Feds are short of provisions, since the failure of the enemy to occupy Texas. Troops at Fort Smith and Gibson, I think will act on the defence. We are now ready to move, only waiting for orders. Quantrell crossed the Arkansas river near the Creek Agency and killed eight men (Creeks) one of them shot a little boy and killed him. Some of the Creeks who were along returned today and brought this news.[9] I have always been opposed to killing women and children although our enemies have done it, yet I shall always protest against any acts of that kind. Two days ago a part of Quantrells men fired on the guard at Boggy. Killed one man and wounded another.

A few days ago a party of Missourians took off Arch Shelton's black boy (Peter) he was recaptured by some men below; in the affray Wiley Forester was killed. No propperty is safe anywhere, stealing and open robbery is of every days occurrence.

I am very tired of this camp we have bad water.

After Parks death all sorts of lies were told that I had planned everything.[10] I am sorry that I should be charged in

[9] W. C. Quantrill was the noted Missouri guerilla. The purpose of his raid down into the Indian Territory is not quite clear, as there was neither any great military object to be attained nor much plunder to be secured by such an expedition. Stand Watie has sometimes been compared to Quantrill, but this letter shows clearly that he did not believe in the methods of that leader and his men.

[10] This refers to the killing of Lieutenant Colonel Robert C. Parks of Stand Watie's regiment, by another officer of the same organization.

public of an act of that kind but it seems that is my doom let me act as I will my conduct is always considered wrong no charity was ever shown me yet I have lived through it and I trust and hope that justice and right will be meeted out to me some day. Although these things have been heaped upon me and (it) would be supposed that I became hardened and would be reckless but it still hurts my feelings. I am not a murderer.

Sometimes I examine myself thoroughly and I will always come to the conclusion that I am not such a bad man at last as I am looked upon. God will give me justice if I am to be punished for the opinions of other people, who do not know my heart I cant help it. If I commit an error I do it without bad intention. My great crime in the world is blunder, I will get into scrapes without intention or any bad motive. I call upon my God to judge me, he knows that I love my friends and above all others my wife and children, the opinion of the world to contrary notwithstanding. Love to the little ones, and my friends.

Let me hear from you, if possible I will write again before I get off too far.

Your Affectionate husband.

STAND

❦ Elias Cornelius Boudinot to Stand Watie

House of Representatives
Richmond May 7, 1864

MY DEAR UNCLE,

I have the pleasure at last to announce definitely your promotion to the rank of Brig. Genl. Your appt. was made yesterday and sent into the Senate for confirmation, but unfortunately the Senate had adjourned until Monday and of course cannot confirm you until then; but for a few moments delay in sending your appt. in I could have sent your commission by Genl. Buckner: but I assure you, *there is no mistake about it* this time.[11] Senators Johnson and Mitchell have been our

[11] Stand Watie's commission as brigadier general was dated May 10, and was to have taken effect from the 6th of May, 1864.

steadfast and warmest friends. They addressed a joint letter to the President upon the subject of your appt. a copy of which I preserved and will show you; their high appreciation of you and your services were there, no personal considerations would command my heartfelt gratitude [but] the interest they have ever shown for our people and country should be noted and remembered by every Cherokee. The news of your brilliant exploit with the Yankees 30 miles from Boggy Depot reached here a few days ago; it has been the subject of much praise.[12] It will now become necessary to choose a staff for your brigade; Lynch I presume is your favorite for Commissary. I think he is as good a choice as you could make. Dick Martin wished to be Quarter Master last fall. I believe he would make a good one; he or Hooly Bell — I throw them out as suggestions merely. You should be *particularly* careful in the selection of an adjutant; *he* should by all means be a man of ability, of good business tact, of military experience and capacity. You should in my opinion select some young man who has served as a Lt. or Capt. of infantry, who has been inured to discipline and understands the duties of a soldier; if you get such a man he should have, under your supervision, the entire management of the police regulations of your brigade, and superintend the thorough drilling of the men. I would beg you to see that your adjt. attends to these matters without fail. I can think of no person more competent to put the brigade in good fighting trim than Andrew Ridge;[13] he is as you know a young officer of fine sense and much experience: he is brim full of courage and ambition. I write these desultory remarks as I would talk to you; and you will appreciate my motives. You have first rate material for a Qr. M. and com. Washbourne might

[12] After the return of the Union forces to the Cherokee country and their re-enforcement in Fort Gibson, the Confederate Indians could do little more than make sporadic demonstrations against Federal herds and supply trains. In raiding and leading foraging expeditions, Stand Watie was at his best.

[13] Andrew Ridge, son of John Ridge, later wrote Stand Watie asking for a place in his regiment. In this letter Boudinot shows that he recognized Stand Watie's dislike for the routine and detail which would be a part of his work in the higher rank of brigadier general.

accept the Qr. M's place[14] — but these are matters of which you are the only judge. President Davis says he will not under any consideration give up any portion of the Indian country. Mr. Scott will soon be in the Indian Country with money for you; I will have $50,000 more by next January I think without fail. The great battle so long pending between Lee and Grant was fought yesterday and today; full official reports have not yet been recd.[15] Enough is known however to convince us that we are again victorious. My regards to all friends. God bless you.

Affly.

CORNELIUS

ᴥ𝔖James M. Bell to Caroline Bell

Hd Qtrs 2nd Cher Regt
Camp Watie May 8th, 1864

MY OWN DEAR ONE

I cannot withstand the pleasure of writing you a line as I know that it will afford you a great deal of satisfaction to receive it. I am nearly well again, have been quite [ill] for ten days, was taken with rheumatism and a very severe chill and Billious remittent fever. Our Scouts start this morning north about eight hundred. I will let you know if anything is done.

The news we have received is all of the most cheering character. We have not recieved official news of the Surrender of the Federal Genl Steele to Genl Price, but there is news continually coming in that he has surrendered and it is generally believed as he evacuated Camden Ark in great haste cutting down his waggons and leaving a great many of his soldiers who were taken prisoners.[16] They broke in on our people while fasting and praying this year and they seem to have had no success. I have always told you that we must be independent. I have as much faith in our ability to withstand the Federal troops now even more than at the commencement of the

14 J. Woodward Washbourne.
15 This was the memorable Battle of the Wilderness.
16 The writer was referring to the famous Camden expedition.

war. Why should we not. Our cause must be a just one and we are only trying to defend our rights — Our homes our wives & our children.

Will you love us the better for doing so or not. I sometimes think you will not. The scout is all eagerness to get off and I must tell you "good bye," kiss all the children and tell them to send me some word. While writing Mr Jerrold came in with the mail from Texas. A letter from Willy. I am obliged tell him, and if I had time would answer it which I will take occasion to do soon he must write often giving me the news. I will take pleasure in attending to his requests. The rings must be made. love to Brock & Jose. Kiss *Watie* a hundred times at least.[17] Tell the negroes all howdy. Lewis is well & sends howdy. they must make a heap of corn potatoes & peas. I am Carrie dearest as ever your most affectionate

JIM

P.S. The reciept for Hooleys corn I sent to you, you can get the corn & I can reciept him here for it, have it measured & send me the amount. J.M.B.

W. T. Adair[18] to Stand Watie

Hᵈ. Qr. 2ᵈ Cherokee Reg'nt
Camp Magruder
Perryville C. Nation
May 20th 1864

MY DEAR COL,

This morning I was pleased to receive letters, or notes, from yourself, Dr. Duval and Col. Bell, and glad to hear you were all well and doing *first rate*. I was sorry tho' that you had no Bread & Sugar to mix along. I have been up today to the Commissary to get some Rations for yours & the Col's Mess. You will find, in the wagon that accompanies the Scout, fifty (50)

---

[17] This was their young son, William Watie Bell.
[18] Dr. W. T. Adair enlisted in the First Cherokee Mounted Volunteers as field and staff surgeon. He later saw service in the second Cherokee Regiment, under his brother, Colonel William P. Adair.

pounds of flour, Twenty five (25) pounds Bacon, Ten (10) pounds Sugar, Ten (10) pounds salt, and five (5) pounds of Soap — all marked to you and Col. Adair. I sent it to you for your mess. I also sent you something over a ½ Qr. paper and a Dozen Envelopes — and your clothes. Do not take a notion into your head that you are becoming troublesome. I would like to hear from you daily and to know what was going on in your part of our Nation, what the feds are doing &c, and what they are likely to do, & our prospects for getting our country again. I have written to Texas since you left and give all the news — wrote *fourteen pages* this time — told them all about you & Col., Scout going out, where you were and as near as I could what you were doing. We received letters from Rusk yesterday Evening, which I will send to you and the Col. There was none came for you or myself — one for Col. & one for Lt. Col. Joe. The letters did not say anything about yours or my family, but I presume that they must have been well or something would have been said in relations thereto. Crops, corn good and promising — will raise plenty of wheat, in that country.[19] So good for our Army. The Conscript Law is being rigedly enforced, in that Country. They have run Starr Bean out, he is now on Red River, in the Choctaw Nat. stopped down there — dont know whether he intends coming on and joining us or not. I suppose he will tho'. Tom Still and Mont. Dial of Bellview have come out — Dial will start back in a few days. But Still will remain with us. I have written to Burton to come. John Harnage will not now come, as he has been appointed ass't Enrolling Officer for the County of Rusk. The young fellows are organizing rapidly also. General Maxey has not come up yet — he and Cooper are both at Doaksville and anxiously looked for him. Maxey furloughed the Choctaws ten days, when he first came back. And it seems to be the prevailing opinion that as soon as he can get together he will march for these parts. "Madame Rumor" or "Reliable Gentleman" says that Maxey brings two Brigades of White Troops

[19] The writer was referring to Rusk County, Texas, where many of the Southern Cherokee were living in refuge.

— Gano's and Cabbell's. I hope it is so. Col. Well's Battalion arrived yesterday evening. The Seminoles are coming, the Chickasaws have gone on to Johnson's Station, I expect with the intention of joining you.[20] It is impossible for me to say when we will leave this place, tho' I hope soon — as I am getting mortal tired of it. My Respects to all of friends and write soon and often, and give me *all* the news down your way.

Very Truly
Your Friend
W. T. Adair Brig. Surg.
1st Indian Brigade

✑ T. R. Harden[21] to W. P. Adair

Camp Mcgruder May the 26 1864

Col. W. P. Adair

In obedience to your order Capt Hendren and myself proceed to Benton Co. Ark to gether up the absentees of our command. on our way to Benton we crossed a trail made by a federal scout of 200 from springfield Mo. They made there rade through benton Co Ark on the 3rd day of May. they killed five men took 3 prisoners. we then notified the men to meet us at a certain place on the 8 day but the 7 day Capt Anderson from Ft Gipson with 130 of his pins came on through the Nation, gethered up some of the independent pins, increased his scout to a bout 200. Capt Hendren with 17 men met them on the 7 at Huffs Mill on spavinaw and they fiered on the advance of the pins killed 2 wounded 7. Capt Hendren got the men away with out any hirt. the pins killed 7 men mosly citizens robing houses and taking all the flour and meal in the country.[22] we

---

[20] The appointment of General S. B. Maxey apparently infused new life into the Southern Indians since Maxey was an able and efficient officer who had their entire confidence.

[21] T. R. Harden was a Major in Company C of the second Cherokee Mounted Volunteers under Colonel William P. Adair. He enlisted in Benton County, Arkansas, and was probably not a Cherokee.

[22] The writer was referring to activities of the "Pin" group of Union Cherokee. The return of the federal forces made it possible for them to regain the upper portion of the Cherokee Nation.

then gathered up our men and remained in camp. on the 12 day of May I taken 4 men and went to take a confederate soldier prisner who swore he was going to Join the feds but we could not find him that evening Capt Hendren moved his camp in two miles of his residence Camped his men and walked over home. about 10 clock in the night of the 12 of May some 40 Militia attacked Capt Hendrens Camp. the Capt not haveing got back yet the men ware all laying down when the Militia dismounted marched up in ten steps of where the men were sleeping opened fire on the encampment hollowed charge at that time the men awoke from sleep with grate excitement leaving there horses and equipage. one man killed there. all the rest got a way safe some five horses ware taken out by our boys. on the next day they killed John Briges got his horse making 27 head they captured on that rade.

W. P. Adair
Comdy 2nd Cherokee Regt.

T. R. Harden, Maj
2nd Cherokee Regt

✑ Sarah C. Watie to Stand Watie

Rusk May 27 1864

My dear husband

I have just come from Susanah Mc Nairs she will not last longer than to morrow. I fell sorry to see her for she was my earliest friends. she was the friend of my child hood. [It was] long before either of us could speak. she says you have come at last. I told her yes, that was all I could say. I have not been well since I saw you, part of the time I was very bad but now I feel a great deal better. I will stay here in this part of the country till July and then I expect to hear from you and if you think there will be peace I will go back as far as I was.[23] It is ten times as hard to get along here as there. I am not well enough to do any thing in the way of making a liveing. I will do well to save my self alive for my children. Nancey is still very feable just can walk about the house, all the rest are well.

[23] Mrs. Watie may have expected to return to the Choctaw Country where some of the refugee Cherokee were living.

163

I am sorry that Oakes could not buy a load but perhaps he can get enough to make a load at sulphur springs. you must govern him. you can tell better than I can but I will watch for a chance to buy but no one will sell any thing for the money. every one wants the new issue. I do not know what they will do with the money if it wont buy what we want. just at this time you can't get any thing with it Borde nor any thing else.[24] I will write all the neighbourhood news by Lucien. I am not well enough at this time to write much. may I use those book[s] for the children to write in it will do them more good than anything else.[25]   from your affectionate wife

S. C. WATIE

⇜ Stand Watie to Sarah C. Watie

Camp Jumper 10 miles north of Perryville.

MY DEAR SALLIE: June 1st, 1864.

In my last I promised to write again soon as I should return from Schullyville. I have been back four or five days found the Pins had left a day or two before and I was not very sorry for it. They had been strongly posted, had a fight come off we would have certainly lost good many men, but it seemed they had taken an alarm and left in a hurry as they had left some commissaries and tools they had been working with on the fortification. A place was picketed near the commissary house behind that large stone house near where you lived, all the houses around that place had port holes cut to shoot out of, the picketing was out of green timber sunk in the ground two feet and large logs rolled against them all around on the outside, two platforms for artillery. The boys burnt every house that had a port hole in it and destroyed the fort much as they could. The Pins are now near the river opposite to Fort Smith, Creeks and few other troops about 1200 at Gibson. Lieut. Col. James Bell took a scout with a hundred men to near Fort

---

[24] The depreciated Confederate currency was another evidence of the hopelessness of the Southern cause.

[25] Some of Stand Watie's ledgers and account books.

Smith, killed one notorious Captain by the name of Gibbons who was a terror to the southern people and brought in three Feds prisoners. Arkansas river is very high, a portion of the cavalry force of my command is on the other side of the Canadian. Cooper with the Choctaws, Gans Brigade, is at Johnsons Station. Maxey is at Doaksville. There are some four thousand men at Fort Smith. The main army of the Federals at Little Rock. It cannot be long before a general move is made in the direction of Arkansas river. The union citizens of Washington and Benton Counties are moving out north. A letter from Mr. Wheeler to John brings the sad news of the death of Mary Ann, her little girl had died a few days before. John took it very hard. Saladin has been sick but is now well ready as he says for a fight. I received a letter from Ann Shelton. I felt better after receiving it, I was very uneasy after seeing Richard, he told me that you was very sick, but Ann tells me you had got better. Tell her that I admire her medical skill, she says she burnt you, how did she do it? did she stick a coal of fire to your side? She must have a *Diploma*. If anything, such as calico or other finery can be had she shall be remembered. Joe Martin and Hooley have gone after cotton and wool cards.[26] I will write whenever opportunity presents itself. Jim has written to Ann, I will write to her at some other time. Write whenever you can. I feel anxious to hear from the children. In my next I may have something of interest to tell you from our country. I rather look for this war to end with this year 1864. The period will then have been times & half a time some where about the beginning of September.[27]

Write Soon,
Your affectionate husband,
STAND

[26] The cards were sorely needed for preparing the cotton and wool for spinning. The opening of the Mississippi by the North had rendered it extremely difficult for the trans-Mississippi region to secure any supplies from east of the river. In consequence they were forced to rely upon their own resources.

[27] This Biblical reference (Daniel 12:7 and Revelations 12:14) shows General Stand Watie's intimate knowledge of the Bible.

165

⋞§ Elias C. Boudinot to W. P. Boudinot

Hos. of Reps
Richmond June 2 1864

DEAR BROTHER[28]

I was glad to get your letter, but think it hardly becomes you to chide me for not writing when you have been so negligent yourself — the fact is I *have* written repeatedly, both to you and others, if you did not get my letters its not my fault. I never suffered an opportunity to slip without writing to somebody in the *Genl's* command. I procured the appt. of Uncle Stand as Brig. Genl; but could have got his promotion two months earlier if you had kept me posted — his commission has gone to him, to make a sure thing I will take an official copy.

You want news! About four weeks ago Genl Lee assured the authorities here that Grant's immense army was advancing; this had been anticipated long before and Longstreets corps from East Tenn. and all the detached portions of Lees army were speedily concentrated. Richmond was comparatively defenseless, there not being 5000 troops of all arms in and around the city. At the same time Grant was making his demonstrations it was known that Baldy Smith and Butler were gathering a large force to menace Richmond by way of Yorktown as we supposed. In this state of things you may slightly imagine our feelings, when at 11 o'clock one night we received the refreshing intelligence that Butler with 4000 men accompanied by a powerful fleet of gunboats and monitors had already landed at Bermuda Hundred, a point on the James river ten miles from Petersburg and about 25 miles from this "hated city." It looked like a sensible conclusion that Butler had only to choose which prize he would take first; two hours march would have given him Petersburg a city nearly as large as Richmond and the possession of the southern railroad — by

---

[28] This informal letter presents an interesting contemporary account of conditions about Richmond in the late spring of 1864. The events and officers mentioned are so well known as to make editorial comment unnecessary.

day light, if he chose, he could have made his head quarters in Jeff. Davis mansion — but like the Jackass who starved to death between two stacks of nice hay because he could not make up his mind which he would eat — so Butler following the tactics of some of our smart Genls. in the Indian Country lost everything by his sloth and imbecility; he quietly went into camp, entrenched and in a couple of days spread himself out took the R. R. between Petersburg and this place, only 11 miles from here, and began to smell around Drewrys Bluff cautiously. All this time wasted by Butler was employed by us in bringing troops from South & North Carolina. In three days Beauregard with ten thousand men had arrived at Petersburg; every body in Richmond able to go was in the trenches — this force kept Butler at arms length — still our troops poured in until in four or five days Beauregard was at the head of *30000* men — we could hear the firing plain in the city day after day, but no general engagement occured until one morning — I've forgot the date, but only five or six days after Butler had landed, the city fairly shook with the thunder of artillery. I was wakened by it — the firing was terrific and very rapid. I counted looking at my watch 30 guns a minute. Beaureguard had attacked the enemy in his intrenchments. About 9 o'clock a yankee Brig. Genl. and 1500 men were brought to town as prisoners showing that Beauregard was doing a pretty good mornings work. Maj. Genl. Whiting was to have acted a prominent part in the rear of the enemy — but he was on a *bust* and failed, so that Butler saved his routed army by falling back on his gun boats which he couldn't have done if Whiting hadn't been drunk. Whiting was promptly relieved, but he ought to be shot, from what *they say.* Just about this time when every armed man almost was south of James river looking out for Butler Genl Sheridan with 15000 mounted infantry and 20 pieces of artillery got around in the rear of Lees army destroyed the R. R. about 20 miles from Richmond and with nothing in his way swept "on to Richmond" — the road was clear, nothing to stop him. Lee discovered the move and sent Stuart with about four thousand cavalry after him — but he was *four hours*

behind. Sheridan anticipating pursuit blocked the roads and
burned bridges behind him — at dark we heard from Sheridan
16 miles from the city — he had stopped to rest his men and
feed his horses — this saved us. He sent word that he would
be here at 1 o'clock, the alarm bells were rung and intense excitement prevailed, the *govt.* packed up. Beauregard sent infantry to the city but it was thought it would be too late. in
this interesting state of affairs, we learned that every R. R.
leading out of the city was cut by the enemy and all who didnt
relish a life of solitary confinement for the rest of the war &
those "grave and reverend seignors" who would escape the
halter were admonished that they must take their feet in their
hands and be ready for locomotion. I was called up at 1 o'clock
by the Arks senators but after going down town and seeing
no yankees, went to bed again. Nobody had any fixed plan
about getting out of the way. I had determined in the hubub
which would naturally take place when the yankees entered
the city to retire to our army, south of James river — a walk of
12 to 15 miles. At day light, we could hear small even firing
just outside of town — Stuart had caught up with the Yankees
and pitched into them bravely — they took our outer works
however, but swerved from the direct line, giving up time to
get troops into position. The fighting was brisk, but troops
poured through yelling vociferously strengthening many feeble
knees; by noon the danger was past, and the enemy lost another good chance of taking Richmond. All this time Grant was
butting against Lees intrenchments — he hurled his masses with
reckless enthusiasm upon Lee, but were as often beat back with
great loss; he succeeded in breaking through Lees lines at one
time and things looked squally. Lee rode to Greggs brigade
of Texas and Arks troops and told them they must recover the
lost ground — he ordered them forward leading with his hat
off — a general cry went up for him to go back but he refused — the men finally swore they would not advance unless
he went back; the line of battle stopped; two officers seized
Lees horse by the bridle and *forced* him from the field amid
the cheers of the soldiers. this is no fable — it is a fact by hun-

168

dreds who witnessed it — the charge was ordered and the Texans and Arkansans swept everything before them. Grant was worse whipped at the battles of the wilderness thenHooker was at Chancellorsville, but he spunkily brought up his reserves, moved down the river towards Spottsylvania C. H. around Lees right. Lee made a corresponding move to keep Grant from getting or slipping round between him and Richmond — the two great battles at this C. H. were fought on the 10 and 12 the heaviest on the 12th. The Feds opened with the advantage, they poured over our works & captured 18 pieces of artillery and 2000 prisoners, among them Major Genl. Johnson, Lees favorite division commander; Longstreet before this had been severely wounded in the neck by our own men. Our loss in officers has been heavy. Stuart was killed close to this city.[29] The battle of the 12th closed decidedly in our favor, we held our own against the most tremendous assaults — the enemy were drunk and staggered up in lines ten deep to the very muzzle of our guns. One jolly fellow reeled over our works and fell upon his back among our men in the trenches. He exclaimed with a hiccup — "here we are boys, let's take a drink," sensible to the last. It is said our boys accepted his invitation and soon emptied his canteen. We recovered all the ground lost and four of the guns captured; our loss in killed and wounded was nothing in comparison with the enemy's — we fought behind fortifications. All Grants reserves were brought into the fight and his loss is estimated by the Yankees themselves as from 25 to 30000 killed and wounded — up to the 13 the loss of Grants army was at least 55000 men, and some of the Northern papers put it at 70000. Grant has not been able to bring his army to the scratch since, tho he has tried repeatedly; he has managed to edge around however, flanking Lee, and compelling him to move towards Richmond to keep Grant still in his front, until today Lees army is in line but 8 or 10 miles from the city. Butler has abandoned his po-

[29] General J. E. B. Stuart, the great cavalry leader of the South, was killed at the Battle of Yellow Tavern.

sition and is trying to make junction with Grant — perfect confidence is felt that Lee will whip the enemy as he always does — You wouldnt dream if you should walk through town and see the self satisfied air of everybody that a hostile army of 150000 men were almost in sight of town, on bloody thoughts intent. Yesterday morning and evening we could hear firing from Lees lines — we gained some advantages. You will see from the slip I send you — During all this fighting about Richmond our old friend Sigel was thrashed by Breckenridge, losing six guns and 2000 men. John Morgan also whipped a column in L. W. Va. which was to perform a part in the Grant programme.

Now I have given you in short all the news of interest hereabouts. I send slips of late papers. Congress has resolved to adjourn next Tuesday, but lest I may be delayed I send this ahead. You must send it to Scales and Hooly Bell both of whom were so kind as to write to me. I have not time to write to them as I would wish, but send them the latest news from the papers.

Laflore was incorrect in his speculation about my approaching *nuptials*. I went to Lynchburg to see your old friend Ciss Chisolm,[30] now the wife of Col Owen, Prest. of the Va and Tenn R. R. I got a letter from Frank[31] by flag of truce the other day — he wrote from Winchester Va — in the yankee lines — he wanted me to meet him at City Point, but of course we couldn't do so, he gave no news of himself — his writing looked like a writing masters — he had the downward stroke very beautiful and his upward strokes were exceptionable.

[30] This was Narcissa Chisholm Owen who was the mother of Robert L. Owen, for many years United States senator from Oklahoma.

[31] This was Frank Boudinot, a younger brother of Elias and William P. Boudinot. He did not return to Indian Territory when he finished his schooling in the East but had remained in the North, as related in a previous footnote. At the outbreak of the war, he enlisted in the Union army and served with credit. It is a bit sad that he and Cornelius were not allowed to see each other, for he was wounded in one of the last battles before Richmond, and died from his wounds. He left a widow and a son Frank, who died in the early 1890's. Both father and son were actors by profession.

170

I pay $450. for board per month — my washing and contingencies run the figure over 500 a month without indulgence in whiskey.[32] Board at hotel 30 dollars per day for regular boarders, single meals $15. I collected for Wm. Alberty by hard work a claim of $18000. I charged him 10 per cent — this enables me to squeeze through without selling my watch. Kirby Smith has made a brilliant campaign against Banks and Steele.[33] Every body hurrahs for the Trans. Miss. Dpt. Love to Carrie[34] and the children.

Truly and affly yr. brother

CORNELIUS

June 3

P.S. Last evening from 5 oc'lk to dark the firing from Lee's lines was rapid and incessant. I counted 45 guns to the minute. Its a little singular but a fact that although we can hear every gun that is fired we know no more of the operations than we do of Johnsons army in Georgia — we see prisoners brought in, and wounded, but dont know anything after all. This morning at day light the heavy firing was reopened. I hear it now as I write. They say we are doing well — at any rate no alarm is felt. The Enquirer is a strong Watie paper; it has given him several handsome notices[35] — the Examiner published as Editorial matter an article on Indian affairs of mine. My object was to commit it to a certain line which may be useful to us hereafter. I have written by request, a long article for the London Herald, on Indian matters. If I get a copy of the article I will save it for you.

Yr. brother

CORNELIUS

[32] This shows the rapid depreciation of Confederate currency. Boudinot wrote the preceding January that he paid $300 a month for board at that time.

[33] Boudinot is referring to General E. Kirby Smith's defeat of General Nathaniel Prentiss Banks and Frederick Steele in the Red River campaign.

[34] Carrie [Fields] Boudinot was the wife of the writer's brother, William P. Boudinot.

[35] This shows that Stand Watie's fame had spread throughout the Confederacy. A brave and dashing leader, he could hardly fail to arouse great enthusiasm among the Southern people.

◄§ Sarah C. Watie to Stand Watie

Rusk Co Texas
June 12 1864

MY DEAR HUSBAND,

I have not been well enough to write much since I come here, sometimes I feel well for a day or two then worse. I dont hear from you at all and that troubles me and all things put to gether keeps me in such low spirits that I cant mend. I been very bad of ever sence I left Jarratts.[36] there is some one coming every few days but none of them can tell me any thing, where you are and tell me whether I had better get a place or not and where. I thought if you thought best I would get a place by the time you could come, if you could come this fall I would go back to Lamar County. I have no idea that you can leave long enough to come here. I do wish you would leave the service and let them see whether they can do so well with out you as some seem to think. as for me I want some to learn how well they will do for I dont feel as if they treat you right, so let them go where they want to go. as for the Nation I believe it is bound to go to the dogs and the more one does to save it the more blame the will have to bear. I dont never expect to sit down in peace among them and if I could I would not for my weight in gold for I am tired of it and if nothing better than the last few years remains for me why I have no desire to live if it was not for Jack and Ninny. I would rather die than always live in dread as we did, it is no pleasure. I would like to live a short time in peace just to see how it would be. I would like to feel free once in life again and feel no dread of war or any other trouble.

you wrote to me you would meet me at Sheltons but I have no ida you will be there so soon, but write to me and tell me when you can be there or in that neighborhood and I will go. I do hope the war will end this year. I will try and get some where close to a school so that the children can go from home, they are *to* small to bord out long at the time. I will try and

---

[36] D. Jarrett Bell was a brother of Mrs. Watie.

have them clothes enough for winter but that is all I can do, for I cant spin a bit my self no do I expect I can if I remain weak as I am. tell Saladin he must shift for his clothes for I cant buy anything at all. Oaks[37] went back with out any load from here. I told him to take what he had from here and buy a load at Sulphur Springs and hurry back to camp. I don't know whether he can buy anything that will pay or not. I will watch and if I can I will buy, that is tobacco. I cant buy any thing with old money, you must send me some that will pass. I told Oks to trade on that he had and sell what he bought for new. I have not sold my horses yet. I dont see how I can do with out them unless I was home and stay there. I had mind to go back to paris. it is far from you. I cant hear any thing but you can tell better than I whether it would be best or not. write me a long letter, you tell me every thing that is going on. sister Nancey is no better than she was last summer. she is very weak but does not cough much like most people with her disease though she does not seem to have the real consumption but it is almost the same. I do not think she will live long though she may last a year or two and she may not last a month. I have not heard any news that would interest you only that Joe Buffington wrote her aunt Nancy an insulting letter. it made the old lady hot and she said they were determined to make her mean just as she going die and if it sent her to the devil she did not want her to come here. she says that they have tormented her what time she has been here. I will write again soon. be sure and write. Jack sends love and a blossom to she say kiss the letter...

SARAH C. WATIE

❧ Sarah C. Watie to Stand Watie

June 21st 1864

MY DEAR HUSBAND

I am still at sister Nancy. I am a great deal better than I was when you last heard of me. I received you letter by Mr

---

[37] Oakes was employed by Mrs. Watie. He was engaged in hauling goods and supplies.

173

Alberty. when I met him at the river I could scarcely walk down the bank of the river. if I could get the right kind of medacine I might get well but there is no cance of getting it here. there is no sarsaparilla in this country. if I could get that it would do Nancy and me both a great deal of good and if you could get me some of that grass I use to tell you of it would cure me. I think it dont grow here, it grows in that country any where. its thorney on the edge of the blade. if you can, send some of each kind by the first chance. well I have told you all I want before I would forget it because every body must talk to one while we write. well it will not do not to tell you some funny thing. Joe Buffington is still at her old trade she has fell out with all of her kin. she wrote sister N. a letter not long ago and give her sut and last week she went over to her sister Charlotte and give her a round for not saying she had acted the lady with her. I dont think Carlotte will live long she ought not to talk so to her. John Thompson has been brought home he was wounde down on the river it will cripple him for life I expect. William P Adair has a fine daughter dont you recon he things he has played the mischief.[38] well I have some funny things [to] tell you but I am a fraid to, some one might get hold of my letter as I have been told they were some examined before you get them. oh dont let no one see such foolishness. oh I must not forget I have not heard of Oakes since he left here. George was to have brought a load for him but could not get it for the money so he started back with the money and thought he could by a load at Sulphur Springs and sell for the new issue which I thought would be the best. you must see to it. he had some 3000 dollars or more. you had better settle with him when he gets there and see that he dont lose it. we cant buy anything with the money here. I want you to send me some of the new and if you want me to buy any thing write and tell me. there is tobaco here at 30 dollars a pound and George would buy if he had new money but he has none.

[38] William P. Adair, later assistant chief of the Cherokee Nation and delegate to Washington on several occasions, was at this time a colonel of one of the Cherokee regiments.

when you send me money send Joe back I can't get along with out him. I let him go with Oakes. you must write and tell me what you think of the times. I want to go back to paris. this country dont suit me. I am afraid our own people will be fussing among them selves and I am afraid that they will have Saladin in it. he got in a difficulty here when he was out here. it troubles me a great deal. Lucian Bell has some trouble about that order you sent down here after those men to return to the army.[39] I can hear it every where I go. dont let one of them come again for it only makes trouble but write me tell me when you will be at or near home for I will be up there before long or as soon as you can be there. I will go back if ther is no danger. I will be at Jarratts in August but I dont know what time. you can write to me and tell me what you think of me going

Jack was awful mad when you did not write her a little letter to her self. you must write each of them one and Wataca dont mind me like he use to. write to him and give him advise. you[rs] till death.   S WATIE

I will write to you by Col Mc Nair.
all well. send me envelopes.

⋙ William Levy to Stand Watie

Pilot Grove, Texas, June 22d 1864.

Col. Commdg Stand Watie,
Principal Chief Cherokee Nation,

Enclosed please find Judge Wheeler's letter, introducing me to you. I have been prevented from visiting you, and even now can only direct myself to you by writing.

Your nephew, Lieut. John Wheeler,[40] can give you all information about myself, as he knew me as long as I was living in Fort Smith.

---

[39] In accordance with the conscript law, Stand Watie had sent Lucien B. (or Hooley) Bell to the Texas Cherokee ordering all men of military age to report for service.

[40] This was John C. Wheeler, son of John F. Wheeler.

What I have to say, Col., is this. The Governors of the Choctaw & Chickasaw Nations[41] have made an application to General E. Kirby Smith to export Cotton to Mexico without interruption or restriction whatever from the Government and import the necessary articles for the *families* of the Indians.[42] This has been granted to them, the Choctaws have a permit for the free export of 500 bales of cotton, and the Chickasaws of 300.

Governor Colbert has appointed me as Agent, I have to buy the cotton and deliver Transportation *for my own money,* and as both cannot be had except for *Specie,* Confederate money will not be received any more for this articles — it will be a little difficult, although I hope to accomplish it.

The principal Idea is: to sell the Cotton again for Specie, and after the *Deduction* of the *Capital* invested in Cotton & Transportation & Expense, to buy for the *Balance* Goods needed by the Indian *families* and sold to them for Confd money or given to them.

You will easily perceive, Col., that it is a very good idea and a splendid plan to provide for the suffering families, and at the same time, it is a good paying business for those engaged in it, as it cannot be expected that we should spend our time and money entirely for charity sake. Judge Wheeler will be with me, he is one of my best friends in the world, and, without saying much, it will certainly be of great Interest to yourself.

I cannot explain more of it in writing — you will understand the whole of it plainly. And again: it is *not for the Soldiers* but for the *families* of the Cherokees.

If you now find it proper, you will write to General E Kirby Smith in Shreveport an application, signed by you as Principal Chief of the Cherokees, in which you request to give you "Permission to export without the least restriction at least Five

---

[41] The governors of the Choctaw and Chickasaw Nations at this time were, respectively, Samuel Garland and Winchester Colbert.

[42] The blockade had cut off the exportation of cotton, but a considerable quantity from the Southwest was exported through Mexico. The writer evidently had in mind the relief of the Southern Cherokee.

Hundred (500) Bales of Cotton to be sold in Mexico, for the *Specie,* the surplus of which, after the deduction of the Capital invested, to be invested in articles needed by the Indians and delivered to them."

I have suggested this idea to Gov. Colbert and the Gov. of the Choctaws has followed.

You will please write the application as *I did style it,* else the Chief Agent of the Cotton Bureau will make difficulties as he has done already to Gov. Colbert, against which he has *protested.* That is: he has granted a permit to export Cotton to Eagle Pass, *to be delivered to the Agent of the Texas Cotton Office to be there exchanged for goods,* And this cannot be done because if I invest *Specie* in Cotton I want my *Capital in Specie* back, but not the goods.

As it is rather late in season and a good while passes in sending to Shreveport — and back — I would respectfully say, not to delay the matter, but send it off as soon as possible, and if it will do, directly by Express.

Colonel! It is important for you and all those interested in, and I would allow me to make it as urgent as possible: and the sooner the better.

Please dear Sir! Let me hear from you soon, and whatever it may be, is a business matter between us alone.[43]

I remain, Colonel,

Very Respectfully Your obedient servant

WILLIAM LEVY

◄§ Mary Starr[44] to James M. Bell

MY DEAR UNCLE   At Home June 22nd/64

I haven't time to write you a lengthy letter though if but a

---

[43] The high price of cotton led many unscrupulous individuals to enter into various profiteering schemes. There is not the slightest evidence that Stand Watie ever entered into an arrangement with the writer of this letter or anyone else to profit by exporting cotton. In fact, later letters show that both Stand Watie and his wife denounced bitterly any attempt to profiteer at the expense of the Cherokee people.

[44] Mary Starr was the daughter of Mrs. Watie's sister Nancy (previously

line so its from home will be appreciated. Mother has been sick ever since you left, she is some better to day. I hope she will soon be as well as she was last Winter. Aunt Sallie is here she has been sick too though she is able to be up and at work nearly all the time. I saw Aunt Caroline last week & hear from her every day. I believe they are all well & doing well. I have no news to write only Miss Mary Estill is married to Captain Terry of Tarrant County.

Hoolie & Capt. Martin started to San Antonia last week Hoolie said that he would be back in thirty five days. They did not take any cotton. I dont reckon they will get many cards as they are selling at $105 per pair.

You must write often for we are always glad to hear from you. When shall we look for you at home? All send their love to you.

Your affectionate Niece
MARY STARR

◄§Sarah C. Watie to Stand Watie

July 2 1864

MY DEAR HUSBAND

I wrote to you a few days ago by ben Goss but I will write again as I promised I would. Matlock will start in the morning to you camps. I would like to see you before you go into the service again but it is impossible. I wish you would resigne and let them all go all they want to. I can always hear some thing said that makes me mad. I never go any where but I hear some thing said about that order you sent down here by Lucien Bell for them to go back to camp by the 25 of March, they all pretend that they did not believe you sent it. I want you to call them all up and tell them for I dont look for any thing else but for hooley to be killed about it. you can ask hooley about it when he gets ther. you have no idia how much

---

referred to) and her husband George Starr. The letter was evidently written from Rusk County, Texas to the writer's uncle, James M. Bell.

talk and fuss that has made among them here. the men write and thrown out hints and then the women go it. it is no place for me for I dont want to hear it. they throw out hints that it's this one and that one that have done the most for you. I would like to know who has done for them. I have got so I dont care if they never do get the old country back and if they do what good will it do such people, none only to fuss over it just let them have command and see what they will do we can live any where.[45] I can find more friends among strangers right now than I can among my owne people. I must account for all that goes on if I dont account for it it must be throwed up to me. if the men dont do it they will put it in the mind of the women and they will, but enough of that. I just want you to know how things are here. I will go back to paris the first of september or sooner for I dont like this country at all. write and tell me when you will come out there. I will go in that neighborhood some where so I can hear from you often. Tell Saladin and Charles that I have been to sick to do any thing so I have no clothes for them and the money would not buy it but as soon as they send me some that will pass I will try and get it. Reports say we gained a great battle in the 19 of this month at Richmond.

I do wish one could have peace once more but I fear that is not for me to see in my day. There is a great many things I would put in this letter but I have heard that my letters were opened sometimes so it would not do to trust every little foolishness in here. keep your eye on Saladin and guide him in the right way and dont let him go astray. I will go to see Charlotte before long. next week I will be at her home for a short time. when you write send by her house. I want to stay at her house in grape time for I never saw so many in my life. I want

[45] The war caused the breaking up of the Cherokee Nation along the lines of its former disturbances and factional differences. On several occasions plans were suggested for the division of the tribe into two groups, with the view of eliminating the factional differences. These plans did not materialize and perhaps it was just as well for the years following the close of the war were to see the death of the former party leaders and a greater unity of the Cherokee than at any previous time since their settlement in the West.

179

to make a barrel of wine for you against you come to see me. I can gather bushels of them in a quarter of a mile of the house. do write. dont wait so long and tell me if I must go back or not. I would not have come if Saladin had not wanted me to. love to all

S C WATIE

write soon. Nancey is very bad. I fear she will not last long. poor woman I feel for her. I know how she feels. her road is a dark one. dont show this.

✑William M. Adair to Stand Watie

Hon. Stand Watie,   Sulphur Springs
Pl. Chief Cherokee Nation   July 4th 1864

SIR,

Yours of the 28th Ins. is at hand, directing Capt Martin to establish a Depot on Gaynes Creek, for Indigent Cherokees.[46] In reply, (I have to say) that a Depot will be established at that point at the earliest convenience. There will have to be a new Roll made out for them and approved by yourself before they can have Rations issued to them. It is impossible to get Rations to them before the 10th or 15th of next month. We are very scant of transportation, not enough to keepe up with our Rations for this place. I will appoint some man to act as Issuing Agent and send him up to make out a Roll and hire wagons, as there are none in this part of the Country to be had.

Hoping that such a course will meete with your approval, I am

Your Most Obt. Servt

WM. M. ADAIR

Act. Chief Issuing Agt for Cherokees

---

[46] The task of caring for the destitute refugees was a very heavy one, taxing to the limits all the resources of the leaders.

[47] It is surprising that Boudinot, in common with so many leaders of the South, should have retained his optimism in view of the conditions confronting the Confederacy.

ᵛᵍ Elias Cornelius Boudinot to Stand Watie

Washington Ark.
July 13, 1864

DEAR UNCLE

I arrived here direct from Richmond a day or two since. I hardly know how to get to you. Everything is clearing about Richmond. Grant has been badly beaten in every fight — his losses up to the 18th of June according to Northern accounts foots up to 100,000 men. Since that time there have been four or five heavy battles which would swell their loss to a frightful number. Sherman has been defeated by Johnson and the latter has assumed the offensive. Chase has resigned — and gold has gone up to 300, Our cause never looked brighter and an early peace is universally predicted.[47] Scott left Richmond with 100,-000 for our Nation last January, I overtook him about the 20th of June at Meridian Miss. I suppose he will get over here a while — he has new issue.

I will send you a late paper. Write to me here, I have an official copy of your commission as Brig. Genl.

Affly yours
CORNELIUS

ᵛᵍ Elias Cornelius Boudinot to Stand Watie

Washington Arks.
July 25, 1864

DEAR UNCLE —

I intended to wait here until I heard from you — but conclude it is too uncertain and will go to Rusk County next week. I have no horse to ride and expect to go with Col Brooks in a buggy. I learn that the dun horse I left at Hoolys is too poor — *dead poor* to ride — I regret this exceedingly as he was in excellent order when I left and I did not dream that my friend in Rusk would use him so badly. Will you do me the great favor of sending my sorrel horse John Wheeler has been riding by some of the boys who would be glad to go to Rusk to

181

Hooly's so as to meet me there by the 10th of August, if possible. Dont neglect this Uncle Stand if you please — If the horse John Wheeler has been using is not in a condition to ride — I shall have to wait a month before I can visit your brigade — Scott has gone up to the Indian Country — he has got $100,000 in new issue that I had appropriated.[48]

Tell Anderson or whoever is your adjutant that I have got all the general orders up to May 4th for him, and whoever brings my sorrel horse to Hoolys place for me can carry them to the brigade.

Affly yours,
Cornelius

I wish you would give Hooly a leave of absence and let him bring me my horse John Wheeler has, either here, or take him to Rusk Co. where I can meet him.

C.

S. S. Scott to Stand Watie

Brig. Genl. Stand Watie,   Fort Towson, C. N.[49]
Prin. Ch'f. Cherokees,   July 27, 1864.
General:

I shall be at Fort Washita on the 8th of next month. You will please notify the Treasurer of the Cherokee Nation of this fact, so that he may meet me there, as I wish to turn over to him the residue of the money appropriated by Congress for the benefit of the indigent Cherokee refugees &c.

With best wishes for your welfare and that of your people,
I am respectfully,
Yr. Obt. Servt,
S. S. Scott
Commr. Ind. Affs.

[48] The Confederate Commissioner of Indian Affairs S. S. Scott had at last reached the Indian Country with money to relieve the destitution among the refugees.

[49] Scott went at once to the Choctaw Nation where many of the Cherokee refugees were assembled, since the greater part of their country was held by Northern troops.

⊰§ S. G. McLendon to Stand Watie

Doakesville C. N.
August 10th 1864

GENL,

In compliance with instructions contained in yr communication of 17th July I & Capt Martin "Commdr." did all in our power to get up the necessary transportation to bring the articles collected by Elder Compere from Miss. river.[50] We contracted with four men who agreed to report here with their teams on 4th Inst. but all failed to comply with their contract except one 4 mule team. The enclosed letter from Capt Martin will explain their reasons. Genl Maxey requested me to write to you on the subject, in order that you may take such steps as are necessary to get up the required number of wagons at an early date. I find that those who have teams manifest but little interest in getting the articles here. Capt M. agreed to pay them in cloth at the rates of one yd cloth per day for two horses and two yds for four horse teams &c as they refuse to go for Co. money. They are of opinions that if their teams should be captured or lost in any way that they would not get pay for them. I mention this in order that you may know their feelings in regard to this step. Capt Martin did not have any funds on hand to turn over to me to defray necessary expenses. I would be pleased for this matter to be given some attention as I have paid out already for necessary expenses until I am running short of money. Probably Genl Smith can furnish the necessary transportation, if it cannot be furnished by the Cherokees.

Hoping to hear from you at an early date I am

Very Respt. Yr. obdt. Svt.

Stand Watie   S. G. McLENDON
Brig Genl & Principal Chief Cherokee N.   Lt. C. S. A.

---

[50] Rev. E. L. Compere, a chaplain in Stand Watie's brigade, had been sent with Watie's adjutant, Thomas F. Anderson, east of the Mississippi River to secure medicines, cotton cards, and other supplies for the refugees. It was necessary to ferry these supplies across the Mississippi River, where they must be met on the west bank by wagons to transport them to their destination.

J. M. Lynch[51] to Caroline (Lynch) Bell

Camp Corser Aug 31st 1864

DEAR SISTER

I have nothing of importance to write Only good news from our army in Virginia. Gnl. Watie in command of about three hundred of his braves crossed Arkansas river a few days a go and attackted a small encampment of negro infantry as they thought but they were more of them than he expected and consequently flaxed our General but among the *whiped* was Col. James M. Bell your beloved husband. Watie killed several negroes took twelve prisoners (white men) only got three wounded. Col Bells horse was shot in the neck in the gallant charge. I was lucky enough not to be in that fight. Our company was not in camp at that time we was on our way from Cane Hill Ark. We stayed about a month in Cane Hill had a fine time had more good apples than I ever saw. The people in Cane Hill are the strongest sothern people I ever saw with exception of a few families who are union. Our company had two fights with the Feds on the road we were victorios in both fights killed sixty in all and lost no men, the luckeyest fighting I ever heard of, we fought on the 12th and 13th of this month we captured the United States mail and two seutler wagons loaded with goods but we could not bring any thing scarcely at all out. Our horses were nearly rode down. I had about fifteen pounds of coffee for you and Frank Adair was to bring it and I was to carrie some things for him but he concluded that his horse would not make the trip if he carried so much and gave the coffee away to Mrs. Danenbergs gals.

I managed to get through with 13 yards of calico for you which I send by Mr. Mart Dial. I dont think we will have a general fight soon the Feds wont came out and give us a fair fight we have tried several time [but] they will not come. I dont think Maxey intends to try to take Ft. Smith. Our army is in fairly good health. We keep our horses rode down scout-

---

[51] The writer of this letter, a brother of the wife of J. M. Bell, was at this time a lieutenant in the second Cherokee regiment.

ing and picketting. two hundred red men left our camps yesterday evening going thru the vicinity of Ft. Gibson to burn
some hay and take in a small squad ... you must send my
mare to me as soon as she is fit for service. dont send her until
she gets real fat, a fat horse will be a show here in about a
month. I want to send my gray horse back and let him rest
and get fat. Tell Brock to take good care of my mare. Salt
and water her regular and get her fat as soon as he can and I
will jahawk him a pony. Tell Ike, Lewis is well and likes
Camp verry well but the soldiers is spoiling him making him
curse ... Write soon tell William Brock to write and write
longer letters than they have been writing.

from your brother

N. B. J. M. Lynch

Direct your letter to Lieut. J. M. Lynch Capt Adair's Company 2d Cherokee Regt.

*Genl Waties 1st Indian Brigade
in the field*

✑ L. P. Chouteau[52] to James M. Bell

Hd. qrs. Osage Battalion
Cherroke Town. C. N.

Col Jas. M. Bell Sept Ist 1864

Dear Col.

Yours of the 15th August last was received and contents no-
ticed with much interest. I was glad to receive a letter from a
friend whom I have not seen for a long time. I have been very
sick this Sumer but However I am happy to say that I am now
able to get about very well. The Osages are all in good Spirets,

---

[52] The Osage, like the Cherokee, Creek and Seminole, were divided in
their allegiance — some fighting with the North, others with the South. L. P.
Chouteau, adjutant of the Osage Battalion, was a member of a prominent
Osage family with a strain of French blood. The Osage at this time knew
far less of white civilization than the Cherokee. They had many points in
common with the Plains Indians farther west, since they were buffalo hunters
who knew little of agriculture. That the Osage were quite unlike the Cherokee is apparent from this letter.

no sickness among us whatsoever at this present time. Last spring we had the smallpox in our camps but very few had it most of them who took it recovered. 2 men Died with it, and four women, none of the Half Breeds had the Small pox, only Gus Hungar a quapaw Boy who [died] with it, this summer. he once belong to Mayes Co. in the 1st Cherokee regiment. My Uncle Augustus Captain is well and in good health, he say he will write to you himself. he Commands the first Company in the Osage Battalion. he has a good Company of men. We want to take a scout up on Walnut in Kansas about the middle of this month it is about 200 miles from here Due North. We have been imformed by some northern Osages who were down here that there was two Store Houses full of Goods and that there was plenty of Fine Horses up in that part of Kansas. They said that all the fine Horses from the East part of Kansas were all taken out By Walnut Creek for safety. I thing that the rade I will make there will pay us well for the trip. Major Dorn[53] our agent was here and informed us the Osage that Col. S. S. Scott, Commissioner of Ind. affairs, has arrived at Sherman Texas and Brot the Osage money anuiety with him and that he was going to perchas goods with the money for us. Major Dorn says the goods are already perchased and Says that we will soon Draw our anuiety in goods and if this is done the northern Osages will Come down here like Geese & Ducks in the fall of the year. I am glad that to see that our government is doing so great a favor to give our poor Osages who are almost necked for the want of Clothing an anuiety of Goods. The women and Children Big & Little are rejoicing. My mother send her kind regards to you She begins to want to see her home in the Osage Nation, it has been three years since we left our homes. Col. Bell I would like very much to hear from you often and I will write you often from this on. I have no more news of interest to write at present. Capt. Anderson told me you wanted to Buck Skins I can not get them now but I

[53] The Osage agent, Major A. J. Dorn.

[54] This shows that the Osage were in fairly close contact with the Comanche, farther west.

will get two for you as soon as the Comanches return from the hunt.[54]

I am Col. with respect your Obt Servt, & friend

L. P. CHOUTEAU
Adjt. Osage Batt.

❧ Sarah C. Watie to Stand Watie

Wood County
Sept 4 1864

MY DEAR HUSBAND

I will have an opportunity of sending you a letter in a few days so I will have it ready. I have been to Rusk since I wrote to you last. Nancy sent after us, she thought she would not live but she was some better and I brought the children back to school. she insisted that I would stay till she got better or worse or I should have said died. poor soul she can not live long. I can not say she is alive now. I left there last tusday but she was just as bad as she could be. I will start back to see her in the morning. I do not think she can stand it much longer. I did think that I would be back at paris befor now but I could not leave her. I came up here to see the children. they are at school near here. they wanted to go and see her and I thought she would not live. I let them go so I had to bring them back to school. You wrote to me you would not be at home soon so I have not been in a great hurry to go up but I must go soon. you must write to me what clothes you need most. I have worked to get some. I will send some of your old clothes and you can give them to Mr. Mac Candlers if you do not need them, every one tells me that he is with out clothes. I feel sorry for all soldiers that are in that situation especially those of my acquaintance. he will not take it as any insult these times to offer them to him. I made some janes for you all. if you can do without it till later in the season I will not send it till you come but if you need it write and let me know. I have been [too] sick this summer to do much but I will try and get through so that you all will not suffer. when the boys get there money tell them to send it home and I will get clothes for them. Charlotte has been very good to me she has rendered me all the assistance she could. I have not stayed with her but a short time I spent all my time with Nancey. God help them when the feds come it will kill them to lose like we all did and if it was not for the reffuges I would pray God how soon some of this country felt the effects of it. I cant believe that God will leave them unnoticed. They ought all to feel the effects of this war so that they would know to feel for soldiers. one half of them wont let one stay all night with them. as for the money no one will have it with out you give them all you have for nothing and as for getting any thing done for it you can't. Saladin wrote to me he would send me a negro woman if she is a good one send and if not keep her. Maginus Matlock said had one perhaps you can hire for me. Susan is in a bad fix for work and I am not able to work so you see the war does not prevent misfortunes of all kinds. I am in hopes that the fortune tellers tale will not be true about me she says that I will have one more heir what will we do with it these times? I must tell you some of the Rusk county news or I will not have room. There is speculation in everything or they wont do at all. I will tell you all I can think of. I do think that people paid to do ought not to speculate of the poor so. When I see you I will tell you a good many things that I do not want to put on paper. I hope you will come as soon as you can. I will be some where in my old neighborhood ready to see you all. I hope the war will close soon and we will get time to sit down in peace but it does look to me as if I could not contain my self any where. I am all out of sorts. this war it will ruin a great many good people, they will not only lose all there property but a great many will lose there caracter which is more value than all their property. you can hardly hear people speak of any of our people but something said that is against there caracter. I am almost a shamed of my tribe. it has got to be such a common talk that they all follow the army and that for bad purposes. I have long since lost all interest in my people. I sometimes feel that I will never be with them any more and it does

188

not make any ods whether or not. I could not do them any good. I want to see the end of this war and then I will be willing to give up the ghost. you will think that I got in the dumps befor I got done my letter, well I do get that way when I think what they are and what they might be.[55] When you go to Rusk it is like going to flint you can hear all sorts of news that is goin, good, bad and indifferent. Well now for the war news

Atlanta was not taken on the 23 of August. we had driven back 15 miles and petersburg was not taken then that is on the 23 but you will get all that kind of news before this can reach you. love to all. the all send love. Ninny has written you.

yours affectionately
S C WATIE

I have filled my sheet with not much of any things you can do the same or let it alone just as it suits you.

⋙ Elias Cornelius Boudinot to Stand Watie

Paris Texas
Sept. 11, 1864

DEAR UNCLE

I leave for Doaksville tomorrow and expect to be at your hd. qrs. in two weeks, unless you should happen to be too far within the enemy's lines. I suppose you have received your commission of Brigadeir General, if not I have a duplicate commission which will answer as well. The President spoke in the highest terms of you in the interview I had with him last — he replied in answer to the remark I made that Stand Watie had penetrated far into the enemy's lines — "Yes he will go as far as anybody."[56] I saw Oaks a day or two since, said he was looking for Aunt Sallie every day. I fear she will not get here before I start off.

We have heard of your destroying the hay made by the Federals — and capturing a sutlers train near Van Buren and of

[55] It is not surprising that Mrs. Watie was despondent and bitter, considering the hardships she endured.

[56] President Davis, a graduate of West Point, seems to have had great admiration for the dashing Stand Watie.

many other exploits too numerous to mention; all of which gratifies me exceedingly.[57] I wished much to see Andrew Ridge as your chief of staff — he is a first rate and ready writer, true as steel and "brave as they make them." You could rely upon him in any contingency. He is well skilled in all duties of an Adj. Genl. and I think would be invaluable to you. You are entitled to three Adgt. Genls — (one as an Inspector Genl) with the rank of Major; have you all of these places filled? Jo Scales and Anderson I hear are appointed as two of your staff leaving one vacancy with the rank of Major, if it is still open send for Andrew; he was a Lt. in Allen's Regt. Walker's Division, and I presume a letter addressed to him as such would reach him.

I shall go to Rusk county when I return from your brigade

Affectionately
Your Nephew
Cornelius

᭏ Sarah C. Watie to Stand Watie

Rusk County Texas
Sept 12 1864

My dear husband

I am at Nancys we have been looking for her to die for several days but she is still living but I do not think she possible can live through tomorrow. just as soon as she is buried I will start for Paris where I hope to see you all soon. I have but a few moments to write. I will write by W. Adair and give you all the news that is any value. I will send Okes with you clothes

[57] Early in September news reached Stand Watie that a federal commissary train was enroute from Fort Scott to Fort Gibson. Union forces accompanied the train and the federals were in general occupation of the country. In spite of tremendous odds, General Watie and his men succeeded in capturing this train of supplies, which consisted of about five hundred wagons loaded with government supplies, and about eighteen hundred horses and mules. From the fruits of this victory Stand Watie provided for the needs of his ragged, hungry army. He generously refused to take any of the spoils for himself, but his men, realizing the need of the family of their beloved leader, loaded a wagon with food and clothing and sent it to Mrs. Watie.

as soon as I get home. I could not get a place here so I went back where I was acquainted, it will suit you and me better than for me to be so far and the people are much harder to get along with here. I have been sick and tired of them long ago but my sister would not let me go as she thought every week would be the last. I will go up as W. Adair goes along I can not tell you what Okes has been doing for I have not seen him since he went back but as soon as I get home I will send him home to you with some things. all the children are well. write them all on separate paper else there is a fus. tell all the boys I will send them some pants that is all I can do for them.[58] if you see any negro woman you can hire send her to me. Matlock has one I think you can get. Susan is not well again and you know that I can not do much on account of my disease. I suppose it is old age that is troubling me so. write soon. I just had a few minutes to write this. excuse so short a letter to you. yours

S C WATIE

[58] About a week after this letter was written General Watie captured the wagon train, previously mentioned, and secured clothing for his entire force.

ᦉ CHAPTER V ᦉ

THE TIDE EBBS

B Y the late autumn of 1864 the condition of the Southern Cherokee was desperate but apparently there was no thought of giving up the struggle. Stand Watie and his men decided to go into winter quarters in the Choctaw Nation near Boggy Depot, and secure a little rest for men and horses. It was sorely needed by both. A summer and early fall of vigorous campaigning had left the grass fed horses poor and thin. The men, worn out by days and nights of marching and sentry duty, often with insufficient food, were ready to welcome a brief respite from active duty.

The condition of the refugees was deplorable. E. C. Boudinot in the Confederate Congress at Richmond made every effort to secure appropriations for their relief but the Confederacy was straining every resource for the defense of the capital and his efforts met with only indifferent success. Even when money was appropriated the great depreciation of Confederate currency made it difficult to secure much relief with the funds so made available. Some men were given furloughs in order that they might care for their families and others were sent East across the Mississippi River to collect and transmit to the refugees various articles and supplies most needed. Attempts were also made to collect cotton and have it sent to Mexico to be shipped from the Mexican ports to Europe. It was hoped that in this way money might be secured for the relief of the suffering women and children in the refugee camps but the great distance to the Mexican border made it difficult to realize much from such ventures. Cotton buyers, and speculative borrowers eagerly sought contracts to purchase cotton for the Mexican trade. Some of them were doubtless unscrupulous profiteers willing to go to any length to fill their pockets. Some of them sought to come into an arrangement with Stand Watie by which he should use his power and influence as chief of the

Southern Cherokee to advance their schemes but the wise and incorruptible old soldier steadfastly refused their overtures.

General S. B. Maxey was replaced in the command of troops in Indian Territory by General Douglas H. Cooper but it was too late to hope to gain anything by a change of commanders. The Confederacy was doomed. Early in the spring Stand Watie took the field again but no great military operations were possible with his scanty force so overwhelmingly outnumbered by the enemy. The best he could do was to wage a defensive warfare. Boudinot's letters show clearly the increasing gloom of that ordinarily buoyant leader. Richmond fell on April 3d. and six days later came Lee's surrender to General Grant at Appomattox Court House.

It was virtually the end of the war but the Trans-Mississippi Department held out until May 26, when the commander, General E. Kirby Smith surrendered the entire department to General Canby.

During the last hours of the dying Confederacy Mrs. Stand Watie living as a refugee in Lamar County, Texas must have suffered agonies of doubt and uncertainty as to the possible fate of her husband and son both of whom she so deeply loved.

"I feel that I cannot live and not hear from you" she once wrote Stand Watie. Now the transmission and delivery of mail, uncertain at best in this region during the war, became even more so. Yet rumors and counter rumors flew thick and fast. It was reported that Jefferson Davis had reached Shreveport, that officers were selling the Confederate property and supplies in their charge and pocketing the money. It was falsely reported that Stand Watie had been taken prisoner, and then that he had not been, but, that a price had been placed upon his head. Confederate currency was now entirely worthless. Rumors of the collapse of the South broke down military discipline and soldiers deserted in large numbers. Among these were some evilly disposed individuals who turned to robbery and pillage. Thieving and all manner of depredations were common everywhere. Through it all Mrs. Watie maintained complete trust in the integrity of her husband and his ability to overcome all difficulties and dangers. She was apparently entirely willing to go with him anywhere and was certain that they could then make a living if only they were left alone and allowed to live in peace.

It must have been a great relief to her to receive from him the letter written on June 23 stating that he had "agreed upon a cessation of hostilities" on that date and was coming home in the very near future. General Stand Watie did not lay down his sword until some ten weeks after Appomattox and nearly a month after General E. Kirby Smith had surrendered the whole Trans-Mississippi Department. He was, therefore, apparently the last Confederate officer to surrender.

Though the war was over Stand Watie's work was by no means ended. As principal chief of the Southern Cherokee he must face the task of assembling his scattered and poverty stricken people and returning them to their home land which must be made a safe place for them to dwell by the terms of an honorable peace. On his broad shoulders, already beginning to bow under the weight of years rested a heavier responsibility for the welfare of his country, than they had ever borne in battle.

⋙ Elias Cornelius Boudinot to Stand Watie

Bonham, Texas
Oct. 1, 1864

DEAR UNCLE,

I send you a hastily written address to the Cherokees.[1] I could not get to you—I had no horse or mule upon which I could make the trip. I went as far as Perryville with Major Rector in his ambulance and of course had to return with him.[2]

I enclose a letter from Dr. Polson[3] — it is full of good sense

[1] The address was evidently Boudinot's report of his activities in behalf of his people as delegate to the Confederate Congress.

[2] This must have been Elias Rector, former Superintendent of the Southern Superintendency under the federal government.

[3] Doctor W. D. Polson, field and staff surgeon in Stand Watie's regiment, served for a time as assistant commissioner to provide subsistence for the indigent Cherokee. It was evidently in this position that Polson was writing to Boudinot.

and suggestions. I would suggest that the Council authorize you to send some person with 10 to 15000 dollars to the other side of the Miss. river and purchase cotton cards and medicines for the refugees — cards they seem especially to need.[4] They can be bought I think for from 30 to 50 dollars per pair. I will get $50,000 appropriated (in addition to the 100000 already paid over), in November or early in December. Polson, I think, would be a proper person to send and I could get such assistance from the County officers in Miss. as would ensure the safe transportation of 3 or 400 cards.

The whole country is alive with the glorious news of your success.[5] I shall take care that due credit is given you across the big river.

Mr. Wm. W. Alberty has volunteered the opinion to Genl Maxey that I "stand no chance of a re-election." I have done all and will yet do all I can for the Cherokees, if they give me no credit at all with it.[6]

Yours

CORNELIUS

Please have my address read to the Cherokees, on dress parade or at some time when they can be got together.

CORNELIUS

৺ Elias Cornelius Boudinot to Stand Watie

Paris, Texas
Oct 3, 1864

DEAR UNCLE,

You may tell the Cherokees that I shall do all in my power to save them from the tax of 33 1/3 percent on the old issue that they hold in their hands, but I doubt if I shall succeed.[7] I

[4] Malaria was prevalent among the refugees and quinine was in great demand.

[5] The writer was referring to Stand Watie's capture of the federal wagon train at Cabin Creek.

[6] Boudinot had bitter enemies but his worry over re-election was needless, since before his term in Congress expired the Confederacy had collapsed.

[7] The tax referred to was on the old issue of Confederate money when exchanged for the new issue.

would advise all who hold the old issue to go to some depository and, if he has not new issue, to exchange at the discount, to deposit the old and take receipts under the direction of the Treasurer of the Confederate States. They will thus get 2/3 of the old in the new issue and establish some kind of data upon which I can ask the payment of the other 1/3.

I will get Genl Maxey to publish the regulations of the Treasury Dept. on this point.

Affly.

CORNELIUS

E. L. Compere to Stand Watie

Copick County, Miss.
Gen Stand Watie,   Oct. 3rd 1864

SIR,

We arrived two weeks ago in Miss. swamps and have not crossed the supplies yet.[8] Everything would have been over and going west by this time, but for the vigilence of the enemy. He has been so active for a few days that we have been afraid to stir with the goods. Had the teams been in readiness by the appointed time everything would have been crossed without the least difficulty and before now would have been to their destination. The country was kept perfectly quiet up to the very river banks, till just about the time we arrived.

This detention and probable loss for the want of transportation leads me to suggest the importance of providing a special train for transportation of the goods which I may collect. Acting under orders as I am, approved by Gen. Smith it is certainly the duty of your Q. Master to provide this train.[9] Perhaps, however it might be well for the Cherokee people them-

[8] This is an interesting letter, in that it tells something of the difficulty under which supplies were transported to the Indian country. Food was plentiful in some sections west of the Mississippi, but manufactured goods were often very scarce and for the most part must come from east of the river.

[9] General E. Kirby Smith was in command of the trans-Mississippi department.

196

selves to purchase a few wagons and teams, to be put in charge of Lt. McLendon for this purpose.

The Lt. has been permanently detailed to cooperate with me, and I request that you have such a Train provided for him or that you authorize him and furnish him funds to provide the Train himself. * * * You see the importance of this matter.

Being sent off without any funds I borrowed from Mr. Wood the sum of $700 seven hundred dollars old issue for incidental expenses. * * * which I assured him you would see paid, and which Lt. McLendon will report to you as to how it is expended etc.

As soon as the supplies are over I will go immediately to Alabama and Georgia and hope it will not be long till I collect another lot. However the winter months being on us now very soon I cannot operate as successfully as I did the first time. Still I think there is no doubt but I will have on hand as large a lot as I now have, by the time the Lt. can get back. As soon then as he can get a Train I hope he will return.

I hope Adjt. Anderson will communicate with me by mail on reception of this.[10] Send to care Rev. F Courtney, Mt. Lebanon, La. — and he will forward to me. Yrs. Truly,

E. L. Compere

Chap. 2nd Cher.

P.S. I have found it necessary to borrow besides the $700.00 from Mr. Wood — $300.00 old issue from the funds in my possession belonging to Missionaries. Please refund to Lt. McLendon $200.00 new issue. He will turn over to the proper agents of the Board.[11]

Most of the funds will be consumed in ferriage over the Miss. River. What is left I will have on hand to commence my purchases with. E. L. C.

Oct. 19th.

[10] Thomas F. Anderson, as Stand Watie's adjutant, would be the one to receive the supplies collected east of the Mississippi by Compere, for the refugees.

[11] Lieutenant McLendon had been detailed to aid Chaplain Compere in gathering and transporting supplies. Compere did not like him and this may have been one reason why Adjutant Anderson was sent.

◀§ A. J. Ridge[12] to Stand Watie

Lampases Texas,

Brigr. Genl Stand Watie,   Oct. 5, 1864

DEAR UNCLE,

I sit down this morning to write you a letter, urged by various reasons. I have not seen you or any of my blood relations for years before the breaking out of the war. I wish to hear from you and my sisters and have written to them since the war began various times, but have only heard from them once or twice. I do not now know where they are or how they are getting along. I have kept up with your movements in the papers and have rejoiced in your success, and think you have well deserved and should have long ago rec'd your promotion. But our Govt. is rather slow in her actions towards some and inconsiderately hasty with regard to the advancement of others.

I have a desire to come to yr. com'd and unite myself with my people, for my experience has proved that with the whites I have not been properly appreciated nor treated honorably.[13] I will briefly give you a history of my course in this war. In March 1861, I assisted one Dr. Ryan of this County to raise a company for the war. He was elected Capt. and I first Lieut., we were mustered into the 17th Tex. Infty. In six months after starting, I was attacked by the measels and have never become strong since. We wintered in and about Little Rock Ark. I returned home in Feby. on sick leave for three months, when I rejoined the Com'd in May. We were marched to La. and fought several battles on Mississippi river in July. The Capt of the Compy resigned, he having been absent from the Com'd very nearly all the time since our enlistment. In Aug. my health entirely failed. I tendered my resignation but owing to infor-

---

12 Andrew Jackson Ridge, son of John Ridge, lived for many years in Texas, away from his relatives. During the war he made several attempts to join the Southern Cherokee forces but was apparently unsuccessful. At the close of the war he removed to Grass Valley, California, where he made his home with his brother, John Rollin Ridge.

13 Due to bad health, young Ridge did not realize his desire to join his uncle's regiment.

mality in the Certificate of the Surgeon it was not accepted but a furlough of 11 days granted. I came home and continued sick, forwarding certificates to that effect, until March 1864, when in obedience to instructions from Brigd Hd. Qrs., I sent up my resignation which was accepted in two weeks after I was ordered to report to the reg't and notified that I was enrolled as a *Private* in the same Regt. I immediately appealed against the injustice of the Order to the Maj. Genl. in June, and just a few days ago received order to report as the order of enrollment could not be nullified. This is all done by the influence of some in the Army who are inimical to me, and for what reason God only knows, save that I am proud of my Father's name and *Indian blood* — which latter *weak* men think ought to disgrace me. I was an honorable, brave Officer and an efficient one and, Uncle Stand, with my Fathers blood running in my veins how could your kinsman be otherwise?

I am not going to submit to this, I am going to forward my Commission as Dist Clerk of this County to which office I was elected, on the first day of August last, by a large majority. According to Act of Congress approved April 2nd 1864 I am entitled to a discharge, but the same authority which refused me justice in the first place are not liable to treat me justly on any terms.

I naturally want to come to your Com'd and unite my destiny with the Cherokees for whom my Father suffered death. I want to strive to give them an honorable place among other nations, with the aid of what little ability I have, and if I am to die in this war I'd rather die amongst my kindred and where my brother died than elsewhere.[14] I want you to give me an honorable appointment on your Staff or arrange Promotion for me otherwise. I had much rather serve on your Staff as my health is not good. I want to see you all, Woodward Washbourne, Polson are in your Brigd — unite us.[15] If the Brigd Commander refuses to discharge me, your Promotion of me on

[14] The writer was referring to his brother, Herman, who was killed in a skirmish at Honey Creek on November 8, 1863.

[15] These were the writer's brothers-in-law.

your Staff or otherwise will take me from their ranks and place me with people of my own blood — arrange this matter as soon as you receive this and forward appointment to me forthwith. Show my friends & kindred This — give my love to all, and let me know where Susan and Flora are.[16] If you have any regard for your Kinsman I know you will make said arrangement.

My family are all well. I send This by a member of Gurley's Reg't who will deliver to you. Let me hear from you soon. I am going to write to Rollin soon, as there is communication between this State and Mexico, from which latter a letter can reach him.[17]

Ever believe my heart with you.

Yours aff'ly

A. J. RIDGE

Lampasas Texas.

⇜ Sarah C. Watie to Stand Watie

Lamar

Oct 9 1864

MY DEAR

I am here in this neighborhood of good old people but we are doing nothing yet. Oakes has been sick for two months. I intend to sow wheat as soon as I can. I do think it is not worth my time to try to do much these times. if you were [only] out just to look around and see how we are to do. I thought I would send you some clothes but I hear that you have done better than to wait on me for them.[18] Well I dont feel a bit like writing because I cannot write what I want to say. I have been looking for you to send me some brown domestic and some callico. I have not a sheet till I make it, it is all I can do to keep clothes on the children. I wanted to send them to

---

[16] Ridge's sisters.

[17] As previously related, John Rollin Ridge had gone to California in 1850, where he was living at the time of this letter.

[18] This refers to Stand Watie's capture of the Sutlers' train previously noted.

Elias Cornelius Boudinot

school but the board is 200 a month apiece and 12 in provision what must I do. I want to have your advise on it. I saw Cornelius Boudinot the other day he will be here in a few days he will start to Richmond from here. He says Lincoln has commissioners at Richmond now and he wants to get back as soon as he can so as to receive our interest there. I want you to be certain and send me some domestic enough to do me two years. I want you to come as soon as you can. I am so tired of this world I cant write it is too cold to sit out doors and the children talk so much that it pesters me to death. If you want Oakes write. I thought I would sow wheat first. if I can make any rise of tobacco I will send them but I cant do any thing for the want of money. I have not a dime of money but old Buck Jones is here at home just as good as can be. he is all right so far. he wont let me want for anything. I guess I can do just about as well as any body else. it is [a] saying that Mrs. W. can get along when others will sink. you know that to be so dont you. I will have to look to you for advise about the children schooling. I dont know how about the board it is high every wher. Cornelius wants Wataca and Ninny to go this winter and the next time he comes he wants to take them with him.[19] you are the best judge. write once a week by mail and I will do the same after this. if you can come this fall do so.

you as ever
S. C. Watie

Elias Cornelius Boudinot to Stand Watie

Washington, Ark.
Oct. 31, 1864

Dear Uncle:

I shall not leave for Richmond before the 10th. of next month, believing that I can be instrumental in effecting more good for the Indians by delaying a few days than if I should hasten on. Senator Mitchell — one of my best friends and one

19 The Watie children remained with their mother and did not accompany their uncle, E. C. Boudinot.

of the truest friends the Indians had, is no more and Col. R. W. Johnson is prostrated by a serious accident and general bad health — he will not be able to take his seat in the Senate this winter. At this particular time our two most influential and zealous friends will not be able to serve us. I will write you again in a week and hope to tell you something that will explain the appropriateness of my remaining.

Don't fail to call the council and recommend the measures I have before suggested — for God's sake and the sake of the naked refugees let some person go across the river and buy cotton cards — and let them do it quick, it will soon be too late.[20]

Affly. &c
CORNELIUS

❧ Sarah C. Watie to Stand Watie

Nov 2 1864

MY DEAR

I have not much time to write but I want you to make haste home. I will just hurry you a little. Mrs. Jackson wants you to inquire about Shelbys Brigade. [She is] uneasy about Mr. J. I wish you would write and tell her soon. I can get a house here soon with three rooms to it tolerable comfortable and ten acres of land, that is if the old man can get a place out in the country on the river and I dont know if that wont be best as I cant get board all the year. Mr. Russel offered me that house that Mr Tol lives in if you could get a black man for him for the rent. it is a good house but it is in the center of town but you can do just as you please about it. Mr. Tucker is not at home yet. I will move as soon as I get a house, let it be where it may I am tired of one room and we have all the company. old man Russel thinks that you are such a great man that you can get a negro just when ever you want it. he wont rent till he hears

---

[20] The vigilance of the Union gunboats on the Mississippi was increasing and Boudinot was eager to secure cotton cards so that the women in the refugee camps might supply the much-needed clothing.

202

from you. I told him I did not have any idea you could make such a deal but he wanted the man so bad that he seamed to think that you could make a negro.[21] write next mail. yours

S C WATIE

all well

⇜Thomas F. Anderson to Stand Watie

H. Qrs. 1st Ind Brig.
Camp on Little Boggy Nov 5th 1864

GENL.

The Brigade got here, through rain and snow, day before yesterday. On yesterday Genl Cooper got in here with the Creeks & Seminoles. I saw him to day for a few minutes. He is looking around for suitable places [for] winter quarters for us.[22] He seems anxious to know your wishes in regard to quartering our Brigade. He proposes either Middle or Clear Boggy or would probably, at your suggestion, quarter us somewhere else. No doubt the nearer we could get to our depot of subsistence, the better it would be. The intention is to send our Horses to Forage Camps in Texas, keeping only enough to keep us a piquet at Lime Stone Gap or Holts. Capt Porum wishes to stay with his company on Little Boggy. They could then do the Picketting and Genl Maxey has promised to furnish forage for one Squadron out of each Brigade for the purpose. Another place, proposed by Maj. Bryan and which appears to me to be an excellent place, is about five miles from Thompsons Cowpen, where there is a large bottom 4 miles wide and range excellent. This would be of advantage to us in several respects. We would be near to our subsistence and for-

21 The dependence of friends and relatives upon Stand Watie has been pointed out in previous footnotes. This is another evidence of the demands made upon him.

22 The horses and mules of the Cherokee soldiers were worn out by the hard campaigning of the summer and early autumn, so that it was necessary to establish winter quarters to allow them to recuperate. While it was not expected that military operations would entirely cease, the Cherokee troops sorely needed a brief period of comparative quiet.

age for our Mules, have a good range for our Beeves &c. I will go over to see Genl Cooper tomorrow morning in company with Maj Bryan & Maj. Mayes and should Genl Cooper wish to ascertain your wishes before locating us for the winter, this letter will be sent to you by Special Messenger and you will please to express your wishes fully and start him back immediately. We have very few men in Camp. Have not heard from Flag of Truce party from Ft Smith but send a few men out tomorrow to meet them.

Anticipating an Order to prepare winter Quarters [on] Middle Boggy, I engaged House Room from Davis which he has reserved for you, should we winter there. Maj. Mayes wishes to urge upon you the necessity of wintering as close to Forage as possible as our mules are failing fast and will not improve during winter if they have to be kept constantly hauling forage. I am sure that your expressed wishes in this respect will have great weight with both Cooper and Maxey and it seems that the Cherokees should be entitled to one winter's comparative rest and have an opportunity of taking care of their Horses which will be hard to replace another year. Should you see proper to decline suggesting a place and leave the selection with Maj. Bryan or the Comdg Officer of the Brigade, no doubt, Genl. Cooper would prefer placing us at such point as would be agreeable to our Comdg Officer. Permit me Genl to make one remark. You are well aware that it is often very difficult if not impossible for the Brig. Q. M., the Commissary and myself to do our necessary work in the cold of winter in our Tents. We need house room for this purpose. No doubt Genl Cooper will go to Washita. Why not establish your H. Qrs at Boggy Depot and let the men put up Houses at a short distance from there. This would not in any manner interfere with the Troops already posted there. I enclose some letters to John Wheeler also one to yourself from Boudinot, which I opened, being marked O. B. No news —   Very Respectfully
                                                Your Obt *Servt*
                                                THOS. F. ANDERSON
                                                AAG

P.S. Please remember me for Christmas in the way of Eggs, Whiskey &c. I would like to have one Christmas Eggnogg during the war.

Thomas F. Anderson to Stand Watie

Verandah Hotel
Shreveport Dec. 16th 1864.

GENERAL,

I wanted to give you some news before I left Shreveport, but as yet I can only send you enclosed Gazette & Extra.[23] Persons who ought to be able to form a tolerable correct opinion seem to be hopeful and think that even should Sherman succeed in reaching the coast he will do so in a very crippled condition. The Delegation had an interview Yesterday with Gen Smith and got everything arranged satisfactorily and without difficulty. They, as well as myself, are now waiting for necessary papers and, as today is a day of Genl Fasting and prayer, all Offices are closed and business suspended and we will have to wait patiently for what tomorrow may bring forth. I will see Col Anderson tomorrow and after seeing him I will complete my letter as I may then have something to write about.

Please take care of Jake for me and make him see to the Old Horse good and not ride him unecessarily as I want his back to heal up good.

Dec. 18th 1864,

Genl. I got my papers last night, but too late to enable me to get off until tomorrow morning as the Office of the Depository was shut up. At the rate of $35.00 a day pr man & Horse, not including necessary bitters, it makes a mans pile grow beautifully less every day.

I got only One thousand Dollars here for myself & Walker as they are nearly out of money, but expect that I can without

23 Captain Anderson's hopes of a comparative quiet winter at Stand Watie's headquarters were doomed to disappointment since it must not have been long after the preceding letter was written until he was ordered to journey east to meet "Parson Compere" to assist in transporting to the camps of the refugees the supplies collected by the latter east of the Mississippi.

much difficulty get more on the other side of the River whenever I may need it. Otherwise I have everything satisfactory, as I am not trammeled with orders or instructions and was given to understand that I had to paddle my own Canoe. I will do my best to return at the earliest date, though I fear that on my return the River will be very full and this side perhaps over-flowed.

One of the chief reasons why our Division is not properly supplied seems to be that necessary reports are not duly forthcoming. And as they can only have such reports to furnish them the necessary knowledge of us, it stands us in hand to make every Officer come up to the mark in furnishing the same promptly. It is not right that the men should suffer from the consequences of the neglect of duty of our Officers.

The Wagons containing the supplies got together by parson Compere ought by this time to have reached their destination as they left here sometime ago — please secure Blank Books for our Brigade as there is a lot of them with these Wagons for Maj. Vore.[24]

I would much desire to receive a letter from you. Please direct to me at Liberty Miss. Care of Landon L. Lea Esq. as he will know where to find me at all times. Put 40 cents postage on it and send by Shreveport Post Office. And above all things, please see that the papers in my office are kept straight.

With my sincerest wishes for the prosperity of yourself and Family, believe me, Genl,

Your friend & Obt. Servt.

THOS. F. ANDERSON

A. A. G.

Genl Stand Watie

◄§ Thomas F. Anderson to Stand Watie

Near Castor Post Office[25]

Caldwell Parish La Dec 26th 1864.

GENERAL

After heading innumerable Bayous and going about 40 miles a day to make 10 miles actual headway, we have got to this point where we have stopped for the day, in order to have a new axle-tree put into a wagon belonging to the Signal Corps on Black River. This wagon has been of material service to us carrying our plunder and will go on to the camp of the Signal Corps below Trinity. Nearly every Bridge has been swept away and since leaving Shreveport John and myself have got to be amphibious animals. Had it not been for a certain Bottle, containing a quantity of Texas Bois d'Arc, we would often have stuck in the mud and the prospect for a Christmas Eggnog this evening is very promising.

We aim to cross the Mississippi at Jackson point below Natchez. I will endeavor to send you a letter after I am safe on the other side.

No news of any kind. Please write to me and direct to Liberty Miss. care of Landon L. Lea Esq. He will know my whereabouts and will forward to me.

I beg to be remembered to your family and believe me, Genl

Your most Obt. Servt.

Brig Genl.   THOS. F. ANDERSON.
Stand Watie

✑Charles A. Hamilton to Stand Watie

Genl Watie   Paris Tex. Jany 18th 1865.
DEAR SIR,

I am just from Washita where I left the Creeks in Council. They have disposed of the cotton arrangement in the following maner. They appoint an agent to carry to Mexico 1000 bales of cotton, one half of the net profits to be invested in goods for the Creek people & to be delivered in the Nation, the other half to the Agent. The agent to purchase the cotton with his indi-

---

24 Israel G. Vore, a native of Pennsylvania, was born about 1825. He served as quartermaster on the staff of General Cooper during part of the war.

25 Compere, as indicated by his earlier letter, was now east of the Mississippi collecting a second consignment of supplies for the refugees. Anderson, who had been sent to assist him, was now about a hundred miles east and a little south of Shreveport and about fifty miles from Jackson's Point where he expected to cross the Mississippi.

vidual money. If it should meet with your approval I should like to become the agent of the Cherokee people & will deliver them the goods in the Nation — will purchase 1000 bales & give them one half of the profits in goods. The following is the calculation —

1000 bales will cost	62 500
Transportation to Mexico	60,000
1000 bales in Mexico is worth	200 000
	122 500
½ of 77,500 to be invested	77 500
& delivered to the Cherokees	

The following *is* about the rate of prices in Matamoras Coffee 35cts pr lb. Calico 28, shoes 2.00 to 2.50 pr pair & so on —

½ of my proffits I should have to give for the use of the money — as would have it to borrow — half of what I realise I am willing to divide with you & net purchase the full amount for you, if you so desire, in goods for your individual use. There is certainly nothing improper in this offer as I take nothing from your people, but only divide with you my individual proffits.[26]

Should my proposition meet with your approval please address me at Waco Texas. Respt. Your friend

CHAS. A. HAMILTON.

✑ Stand Watie to Sarah C. Watie

DEAR SALLIE: Boggy Depot[27] Jany. 20 1865

We were three days on the road, came by Jarretts, all well there. I find that I can't get along well here without help. I

---

[26] This clever attempt to influence Stand Watie to give the writer of this letter a contract as agent for the Cherokee people, of course, entirely failed. Stand Watie had a very keen sense of honor and there is not the slightest evidence that he ever at any time derived a personal profit at the expense of his people.

[27] The Confederate Cherokee army was now in winter quarters in the Choctaw Nation, where Stand Watie's headquarters were located at Boggy Depot.

have a house without anything. Send Marye Andrews, my box with what clothes you may judge to be sufficient, few cooking things if you have any which you can do without, don't forget my big tin cup & whatever you may be able to send me which you do not particularly need at home. Send the Federal Order Books, I find I shall need them. I will not need the tent for a while yet. If Oaks can't come better send for Swearingan, he lives about 15 miles from your place. I think tho' Oaks had better hire some one to work until he returns, either of the waggons will do, it can be taken back. if you can get it send about 400 lbs of flour. I can trade it for pork 1 lbs for three. John Alberty killed on the way. John Wilson is still on the Canadian. Try to come and stay with me a few days, stay long as you can as we can live in a house without sponging on any of our friends.

Yours as ever
STAND

Charley will tell you the rest.

⊷§L. P. Chouteau to James M. Bell

Head Qrs Osage Batt.
Camp Dorn C. N.
Jany 21st 1865

DEAR COL,

You must excuse me for not writing to you Sooner. I have been Very Sick Sence I come home from your Hd Qrs. all is going on right Side up With Care up here. Capt. Augustus Chouteau & my Mother Sends You there best respects, give my Kind regards to your Boys and to all my friends and In particular to Lt Patrick Patten, Who I long to See. The Commanches & Kawiowaies of the Plains have all come in and Want to Join the South and fight the federls this comming Sumer & Spring. They went up to there Camps, which are at the Antlope Hills about 200 miles west of this place. They will be here in or about the 25th of this month to Hold a council With us at this place. We have no Wild tribes now to contend against.[28] I hope next Summer We will give Kansas Hell.[29] My Dear friend I have them Buck Skins for you.[30] I will be down in a few days. Tell Major Mayse to remember the Osage Battalion in the Clothing Line. no more news. I Wish I had more news to write to you all our troops are in good Spirits, all they Want is Clothing

I am Col your

Friend & obdt Servt

L. P. CHOUTEAU

To Col J. M. Bell   Adj't & Q. M. agent

Comdy 1st Cherroke Reg.   Osage Batt

C. S. A.

P.S.

I have them peccons for Doctor Adair but no Convance to send them by

L. P. C.

T. M. Scott[31] to Stand Watie

Hd Qs Dist Ind Terry

Fort Towson C. N.

February 1st 1865

GENERAL.

The Maj General Commanding Directs me to say to you that he is in receipt of a letter from Genl McCulloch in refer-

---

[28] Several tribes of the Plains Indians in the western part of the Indian Territory had made treaties of alliance with General Pike at the outbreak of the Civil War. They had done little to help the South, however, and as the fortunes of the Confederacy grew more and more desperate the Northern officers on the border sought to point out the situation to the plains tribes and to detach them from their alliance with the Confederates. At the very close of the war, however, the Plains Indians became vexed with the United States and they made another treaty at Camp Napoleon with the tottering Confederate government.

[29] The war was to continue only a few months longer and these plans to raid Kansas did not materialize.

[30] Referred to in a previous letter.

[31] T. M. Scott was assistant adjutant general for General S. B. Maxey. Soon after Maxey was replaced by General Douglas H. Cooper, which occurred on March 1, 1865. Scott was promoted to the position of adjutant general.

ence to depredations committed in Texas represented to have been done by men of the Indian Division, containing enclosures of letters written to him (Genl McCulloch) by citizens living in the vicinity of where the outrages were perpetrated.[32] Genl McCulloch writes that he has forwarded like papers to you direct, so that it is unnecessary to forward you copies from these Head Quarters.

The Maj Genl. Commanding had hoped that the men of your command had by this time learned the importance of keeping up the best of good feelings between the troops of this Dist. and that portion of Texas immediately south of Red river.

It is well known to you, General, the great importance that the Northern Counties of Texas are to this District in furnishing us the whole of the supplies for the army as well as the indigent and refugee families, and how necessary it is to preserve amical relations with the citizens of that section, and rather than suffer them to be depredated upon every effort should be used to protect and sustain them in their persons and property.

When these men go over to Texas and commit their depredations they represent themselves as "Waties Men, Coopers Men &c" and bring disrepute not only upon your Division but the whole district.

The Genl Comdg. therefore directs me to urge upon you the great necessity of finding out if possible the party representing themselves as belonging to this District, Who forcibly took the Whiskey at the house of Mr Briscoe from the guard in whose charge it was, And afterward at the farm of "Butts" killed a Mr Davis while peacibly in his house.

Such things as these go a long way to discourage our best friends in their efforts to aid us. And provoke retaliation, and if not suppressed will likely end in a border warfare terrible to contemplate.

[32] General Stand Watie's troops were in winter quarters not far from the Texas border. It is not surprising that during the weeks of enforced idleness the restless soldiery should become involved in difficulties with the nearby Texans.

This "Capt Savage, of Clarks Indians," I have not before heard of, or the Command, and think it a false name, but let it be whom it may, I would urge upon you General the necessity of bringing if possible these men to punishment, not only in justice to the District but to yourself as Commander of the Indian Division.

The Maj Genl Comdg directs me to further say that if you discover who the parties engaged in these late outrages are, to make application for a Genl Court Martial to sit in your Division recommending suitable officers and he will at once Order it to assemble, when charges will be made out and the above parties brought to a speedy trial.

In carrying out the instructions herein contained and the effort to suppress such like occurences in future, the Maj Genl Comdg directs me to say he feels confident of your hearty aid and support in the matter.

I am General

Very Respty &c
Yr Most Obt Sevt
T. M. Scott
A. A. Genl.

Brig Genl
Stand Watie
Comdg Division

⋘T. M. Scott to Stand Watie

Hd. Qs. Dist. Ind. Terry
Fort Towsen C. N.
Febry 12th 1865

Genl.

The Maj. Genl. Comdg. directs me to acknowledge the reciept of your letters of Feby 7th and 9th.

And directs me to say to you that your hearty co-operation in regard to the suppression of lawlessness along Red river, so plainly shown by the steps you have taken to suppress it, is what he expected of Genl Watie.[33]

---

[33] This indicates that Stand Watie took prompt steps to suppress the lawlessness complained of in the preceding letter.

You had been advised previous to the writing your letter of the 7th inst, (which I suppose had not reached you) what steps had been taken in regard to forage for the compy of Cavalry to be under your immediate control at Boggy Depot. I however herewith enclose you a special Order for Maj. Vore to forage the Company, with instructions in regard to a pass if necessary to send the transportation to Texas for the same.

The Maj. Genl. further desires me to say that the steps you have taken to ascertain what you can do are judicious.

In the meantime from a letter this morning received from Dept Hd. Qs. a copy of which I send you, the Maj. Genl. Comdg. apprehands the emmergency named in Genl. Magruders letter has passed by. I will fr'd copy of your letter to Genl. McCulloch.

I am Genl.   Very Respty &c
                                     Yr. most Obt Sevt
Brig. Genl.   T. M. Scott
  Stand Watie   AA Genl
    Comdg. Div.

◆§ O-hop-ey-a-ne to the Chiefs and Headmen of the Creek Nation

Cherokee Town Feby 21st, 1865[34]

To the Chiefs and Head men
of the Creek Nation
FRIENDS AND BROTHERS

We have lately been visited by the Prairie Indians, Viz Commanches, Kiowa's and Arapahoes. As soon as they ar-

[34] This letter is interesting as showing the conditions among the wild Indians of western Oklahoma as the Civil War drew to a close. On the back page (in one of the squares, as the letter was folded as an envelope) is written the following note from the principal chief of the Southern Creeks, which explains how General Watie came to receive the letter:

                          At Council on Washita River
                            March 11   65
GENL.
  The within is a letter from the 2d chief of the Comanches the purport of

213

rived at our Camp, they requested our Agent to send an express to the Chiefs of the Confederate Nations and envite them to come to this place and meet them in Council, he did, so they waited several days but no one comeing they have returned to their camps. They were anxious to see you all and expressed disappointment at your not comeing to see them. We can assure you our Brothers of the Friendship of our Red Brothers of the Prarie. The Comanche Chief who visited us says that they made a Treaty with Genl Pike on behalf of the South but still wished to be friendly with the North but early last spring they were called to a Council of the Northern Red men. In that Council Jesse Chisholm acted as Interpreter for the Comanches.[35] Several speeches were made some in favor of peace some for war on the Southern and Texas. The Chief of the Tahaaccano's made a strong war speech. The Commanche Chief spoke last. He told them that here in Council was assembled Creeks, Chickasaws, Cherokees, Seminoles and others who all had friends and relatives in the South and he thought that the men who made these speeches for war had been drinking strong water and were drunk for he did not think that sober men would propose to war on their friends and brothers. In this Council Jesse Chisholm opposed making war and said all these people in the South were his friends so the Council broke

---

which shows their feelings toward us. I wrote a letter a short time since to Col. John Drew stating to him to forward the same to you after reading it, if you have received it you will please attend to the matter referred to in it.

Your friend

TUCKABATCHE MICCO

Prin. Chief

[35] Jesse Chisholm was a Cherokee Indian trader and one of the best known characters of the Southwest. He was born in Tennessee in 1806, his father being a Scotchman and his mother a Cherokee. He came to the West when hardly more than a boy, married a Creek woman and engaged in trade with the western tribes. He was said to speak fourteen different languages and in consequence was often called upon to act as interpreter. He accompanied Pike as guide when the latter came to the Indian Territory in 1861, but later was to be found among the refugees of the North on the border of Kansas. Chisholm was very influential among the Plains Indians. He died in 1868. The Chisholm Trail was probably named for him.

up with out concluding to make war on the South. Some time after this Council was held the Commanches, Kiowa's and other Prarie Indians were called to another Council by some white men Northern Officers at which place they had a large amount of goods or presents to the Indians also a large number of guns and ammunition. The Officers told them that they would give them all these goods and guns if they would make war on the South, he told them to kill all the men and boys and take the women and children prisoners and drive off all the cattle and horses and when they returned from their expedition they must give up the white women and girls but the Indian women should be theirs; also all the mules and horses, the cattle they would buy from them. When the white Captain was done speaking the Commanche Chief spoke. he told them he had friends and brothers in the South and he would not make war on them. He said he had made a Treaty with Pike and he held out one hand to the North and one to the South, he would not strike either unless he was struck first. The white Captain then told him if he would not help to fight the South he should not have the guns. The Commanche Chief then said that he would do without the guns that he still had his bow and arrows and with them he could kill buffaloe and live on the Prairie. It may be proper here to say that Chisholm was Interpreter at this Council and advised the Indians not to listen to the Northern mens bad talk. The Council broke up. few goods and no guns were given to them. afterwards they refused to let the Indians trade with their suttlers this soon resulted in a fight since then several battles have been fought.

There is a perfect estrangement between those people and the North and they may now relied on as true friends to the South. They are now encamped in the vicinity of the Antelope Hills some Fifty or sixty miles north west of Fort Cobb.

My friend and Brothers none of the other Chiefs are here but I send the words as they were told me by our wild Brothers.

Your Friend & Brother

O-HOP-EY-A-NE [his x mark]

Second Chief Commanches

৬§ B. F. Farley to S. B. Maxey

Gen'l.

Sir:

Levier Co. Arks.
Feb. 27th, 1865

I will give you a short detail of my Scout. We had a fight with the mountain Fed's.[36] We lost one man and killed two Fed's, next we captured four fine horses and Ambulance on the Van Buren and Ft. Smith road, within half mile of Van Buren. I left the Ambulance.

It is supposed the horses were Gen'l Thayers. They were in fine condition. I lost three men. They were at houses contrary to orders. I had another fight with some Infantry. I had one man wounded and three horses killed.

Please give the bearer Lt. Andrew Tyner leave of absence for the purpose of getting a horse. His horse was killed in the last fight.

Very Respectfully
yours & &.
B. F. Farley

৬§ William A. Musgrove to Stand Watie

General Watie

Dear Sir

Feb. 27 1865

The weather has been such that it was out of My Power to come up to see you. I have succeeded in getting (300) three hundred Bales Cotton and have the offer of more.[37] I have sent My papers to Shreveport by Major Norris who was kind enough to take them. He is expected back in a day or two. Should everything work rite I will be up to see you or let you heare from me by mail.

---

[36] "Mountain feds" evidently means the mountaineers of the Ozark region who favored the North. This brief letter shows the type of fighting common in this area during the latter part of the war.

[37] Apparently the Cherokee were making a desperate effort to transport cotton to Mexico in order to get money to feed the starving refugees.

General Cooper is expected per steamer tomorrow. I was at youre house a few days ago all was well.

Youre Friend
WM. A. MUSGROVE

I have some (40) or (50) wagons engaged and I think their will be no difficulty in getting all the transportation needed.

W. A. M.

⌐§ T. M. Scott to Stand Watie

Hd. Qs. Dist. Ind. Terry.
Fort Towson C. N.
March 15th 1865

GENERAL

The General Commanding directs me to say to you that all accounts from Fort Smith concur in the report that the Enemy are throwing large supplies both of forage and subsistence into the place.[38] And that he desired that at the earliest practicable moment that grass will do to forage the stock on, that you have both men and animals in Camp.

Johnsons and Burnets Battalions have been ordered by Dept. Hd. Qs. to Texas and the Genl Comdg. has directed the 1st Indian Brigade to move to Boggy Depot and relieve Burnets Battalion. Capt. Frank Colberts Company has been ordered to Fort Washita as a guard at that Post, and Capt John Miller of Bryants Battalion been directed to move to Doaksville to relieve Capt Smith in charge of prisoners there.

The Genl. Comdg. thinks that by the middle of April the grass will be sufficiently advanced to forage the horses, when not on active service, and that you will have but little time to spare in getting the horses from the most distant camps in Texas, if you were to give the necessary directions now to have them brought in.

---

[38] From this it would be inferred that the North expected to use Fort Smith as its base in an active campaign in the Indian Territory, as soon as spring should be sufficiently advanced to make the movement of troops possible.

217

The Genl. Comdg. further directs me to say that the source from which he received the intelligence in regards to supplies at Fort Smith is reliable, and direct from that place. And a reasonable supposition is that we must have everything in readiness to meet any movement the Enemy may make, by the latest the first day of May. You will therefore please give your Quarter Masters the necessary directions to have their trains in readiness and engage in moveing supplies to the front to be in readiness for the troops by the time they rendezvous. Also to the Commissioners & Ordnance Officers to make necessary preparations in their Departments.[39]

I am General very

Brig. Genl.   Respty & Yr Obt Sevt

   Stand Watie   T. M. Scott

     Comdg. Div.   A. A. Genl.

✥ Stand Watie to Tuckabatchee Micco[40]

Head Quarters Indian Division

Tuck-a-batch-ee Micco   Boggy Depot, C. N.

   Pl. Chief Creek Nation   March 19, 1865

Friend —

The letter from the 2nd Chief of the Comanchee Tribe of Indians, dated Feb. 21st/65 with your note on the same, dated March 11th/65 has been received. In reply I can assure you that it is a source of great pleasure and satisfaction to me to hear of the friendly disposition manifested by our red Brothers of the Prairie, and hope soon to have that perfect understanding and good will established among all the red Brethren of the south & West. The letter you mention of having written to Col. Jno Drew, and requesting him to forward the same to me,

[39] By this time the Confederacy was tottering to its fall but the Indians apparently had no idea of surrender. As spring approached they began to make active preparations for a vigorous defense against the expected advance of the North.

[40] This is in response to the letter of February 21, 1865, which was forwarded to Stand Watie by Tuckabatche Micco, principal chief of the Creeks.

did not come to hand but I received a letter a short time previous from the Confederate States Agent for the Reserve Indians, stating in substance that the Prairie Indians had come to their camps and expressed a wish for a meeting of Delegates from the Confederate Indian Nations. On receipt of said letter I immediately notified the General[41] commanding the Indian Territory, who is "Ex-Officio" Superintendent of Indian Affairs, and who Thereupon appointed Maj Vore Q. M. of the Confederate Army to proceed to the place designated and have an interview with them; but on his arrival there he found that the Prairie Indians had already left, and nothing more can now be done only to wait until the 15th day of May next, the day appt. according to the agreement of the different delegates, who were appointed last summer for that purpose, when a General Council of All the Tribes of Indians, in friendly relations with the Southern Confederacy, will meet for the purpose of entering into a closer combination and a more intimate acquaintance of the relations which shall hereafter govern their intercourse with each other and also to adopt the plan for united and more efficient and vigorous prosecution of the War in which we are engaging and for a unity of action — that when we strike it may be felt to our satisfaction until we shall have conquered and obtain peace on terms which we can with honor, accept.[42]

Resptfully
Your Friend
STAND WATIE
Pl. Chief C. N.

ᏎᎦT. M. Scott to Stand Watie

Hd. Qs. Dist. Ind. Tery
Fort Towson C. N.
March 22'd 1865

GEN

The General Comdg. desires [me] to say that he has been shown a letter [from] Capt Welch A. Q. M. in charge of sub

41 General S. B. Maxey, in addition to his military duties, acted as ex-officio Superintendent of Indian Affairs for the Confederacy.

[sistence] train, in which he says that he [forwa]rded [19500] Nineteen thousand five hundred pounds of [bread] stuff to Boggy Depot and that this is all he [will] be able to forward until after the middle of April or near the first of May Next.[43]

The General Comdg. further directs me to say that to prevent the troops from being entirely without bread, you will reduce the issues of breadstuff to the troops to half rations until such time as they can be supplied more abundantly.[44]

Very Respectfully
Yr Obt Sevt
T. M. Scott
Ad Genl.

◆§ A. J. Ridge to Stand Watie

Lampasas Texas
Apr 14, 1865

Dear Uncle

I received yours of Feb 27th by last mail and hasten to reply. I had given over all expectations of hearing from you and was fully persuaded you had not rec'd my letter. I can only answer your letter briefly at this time and in relation to the acceptance of the appointment have to say that I am, by bad health and not from inclination, forced to decline.[45]

I am, dear Uncle, anxious to be with you all, and will say that if this war continues and I am alive, I will come up to your country and give my own to the cause. If my health improves I will no doubt come in the Fall. I have been solicited to procure an order from Genl Smith and endeavor to raise a

[42] The Camp Napoleon Conference closed with the adoption of a treaty between the Confederacy and the Indians on May 25, 1865.

[43] The general commanding referred to was General Douglas H. Cooper, who had succeeded General S. B. Maxey on March 1, 1865.

[44] The original of this letter is very fragmentary and it has been necessary to make insertions. The letter has been included because it shows that great efforts were made to keep the troops supplied with foodstuffs.

[45] As earlier letters indicate, Ridge had sought an appointment to Stand Watie's staff and it had been urged by E. C. Boudinot.

Regt in my old Country, Arks. I have been assured of success. I have not heard from Rollin since the war began, expect to write him shortly, will do what you request. Receive, dear Uncle, my thanks for the appointment with the assurance that I will be with you as soon as practable, to serve as Private or officer. I wish to serve the Cherokees to the best of my ability. If I have mental capacity which merits a position of importance of course I should have it. I am the last of the Ridge name in the C. S. and by joining with you could benefit the nation. I have a good standing in this Country and possess influence, am regarded as a man of honor and talent.

But I've said too much perhaps of myself already. I will only say that the Authorities, Military have acknowledged by letter to me their error in respect to my affair in the army of which I wrote you. Where is Cornelius Boudinot.[46] Give my best love and tell him I would be happy to hear from him directly. My best respects to all my friends in your Div. and also my Father's friends in the Nation and tell them his *son* does not feel indifferent as to their struggles and will ere long be with them and willing[ly] would shed his blood in their cause if necessary. I will write you again. Please let me be posted as to your welfare. You are well thought of in Texas. Goodby. Success to you. In war or Peace Dear Uncle believe me

truly your Nephew
A. J. RIDGE

⮑ William A. Musgrove to Stand Watie

Paris Lamar County Texas
May 2 1865

General Watie

DEAR SIR

Things are progressing as fine as I could expect under the existing circumstances such as bad weather and muddy rodes. Some teams have already started some 250 or 300 Bales will be

---

[46] Boudinot was on his way home from Richmond, having left that City on the 18th of March. Richmond had been occupied by Union troops about ten days before this letter was written.

on the rode by the 15 of this month. Others getting ready you shall be advised at every movement from this to Matemoras Mexico. I could have taken one Thousand bales if I had known it sooner as easy as I can take the 500. My arrangements are all made.[47]

Tell Saladin we must get off by the 15 in order to meet the Cotton trains at Matamoras. General would you be so kind as to send me a pass by mail for transportation [for] my son as he is in bad health and has been for a year. I think it would be beneficial for his health and oblige

Your Friend
With Due Respt
WM. A. MUSGROVE

⊷ Elias Cornelius Boudinot to Stand Watie

Shreveport, La. May 11, 1865.

DEAR UNCLE,

I arrived here two days ago, and will probably leave to day for Washington Arks. where I shall leave my extra bagage, and as soon thereafter as possible will proceed to Doaksville where I understand you are now.

I have had a long and tedious journey from Richmond, having left there on the 18th of March and lost no time unnecessarily on the way.

I got a bill through Congress requiring Genl Smith to turn over to the Cherokee — worth of cotton, specie value.[48] Another was also passed making the same provisions for the other nations to the extent of their annuities. I have seen Genl Smith, who promises to conform speedily to these provisions of the bill, he has gone to Marshall to see the Treasury Agent and will write to me, where, and how soon the cotton can be delivered.

---

[47] William A. Musgrove was evidently meeting with considerable success in the enterprise of securing cotton to be sold in Mexico for the benefit of the refugees.

[48] The exact amount is illegible.

It is important that we secure this cotton and export it if possible before the general crash on this side of the river, which, between you and I will take place this summer. I have nothing to do and am willing to devote my time and energies to this business if you will call your Executive Council together and give me the requisite authority.

It is a herculean task, and the probability is, nay the certainty is, we will have to find our transportation. I think I can do this and turn over for the benefit of our people the full amount of this years annuities in coin. I suggested to Genl Smith an arrangement by which the cotton could be taken out of Red River and thus save time and expense, but he anticipates a movement of the enemy up the river soon, which would render such a scheme impracticable. If you see fit to intrust the matter with me I must not be trammeled by any superior authority, but must be allowed to carry out my own plans without dictation.

The surrender of Lee and Johnson virtually puts an end to the war on the other side of the river.

The people from Virginia to the Miss. river are willing to try the experiment of absolute submission and return to the old Union. Gen Smith in my opinion will hold on if possible a month or two yet, until the hopelessness of further resistance is apparent to the world, before he will yield the contest.[49]

From all that I learn his army will fall to pieces. The war will close in some shape by the 1st day of August, unless the old story of foreign intervention should be verified. Our policy should be to remain still and watch the current of events. Cooper is Superintendent.

Aff'ly Yr. Nephew,
CORNELIUS

Congress voted you thanks for the capture of the train last fall.[50] I had a bill passed also redeeming all the old issue, but that is of but little moment now.[51]   C.

---

[49] The surrender of General E. Kirby Smith, Confederate Commander of the trans-Mississippi Department, to General E. R. S. Canby came on May 26, fifteen days after this letter was written.

⚜ William P. Adair to Stand Watie

Camp. New Cherokee Town,
May 13, 1865.

GENL.

I send you what news we have. All the Delegates have not yet arrived. The Choctaws & Chickasaws are yet behind and are looked for tonight. We held a Council today, and decided to hold our Grand Council at Council Grove as already agreed upon.[52] We leave here tomorrow for that place and will get there about the 16th. We have sent out runners to notify the Indians to meet us at the place appointed.

The following named Tribes are uncertain [but] from information will meet us —

The-No-Coo-No
Coosh-Ta-take-ken
Lick-ah-Ka-Nah
Yamparekah
Tah-ne-nah   *Commanches*
Po-ho-teh
Moo-Chah
Ruahrhrey-dit-Suche-Co
Araphoew
Lapans
Ki-a-wa
Chi-ans
Caddoes

The most of the warriors of their Tribes are now said to be fighting the Federals in Kansas. We have sent for several of the more Northern Tribes who we are informed wish to join us. Such as the Soux-Pawnees &c &c. In fact from information

---

[50] This was the capture of the wagon train at Cabin Creek in September 1864, to which reference has already been made.

[51] The redemption of the old issue of Confederate currency was of no importance now since all Confederate money was worthless.

[52] This grand council consisted of delegates from the Five Civilized tribes and representatives of the Plains Tribes farther west. Council Grove was located a few miles west of the present Oklahoma City, near Bethany.

recd from Indians here, I am induced to believe that all of the Indians of the plains are at war with the Federals and with proper management and energy used on our part they will meet us in Council where we can make any arrangement with them desirable.

Enclosed I send you endorsement of Genl Cooper on your order for your information & from which you will see that Col. Lee is in command of all the Reserve Indians, Osage Batt. and such of the wild Tribes as may hereafter join us.[53]

Your friend &
Obt Servt
W. P. ADAIR Col
Comdy Detchmt 1st
Ind. Brig P. A. C. S.

❧ Sarah C. Watie to Stand Watie

Lamar Co. H.
May 21 1865

My —

We all feel disapointed at not hearing from you as one week has passed and no word yet. we hear all kinds of rumers and none satisfactory to us. we heard you was captured and have not heard any thing to the contrary. we heard that Gen K. Smith has surrendered and than we hear that he has not. So we dont know what to believe and do let us know all that you know for certain. if it for the worst let us know it so we can be prepared for it. if I have to fall among the feds I do not want to be amonge old Blunts set for the pins will be mean enoug and what is you prospect? I hear that they have set a price on several of there heads and you are included. that is the rumor.[54] I do not want people to believe it for some of them would be after it. I hear that Cooper will not give you any

---

[53] The Reserve Indians were the Comanches, Kiowas and Wichitas who lived in what was known as the "leased district."

[54] Rumors of all kinds were circulating throughout the Confederacy at this time.

thing. if he does not I believe that they all are speculating of it and I hope that the last of them will sink. I do not want you to do any thing of that kind. I would live on bread and water rather than to have it said you had speculated of you people. I believe you have always done what you thought best for you people and I want to die with that last belief. if [I] thought you was working for nothing but fill your pocket it would trouble me a great deal but I know it is not, else it would have been filled before this time.[55] I know that you are capable of making a living any where if we are let alone after the war is over.

S. C. W.

write soon and send it. I do not know what to believe. If you can get any specie get it for we cant get any thing for confederate money here and if we have to get away from here which I fear we will I dont know what we will do. my notion is that we can not stay here for the robers. my black horse is not found yet. I am all the time afraid the mules will be gone. write all. we are all sold out I believe.

report says Jeff Davis is at Sreavesport.[56]

⚬⑧Richard Fields[57] to Thomas F. Anderson

Hd. Qrs. 1st Cherokee Regt.
May 22nd/65

CAPTAIN

In obdience to orders on 14th Inst I moved with a scout in direction of Fort Gibson. went on as far as Canadian River Main ford between Scailsburge & North fork Town. found the River unfordable verry full. There I found some fourteen

[55] The speculating referred to doubtless means in cotton or army supplies. Stand Watie, who was quite wealthy before the war, came out of that struggle virtually penniless, which is the best indication that Mrs. Watie evaluated his character correctly.

[56] Jefferson Davis had been captured at Irwinville, Georgia on May 10, 1865.

[57] Richard Fields was with the Texas Cherokees for many years. He later served as a member of the delegation of the Southern Cherokees that went to Washington in the summer of 1866.

226

Creeks. from them I learned they had been over between North fork & the Canadian & had saw federal signe over ther, plenty. lost four men supposed to have been killed or captured by the federals. A [number] of this band went with me to try to cross the River. we again found the River impassable from thence we came back [to] Scailsburge & staid all night, again that night the four men supposed to have been lost came in and they reported they had been all between the two Rivers up as far as Hillaby & Country arround & came on back by Chillie McIntosh's[58] place. saw no sign of federals. Next Morning My scout & the Creeks started together to cross the River went & found it still rising. I then turned back left 18 Creek & two Lieuts & they promised [to cross] the River next day if they had to swim it. I instructed them to watch the fort Gibson road bend [as near] North fork as they thought would be safe. I ordered them if [they] made any discoverys to report immediately. Gave them all the amunition I had & returned.

I am Capt Your Obt sevt

Thos. F. Anderson   RICHARD FIELDS
  Asst Adj Genl   Capt. Comd. Scout

✑ Stand Watie to Sarah C. Watie

Boggy Depot May 27th 1865

DEAR SALLIE:

No definite news yet great deal of confusion amongst the troops more particularly with white portion. I have thought best to send off the majority of them home on furloughs hints have been thrown out that they would help themselves to the public propperty.[59] I have sent off enough of them so that I think I can manage the rest. John will start back perhaps tomorrow. I do not know how much your relatives will send

---

58 Chilly McIntosh was a famous Creek leader.

59 The news of the collapse of the Confederacy east of the river caused great confusion and general disintegration of the forces west of the Mississippi. As a matter of fact, General E. Kirby Smith had surrendered the trans-Mississippi Department the day before this letter was written.

227

you. I will instruct John to bring the carriage. I can have it fixed up here. We have great deal of Iron. We hear that there is great deal of confusion about Bonham, report is McColuch & his adjutant hid themselves from the fury of the people. The man that takes this is waiting, he lives near Davis's mill and has promised to send it to you. I only write to let you know that I am still in the land of the living — love to all. Please write again by John or Smith, let the Waggon which John takes remain. I have promised it [to] Smith. yours as ever —

STAND WATIE

✑Stand Watie to Sarah C. Watie

Jones's June 23rd 1865

DEAR SALLIE:

We leave this morning; intend to go as far as Jarretts. Have agreed upon the cessation of hostilities with the Comrs. they will leave tomorrow — Genl Smith had surrendered the whole department on the 26th day of May — The Grand Council will convene 1st day of Septr. when a comr. from Washington is expected to arrive.[60] I will return home soon as our council is over at Nail's Mill. Jumper and Checota are expected in today[61] try to have Cornelius at your house next week. I must see him.

STAND[62]

---

[60] The Indians had hoped to meet the commissioners from the United States at a council at Armstrong Academy, but it was later determined to meet at Fort Smith.

[61] John Jumper and Samuel Checote were Seminole and Creek leaders.

[62] The war had closed. Stand Watie was apparently the last Confederate officer to surrender. His brief note must have greatly relieved the fears and anxieties of Mrs. Watie as expressed in her letter of May 21st.

⌐§ CHAPTER VI §⌐

THE STRUGGLE FOR PEACE

THE surrender of Stand Watie and the close of the war left the Cherokee, in common with all other tribes in the Indian Territory, gravely solicitous as to the future policy of the United States toward them. They were eager to know to what extent they were to be punished for fighting on the side of the South and just how far the victor would prove generous to the vanquished. A grand council was called to meet commissioners of the United States at Armstrong Academy but the meeting place was later changed to Fort Smith. To this place the Indians were told to send delegates to meet the United States commissioners who were authorized to make peace with the various tribes, and to explain to them the terms upon which they would again be admitted to the good graces of the government of the United States.

The Federal Commission was composed of Dennis N. Cooley, Commissioner of Indian Affairs, Elijah Sells in charge of the Southern Superintendency, General William S. Harney, Colonel Ely S. Parker, and Thomas Wistar. Accompanied by several secretaries and Indian agents they reached Fort Smith early in September. Here they met representatives of the loyal factions of the various tribes in the Indian Territory and the council began its work.

Delegates from the Southern Indians did not reach Fort Smith until after the council had been in session for several days, since they had first met for an inter-tribal council at Armstrong Academy.

The work of the Council of Fort Smith was greatly complicated by the fact that two delegations appeared from some of the larger tribes, one representing the Northern and the other the Southern wing of the tribe. John Ross was present and appeared before the commissioners to defend himself against the charge of disloyalty and to assert that he had signed a treaty with the Confederacy only in order to save his country from

229

destruction. Both the Northern and the Southern group claimed to be the real Cherokee Nation and asserted that the other was only a faction.

The United States commissioners declared that the Cherokee and all other tribes that had joined the Confederacy had thereby forfeited their lands and all rights granted them by former treaties. They were told that, in consequence, they must make new treaties and these must include certain specific provisions. Some of these were that all slaves be freed and adopted into the tribe or provided with land, and slavery declared forever abolished. Also they must give up a part of their lands for friendly tribes of Indians in Kansas and elsewhere. It was further declared that the policy of the United States government was to consolidate all tribes and nations in the Indian Territory under one government.

The terms seemed very harsh to the Indians and most delegations declared, moreover, that they had not been authorized by their people to sign treaties but merely to make peace. Accordingly, the various Indian representatives merely signed a treaty of peace and it was agreed that delegations should be sent to Washington the following spring to make treaties with respect to matters involved in the various demands made by the United States commissioners.

Most of the Southern Cherokee remained in the Choctaw Nation along the Red River during the winter of 1865-66. They dared not return to their old homes because of the bitter hostility of the Northern group which had passed a law confiscating the lands of the Southern Cherokee. Many of the latter group felt that the two factions of the Cherokee people could never again live together in peace and harmony in the same country and under the same government. Stand Watie made every effort to relieve the suffering of his needy people who must spend another winter as exiles living, in many cases, in dire poverty.

When spring came the delegation from the Southern Cherokee set out for Washington. It was composed of Stand Watie, Saladin Watie, Elias C. Boudinot, William P. Adair, J. A.

230

Scales, and Richard Fields. From far off California came John Rollin Ridge as the seventh member of the delegation. He was chosen as chairman probably because of his reputation as a scholar and writer and possibly also because he had been living in exile for many years and, in consequence, would be likely to prove unbiased and free from personal prejudice.

The Northern Cherokee, or Ross wing of the Nation, also had its delegation in Washington. Chief Ross was so old and ill as to be physically incapable of attending many of its meetings or of actually leading it in person but behind its every move was his clever and alert mind. From a sick bed he skillfully directed its work bringing to its difficult problems all the experience in diplomacy that he had acquired in nearly half a century of active political leadership.

Stand Watie's presence among his people in the Indian Territory was sorely needed. In consequence, after some weeks he took Scales with him and returned home, leaving only five members of the Southern delegation in Washington. Primarily a man of action rather than a diplomat it seems probable that he grew tired of the constant conferences and interviews; the endless plotting, planning, and scheming in which Boudinot excelled, but which must have been very distasteful to the old soldier.

The question before the Southern delegation was how to secure from the United States government their own recognition as the rightful representatives of the Cherokee nation. If they could do this they would make the treaty and the Northern delegation would be left out of the negotiations. To this end they bent every effort and, for a time, it seemed they would succeed. The United States commissioner at Fort Smith had sought earnestly to discredit John Ross and to show that he and his adherents had been quite as disloyal to the Union as had the Stand Watie group. If this position were taken by the officials of the United States the Southern delegation stood at least an even chance of having their credentials accepted as the rightful representatives of the Cherokee Nation authorized to make a treaty. But the position of the Fort Smith Commission was hardly tenable. The Ross delegation pointed out that they had repudiated the treaty with the Confederacy and returned to their allegiance to the North at the earliest opportunity and that many of the old Chief's adherents had never accepted an alliance with the South at all. Certainly it was difficult to regard as disloyal those Cherokees who had fled to Kansas to escape the vengeance of the Southern group and had later returned as soldiers of the United States in the invading Northern army. These all recognized Ross as chief and there was no question but that they had fought bravely for the Union. Perhaps Chief Ross, even as the sands of his life ebbed away and the shadow of death hovered over his pillow, was too clever for the Southern delegates. At any rate the Northern delegation pushed every advantage to the limit and was at last recognized as the group with which a treaty should be made.

Bitterly disappointed, the Southern delegation then sought to have the Cherokee Nation divided into two parts. In panic stricken haste Boudinot and the secretary to the delegation J. Woodward Washbourne wrote Stand Watie urging that he immediately organize a government of the Southern Cherokee in the Canadian District which should include a national council, judges, and local officials. Evidently they believed that, if a government were an accomplished fact at the time the treaty was signed, the United States would be forced to recognize it.

They declared to United States officials in Washington that it would be impossible for them to live under the same government as that of the Northern Cherokees and that the only way to secure peace and harmony was by a division of the Nation. They insisted that otherwise a repetition of the disturbed and lawless conditions of earlier years was inevitable.

Again, however, they were doomed to disappointment. The policy of the United States government looked to further consolidation of the tribes of the Indian Territory rather than to division. On July 17, 1866, the treaty was signed with the Northern, or Ross, delegation, leaving the Cherokee country undivided.

Chief Ross had been too ill to join in the final negotiations and died on August 1. Ten days later, on August 11, the treaty was proclaimed.

Desperately as they had struggled, the Southern delegates had been able to accomplish comparatively little. It is true the law confiscating the lands of the Southern Indians had been repealed and they were free to return to their homes in the Cherokee country though some still entertained grave doubts as to whether they might be permitted to live there in peace. A bitter quarrel had developed within the ranks of the Southern delegation and it is not impossible that this may have somewhat hindered its efforts. Boudinot had engaged in a violent quarrel with John Rollin Ridge and, to a less extent, with Adair, and did not fail to voice his grievances in positive terms.

The treaty of 1866 was a hard blow to the Cherokee even though it may have been somewhat more favorable to the Indians than were similar treaties made that year with the remainder of the Five Civilized Tribes. No absolute provision was made for the consolidation of the tribes of Indian Territory under a territorial government but a provision was included that an intertribal council might be held annually looking toward such end in the future. The Cherokee were required, however, to free their slaves and adopt them into the tribe as citizens who should be permitted to share in the lands. They were further required to grant right of ways to railroads across their country, to give up the "Neutral Lands" in Kansas, and finally to allow the United States to locate friendly Indians upon the lands of the Cherokee Outlet. Until such friendly tribes were so located, however, the Outlet was to remain the property of the Cherokee. The Cherokee Nation, however, still retained sovereignty over its people and remained as it was before the war, virtually an independent republic.

With the signing of the treaty the Southern delegates returned to the Indian Territory, with the exception of John Rollin Ridge, who set out for his home in California where he died some two years later.

The Cherokee living in the Choctaw Nation, or in Texas, soon began to return to their own country. They found, in

233

many cases, that their old homes had been destroyed since the Cherokee Nation has been described at the close of the war as "one vast scene of desolation where only chimney monuments mark the sites of once happy homes." Stand Watie lingered for a time to assist his people in removing and to gather his crops and assemble the little property remaining to him. Eventually he too returned, however, to settle near Webber's Falls. It is refreshing to note that Mrs. Watie so long an exile, suffering from illness, hardship, and anxiety for her loved ones soon recovered her health and spirits, when safe in a home of her own within the limits of her own country. "Mother steps about like a sixteen year old girl" Saladin wrote to his father.

A great sorrow, however, was soon to come to her and her husband. Saladin, the deeply loved oldest son, died in 1868 when only twenty-one years of age. His death cut short a very promising career and must have been a terrible blow to his devoted parents who looked to him as a prop to their declining years. Cumiskey having died in 1863, only one son and two daughters were now left to them.

Stand Watie was by this time growing old, and hardship and exposure had left him not in the best of health. The freeing of his slaves, and the destruction of most of his other property had, moreover, left him poor. Yet the old General faced the future with the same courage with which he had so often faced the enemy on the field of battle. Bravely he set to work to recoup his fallen fortunes, to provide for the comforts of his family and to give to his three children the education they had not been able to receive during the troubled years of the war.

◄§ Stand Watie to W. P. Adair & James M. Bell

Executive Office for Cherokee Nation
Ft. McCullough C. N. June 29th 1865

Cols. W. P. Adair & James M. Bell will proceed to Shreveport La. to H. D. Qrs. [of] Major Genl. Herron U. S. A. and confer and make such arrangements with him (as practicable) for the benefit of the Cherokees in this Territory and in the states, as their condition requires and as will not be incompatible with the Convention entered into between Lt. Col. A. C. Mathews and Adjt. W. H. Vance Commissioners on part of U. S. Govt. and the undersigned of the date of June 25th 1865.[1]

On completing their mission Cols. Adair and Bell will return and report to this office.

STAND WATIE

Principal Chief

Cherokee Nation

Attest

W. P. Boudinott

National Secretary

⇜James L. Butler[2] to Stand Watie

Mount Pleasant, Lotus Co, Texas

July 13th 1865.

Brig Genl Stand Watie

DEAR SIR

I have the honor to inform you, that I am still in the land of the living. Since the Surrender of the C. S. Army my spirits have been so low that I did not wish to see My Old Officers knowing that they were in low spirits. I do hope you will succeed in doing something for the Southern Cherokees for some of them are in great need. And some who call themselves C. S. are not entitled to respect from anyone as they have never done one thing *only* to Slander the defenders of the Cher. Nat. I have found out many of them since I left your command & will recollect them. I left your command not wishing to implicate or bring my friends into a difficulty, that was my own and one I was able to settle myself. As I wrote to Bill Alberty that the Cherokees *knew* that Jim Butler needed no one to *help* him to meet one man. Should you succeed in getting our

---

[1] Stand Watie was ever solicitous for the welfare of his people. To negotiate with representatives of the United States government in an effort to bring immediate relief to the Southern Cherokee refugees, Stand Watie sent his two most trusted officers, William P. Adair and James M. Bell.

[2] The writer of this letter served throughout the war period in the command of General Watie.

rights in the Cher Nat Please recollect me and family for I expect to live in the Cher Nat yet.[3] I think it will take about one year to run the Pins out And then Jim Butler can ride up to Maysville in safety and pay my respects to his old Commander.

If you will speak to bearer of this letter, Hon. Henry Jones or Judge Grey, all of this County, no doubt they would furnish some Rations for the destitute Cherokees as they have influence in this County. I am here and would attend to it for the said destitute, They are abusing the kindness shown to the true Cherokees. Bill Alberty, Jim McKay, John Drew, Sam Taylor, Clem Abner — such men drawing rations as destitute when the poor are suffering for something to eat.[4]

Traitors, Cowards, villians should be set opposite each of their names. I expect to live in Texas one year, then return to Grand River where I hope to enjoy your company.

Your true friend

James L. Butler

Genl. I am nearly broke. Did not get one thing from the C. S. and I see several fellows of your command with more mules than the Law allows them. And altho some times they are men that did nothing for their country or towards obeying your orders.[5]

I would like to call on them for about two mules with your permission.   J. L. B.

---

[3] Butler raised a question that was common in the minds of all of the Southern Cherokee: their position in their Nation since the termination of the war. This problem was, of course, one subject of the peace negotiations to be held at Fort Smith and, later, in Washington.

[4] In the months following the close of the war it was necessary to feed at public expense the destitute Cherokee. Under such circumstances the question was often raised as to whether or not some were receiving help who did not need it as much as others.

[5] It seems that when Stand Watie surrendered, the horses and mules used by his little army were distributed among his officers and men.

[6] This letter, which is explanatory in itself, is a report on the efforts of Adair and Bell to secure supplies for the destitute Southern Cherokee.

✑§ James C. Veatch to Stand Watie

Head Quarters Northern Division
of Louisiana

General Stand Watie, Shreveport La. July 21st, 1865.

Principal Chief of the Cherokee Nation,

GENERAL,

Your Commissioners, Colonels Adair and Bell, have been received at these Head Quarters and a full and free conference held with them in relation to the wants of your people.[6]

Colonel Bell will leave today for New Orleans with adjutant Vance who I send as a Special Bearer of Despatches to lay the whole matter before the Major General Commanding the Department of the Gulf. Colonel Adair leaves here today on his return to you. I send by him my answer to the questions submitted by your Commissioners.

With high consideration, I am, very respectfully

Your Obt. Servant

JAMES C. VEATCH

Brig. General Comdg.

✑§ Richard Fields et al to Honorable Commissioners[7]

Ft. Smith, Ark.

To the honorable commissioners Sept. 20, 1865

GENTLEMEN,

We the Delegates on the part of the Cherokees South would respectfully represent that there are about two hundred families of our people within the limits of the States of Arkansas & Texas driven thence for safety and subsistence before & during the war and expect to return to the Territory under the provisions of the Treaty just signed by us but in consequence of the still unsettled state of our business & their having raised crops

[7] To represent the Southern Cherokee at the peace council in progress of Fort Smith at the time of this letter, Stand Watie had appointed a delegation of seven men. This rare document is an early request presented to the United States commissioners by the Southern Cherokee representatives.

which they cannot dispose of advantageously in the country in which they now reside, we would respectfully ask that they be exempted from any and all species of taxation during their residence within those states or from being subject to any confiscation act either of these States or the United States, We promising that they will remove from those states [at] as early a period as practicable.

R. Fields
W. L. Holt
Jo L. Martin
D. M. Foreman

✑ Henry J. Hunt[8] to W. P. Adair

Head Quarters, Frontier District.
Hon. W. P. Adair   Fort Smith, Ark., Sept. 30, 1865
   Delegate Southern Cherokees,
Sir:

I have the honor to acknowledge the receipt of your letter of 27th inst., respecting the destitution which threatens and now partially exists among the southern Cherokees, and the necessity of making some provision for supplying, until agricultural operations can be resumed, those who are in want and have heretofore been supplied by the late Confederate authorities.

The subject has already been brought to the notice of the Commissioner of Indian Affairs and forms part of the record of the late Council assembled at this place.

I will, however, address a letter to the Commissioner especially inviting his personal attention to the matter at an early day and will, in the meantime, forward your letter to Maj. Gen'l. Reynolds,[9] commanding the Department of Arkansas,

[8] In 1865 General Henry J. Hunt was sent to Arkansas to command the frontier district that embraced the Indian Territory. To him Adair appealed for means to relieve the sufferings of the Cherokee, still in refuge in Texas and in the Choctaw Nation.

[9] The writer was referring to General J. J. Reynolds who had been assigned to the Department of Arkansas in 1864 to succeed General Frederick Steele.

for authority to issue from time to time such supplies as may be indispensable before the Indian Department can act. I do not know what will be the policy pursued by the military authorities on the subject, but my best efforts will be exerted to procure from any source, the supplies which the condition of your people requires.

Respectfully

Your Ob't Servant

Henry J. Hunt

Bv't. Maj. Gen'l. Com'dy.

⋞§ Elias Cornelius Boudinot to Stand Watie

Boggy Depot

Genl. Stand Watie   Dec. 8th 1865.

Chf. Cherokees.

I was requested by the Commr. of Indian Affairs[10] to come to Boggy Depot and procure information that he considered necessary to let out a Contract for feeding all the destitute Indians, and to aid the Special Agent who will be here tomorrow or next day I think, in establishing such depots as will most effectually supply all. I have been delayed by law matters in Ark. and it is necessary that I should return, as soon as possible, so that this important matter can be systematised and settled definitely and finally. Mr. Smith the special agent (was) appointed to establish these depots and to see that the contracts are carried out in good faith.[11] You had better come to this place in a few days and call upon him; I shall advise him to stay at Maj. Armstrongs.

I have been doing all that I could and am still working for what I believe to be the best interest of the Southern Cherokees

---

[10] D. N. Cooley, appointed Commissioner of Indian Affairs by President Johnson in 1865, created a commission of special agents to go into the Indian country and administer relief to the Southern indigents.

[11] Egbert T. Smith, one of the special agents appointed by Commissioner D. N. Cooley, was directed to distribute subsistence from Boggy Depot in the Choctaw Nation.

239

and all other Southern Indians. I have already expended $600 on my own account for which I ask and expect no return.[12]

Truly yours, &c.

E. C. BOUDINOT
Delegate &c.

ᑌᔕ Thomas F. Anderson to Stand Watie

Near Waco, McLennan County
Genl. Stand Watie Texas, Febr 19th 1866.
DEAR SIR

I saw a Mr. Conway from Greyson County a few days ago on his way to Austin, from which place he will return here in two or three days. He informed me that you were living in the Choctaw Nation a few miles west of Armstrong Academy and promised me to have a letter forwarded to you.[13] Personally I have no other motive for writing than such as would induce one to write to a friend, if you will permit me to include myself in the number of those who truly esteem you. But I have been requested by Adam Bibles and Downing, whom you both know as citizens of your Nation, to endeavor to get them authentic information in regard to the prospects of the Southern Cherokee.[14] Both wish to return to the Nation this Spring but, on account of the thousand and one rumors in circulation, do not know what to depend upon and would like to see their way clear. And I confess as much anxiety on the subject for my own part as they or anybody else can possibly feel. I find it hard to shake off old associations and cannot help feeling identified with the people among whom I had the honor to serve during our late war. And when, homeless as I am, I think of a future home I am bound to say that the United States proper

[12] Boudinot was endeavoring to assist Smith in the administration of relief to the destitute Cherokee.

[13] At the close of the war, Mrs. Watie joined her husband in the Choctaw country where they lived until late in 1867.

[14] The peace council held at Fort Smith in September, 1865, having ended in disappointment, negotiations were resumed in Washington the following spring. Anderson was anxious to know what was being done for the Southern Cherokee.

possesses no attraction and holds out no inducement to me to live there in future and to live contented.

I have had a very tedious time of it here with my Shattered leg, but am now doing as well as I could expect and can now begin to use it some.[15] I would like very much to see you again before I go home this spring, and will probably come up with Mr. Bibles. He is anxious to learn at what time you will all start up to your old home, so as to be there in time to go up with you. If however matters are not so arranged as to induce the Southern Cherokees to return he desires to know, so as to enable him to shape his course accordingly.[16]

Since I came here I have written several letters to you and fear that I have annoyed you. But I beg you to believe that such has not been my intention. Outside of my own family, such as I look upon as my best friends are among your people and among them I can say in all sincerity that you hold the first place. I know that you will understand me and receive this as a full apology if you have thought me guilty of any boring.

I would like to hear from Saladin and other friends. If you know P. G. Lynch's address, please give it to me.

I have no news whatever. I hear frequently from my family, since the Mails have again begun to go with something like regularity. They are well but getting along about as bad as the majority of impoverished families east of the Mississippi.

There are now a company of U. S. regular soldiers stationed at Waco, and the probability is that they will remain for an indefinite time or untill Messrs. Sumer, Stevens & Co. choose to admit Texas as a State into the Union. The Convention here is in session but I have not heard from Austin lately.[17]

[15] Anderson's reference to his shattered leg leads one to believe that he was wounded late in the war, as he was apparently hale and hearty early in 1865.

[16] Public sentiment among the Northern Cherokee who were now in possession of the Cherokee Nation was quite hostile towards the Southern branch of the tribe. In consequence, the Southern Cherokee were in most cases afraid to return to their old homes, especially since the entire country was in a lawless condition.

[17] The writer was referring to a convention, held for the purpose of forming a new government for the State of Texas.

Please answer this as soon as possible and address to me at "Waco McLennan Co. Care of Danl Acre."

With my sincere respects to your family and begging you to remember me to other old friends, believe me Genl.

Your friend & Obt Servt
THOMAS F. ANDERSON

ᎦᏍ Stand Watie to Saladin Watie

Fort Smith May 12th 1866[18]

MY DEAR SON:

I have come on this far — arrived night before last on the Steamer J. S. Hales, will leave this evening in an ambulance furnished by the 5th. I had the address of the delegation to the Southern Cherokees printed and will be distributed to the people. You may tell the Delegation that our people are steadfast, none have taken or will take the obnoxious oath, only those that we have hereto heard of. A large sale of cattle confiscated from the Southern Cherokees were advertised to be sold last Tuesday, which was countermanded and the cattle turned loose. I have sent word to the people on the Canadian to defend their rights from the unauthorized laws of the Pins affecting the constitutional rights of the Cherokee people. I have met with many of our friends here, amongst them is Anderson, Johnson, Dawson, Hill & others.

Every one I have seen agrees to [what] has been done by their delegates. Our people are settled from Little Boggy to the Canadian & Arks. rivers and they are all true notwithstanding the report of the opposite delegation to the contrary.[19] Tell

[18] Stand Watie had gone to Washington as a member of the delegation of Southern Cherokee and was returning home accompanied by J. A. Scales. He had left the remainder of the delegation, consisting of Saladin Watie, E. C. Boudinot, Richard Fields, and William Penn Adair, in Washington. John Rollin Ridge, the other member of the peace delegation, who came from California, had not yet reached Washington when Stand Watie left that city.

[19] Evidently the Ross delegation had sought to create the impression that large numbers of the Southern Cherokee were withdrawing from the Stand Watie group and aligning themselves with the Ross faction.

Judge Fields that I am [not] able to learn whether his family have moved out or not. I will instruct Scales to give them assistance in case they should be on the Canadian. He goes to that region of the country. I go through Boggy. If they are still on Blue I shall take pleasure in giving them all the help I can.

Tell my friend Majr. Page that I saw his wife, in her anxiety to hear from him she came to town to see me in order to hear from him. She says they are all well but have a rather hard way of making a living. She requests him to write home.

Dr. Spring & his wife sends love to you — my son write to them. They are your true friends, also Dr. Main & family.

Cornelius has gained a name which will hold good all his days.[20]

Our folks were well when Dawson left. I will write to [you] from Boggy. I take a few things to buy a start in cattle. I had an offer in Memphis by an agent in Ohio to furnish me a saw mill which I think I will accept.

My dear son write to us often.

Your affectionate Father
STAND WATIE

P.S. Wheelers family all well. John is going with me.

∽§ J. W. Washbourne[21] to J. A. Scales

Little Rock, Arks.
June 1st, 1866

DEAR SCALES:

Our matters are going smoothly in Washington. By the 10th and 14th I learned that Rollin Ridge had arrived.[22] He was immediately elected Chief of the Delegation. He is recog-

---

[20] Elias Cornelius Boudinot seems to have been the most aggressive and resourceful member of the delegation.

[21] J. Woodward Washbourne was secretary of the Southern delegation but had apparently left Washington and returned to Little Rock on matters of business.

[22] John Rollin Ridge, who had been living in California since 1850, made the journey to Washington to assist in the negotiation of the Treaty of 1866. Upon his arrival he was promptly qualified as a member of the Southern delegation, of which he was made chairman.

nized by the Government as the loyal chief of the Ridge Party. Ross had relapsed and was expected to die tho he was alive the 22 ult.[23] The Ross delegation has been dismissed by the Commissioner because they would not agree to a division.

Ridge, Adair, Fields, and Boudinot, with Fuller and Vorhee had an interview with the President. They are all in high spirits.

The President has ordered that a treaty be made with us for our pro rata share of the nation.[24] This is positive. On the 22d May they were drawing up the treaty. It is probably signed before this.

Ross is going to try to beat us in the Senate. His only show is what it was when you left. He will be beaten there. He is trying to make public sentiment through the N. Y. Tribune. Rollin has answered it in a scorching reply and went himself to see Greeley, of the Tribune, about its publication. Ross will be beaten there. His day is done. Ours is rising fast and bright. We will get all we asked for, with, perhaps, not so much money.[25] I have been appointed to write to Gen Watie to urge him at once to organize the Southern Cherokee Government in the Canadian District. In God's name be swift about it. Let Genl. Watie issue his proclamation in the Canadian District declaring the existence of the Southern Cherokee Nation, whereever they are, to hasten to the Canadian District and there hold election for members of Council, Committee, Judges and all the officers of the Government of the Southern Cherokees.[26] Hurry this up. I write this to you be-

[23] Chief Ross died two months later, on August 1.

[24] The Southern Cherokee delegation was seeking to have their Nation divided into two parts, asserting that they could not live under the same government as the Northern faction.

[25] The plan involved not only a division of lands but a division of the money due the Cherokee from the United States for their lands in the East and from the contemplated sale of the neutral lands in Kansas and portions of the Cherokee Outlet.

[26] Washbourne and the Southern delegation believed that if the organization of the Southern Cherokee government were an accomplished fact, it would strengthen their position.

cause I want you to know, to act, and because I want it got to Gen. Watie as soon as possible.

Organize the Government as soon as it can be done. You will be protected against any interference.

Send this letter to Gen. Watie as soon as possible.

Yours truly,

J. W. WASHBOURNE

Cherokee Delegate

◄◙ J. W. Washbourne[27] to J. A. Scales

Steamer "America" June 20, 1866.

DEAR SCALES,

Don't neglect to have the Southern Cherokee Government organized Immediately. Have it done by all means, even should Gen. Watie's Proclamation not be able, in time, to collect a thousand voters. Organize it with a few hundred votes if you can't get more, or less, but organize, and afterward we will settle elections again.

We have won the day and delay must not be suffered to endanger our work. Ross is appealing, lamely, I admit, but still appealing to the sympathies of the Radicals and the ignorant. He will appeal also to the sympathies of the ignorant Cherokees. He is an artful man and tho' he is personally powerless, he can work through agents, as you and I know to our cost.[28] I entreat you as a representative of the Cherokee South to lay all this before Gen. Watie, our Chief. I write to you for that purpose. Don't let any delay avoidable hinder the organization. Preserve the copy of this and my other letters, as public record.

I shall return to the Rock soon.

Yours truly,

WASHBOURNE

27 Washbourne was evidently returning to Washington from Little Rock.

28 Ross and the Northern delegation were, of course, entirely unwilling to see the Nation divided and did their utmost to prevent it.

E. C. Boudinot to W. P. Boudinot

Washington D. C. 2nd July 1866

DEAR BROTHER

I wrote you some time ago that we had signed a satisfactory treaty and that we were in high hopes of its speedy ratification. Since then things have taken a change, under a mistaken apprehension that a compromise can be made. The President directs that another Treaty shall be made. I have no idea we can sign it. I have an idea the best thing to be done is to leave the question of division unsettled.[29] But to secure few simple titles to all our improvements and the restoration of all our property sold under confiscation, we can then bid over them and rent our places.

CORNELIUS

Saladin Watie to Stand Watie

Washington, D. C.
July 24th 1866

DEAR FATHER

Mr. Brown will start this evening for the Nation and I therefore avail myself of the opportunity to write you a few lines, and the news I have to communicate I know will be very unwelcom to you, and a sad disappointment to our people. The Ross Deligation have made a Treaty and it has been approved of by the President,[30] at least it was sent up to the Senate by him for ratification, and yesterday we had an interview with Senate Committee and I infered from their remarks that it would be ratifyed, for the way they talked to us was abserd and rediculous. Their was sevorald questions asked us, one was by Chr Lumbuer, where do your people now reside — answer was

[29] This letter was in a very fragmentary condition, but it seems that E. C. Boudinot was still unwilling to give up hope of eventually securing a division of the Nation.

[30] This treaty, when ratified with amendments, readjusted the relations of the Cherokee Nation with the United States. John Ross was recognized as the principal chief of the Nation and the plan for dividing the tribal domain was discarded. The loyal Cherokee agreed to repeal the confiscation laws and to restore their secessionist brothers to full rights.

246

partly in the Choctaw Nation, and partly in Canadian District, to which he replyed why not let them stay whare they are.[31] I am compelled to go to the Depo with Brown or I would write more but will write again in a day or two. My love to all.

from your dear son
SALADIN WATIE

✑ Elias Cornelius Boudinot to Stand Watie

Washington D. C. July 25, 1866.

DEAR UNCLE:

We have been beaten; that is to say we have not been successful in securing an absolute separation.[32] I am in doubt as to the proper course to pursue. Adair and the others wish to defeat the treaty the Rosses have signed, but I incline to the opinion that the better policy would be to accept what he put in their treaty as it does not commit us to anything, and gives us a good chance to renew the demand for a division at a more favorable opportunity.

The treaty grants a general amnesty, declares confiscation laws void, and gives the Ross party no jurisdiction over us in civil and criminal cases before the courts. They shoulder all the responsibility of the negro matter. We get none of the money.[33] I haven't time nor patience to explain. Yours,

BOUDINOT.

✑ W. P. Boudinot to Stand Watie

Webber Falls Apl 9th 1867

DEAR UNCLE,

I have written to you twice within a week in regard to a matter of business between myself and George Buffington who I hear lives near you; in both of which letters I have requested

[31] The reply, by the chairman of the Senate (Indian) Committee is indicative of the lack of understanding of the Indian problem and, to a great extent, of the Senate's lack of interest in its solution.

[32] The writer was referring to the proposed division of the Cherokee Nation.

[33] See 14 Stats., 755-99, for this treaty.

you to give yourself some trouble on my account. I sent one by hand, which may likely meet the fate of such epistles, i.e. be worn out in some ones pocket. The other I have sent inclosed by mail to Col. Harkins, Boggy Depot, with a request to have it forwarded to you. It may also miscarry. To make sure, as the matter however small is in my present circumstances important to me, I write this third one with a design to address it to Parris from which place you may get it direct.

On my way up while camped near Nails Mill I loaned Buffington a large old bay work horse to assist him in getting off. It was agreed between us that the horse should be returned to me last fall after his arrival in this country upon my applying for it or, if the horse should die or become disabled in his charge, that he should pay me seventy five dollars in Greenback. The latter part of the arrangement I purposed solely to ensure fair treatment to the horse which I intended to use and was certain I should stand in need of. B. did not move as promised and expected and, Saladin tells me, has since sold the horse to you. It is plain that if he has not acquainted you with the circumstances under which he got possession of it, that he is not acting honestly in the business and, unless some friend will see to my interest, that I must suffer. Will you be kind enough to do it? If you wish the horse to match Mountain or for any other purpose convenient to you, Keep him; but secure for me the one you let Buffington have or some other work animal. For I really need one and may be compelled to send or go to Red River to supply ourself. At the same time B. got the horse, I let him have four half grown sows with the understanding that he would take good care of them, bring them to this country and take half the stock for his trouble. I enclose an order for all. Please do what you can without putting yourself to too much inconvenience. I want to get my property out of Buffington's hands and if successful will have, under favor of Providence, nothing more to do with him.[34]

---

[34] It is interesting that the men, who only the year before had been engaged in matters of State, were now faced with the serious task of making a livelihood by farming.

Southern Cherokee Delegation to Washington, 1866

Left to right: John Rollin Ridge, Saladin Watie, Richard Fields, E. C. Boudinot, W. P. Adair

I had been sick since I crossed Canadian last summer but am getting better I think. The rest are well. No law business yet. I don't like the idea of throwing myself in the arms of Pins across the river and have therefore rented twenty acres here.[35] The Pins I hear are going it pretty lively on the Head right question pro and con. Downing expecting to win next August on that hobby in a canter over Ross.[36] You have probably heard that J. M. Hildebrand went crazy and disappeared last Fall. Jack Candy has gone crazy and *appeared* to me this morning. I am sorry to say this is no Joke. He is really out of his wits. Cornelius wrote you early last winter a full history of the split with Ridge and Adair. Did you get it?[37]

The Pin ticket for Chiefs next election is Bill Ross and Jim Beam (Csomana-tah) on one side — Louis Downing and Crabgrass on the other.[38] The offices are worth a little *now* and with Jones and Ross in the forground to intrigue, backbite and blarney, the race is expected with some interest by Southern lookers on.[39] Serge Beck and wife were lately killed by Charley Rootdigger near Hildebrand's Mill. So reported direct from Ft. Gibson. Little Dick Fields is warned from entering Flint and keeps rather shy.

[35] William P. Boudinot knew that he was quite unpopular with the Northern Cherokee, and for that reason he preferred to live at Webber's Falls, as far away from them as possible.

[36] William P. Ross, nephew of John Ross, and Lewis Downing, both Northern Cherokee, were candidates for the office of principal chief.

[37] The Southern delegation in Washington became involved in a controversy during which Elias Cornelius Boudinot became bitterly angry with John Rollin Ridge and, to a less extent, with Adair. This controversy probably hindered somewhat the efforts of the Southern Cherokee delegation.

[38] Following the usual Cherokee tendency towards factionalism, the Northern wing of the tribe itself became divided into two parties, the "Pin" element declaring that William P. Ross had not been favorable to their interests. The Reverend Lewis Downing and Captain James Vann were elected principal chief and assistant chief, respectively, at the general election on August 5, 1867.

[39] More interest was taken in the election for the chieftaincy of the Nation after the death of John Ross. The Southern wing realized, however, that as yet they had no chance of choosing a chief from their own party.

The Pins generally are friendly but are organized in each Dist. with a fair supply of arms ammunition and speeches.

My regards to Charley and the rest.

From your affectionate Nephew

W. P. BOUDINOT

◄§ J. W. Washbourne to Stand Watie

Norristown, Arks,

May 2nd 1867.

DEAR GENERAL:

I write you a hasty note by Maj. Boudinot. I wish I could have seen you as you passed and that you had stopped here at my house and waited for Boudinot, who I knew would be here soon. I think it would have been to your advantage.[40]

I wrote to you at Little Rock but the letter got there just as you left. Col. McDonald forwarded the letter to you at Fort Smith. I hope you got it and that you remained there to see Boudinot.

In that letter I mentioned concerning my pay as Secretary to the Delegation and hoped you would confer with Maj. Boudinot thereupon. I yet request that you would. He acts for me and can tell you all. He has been most shabbily treated and so will you be if you dont look Sharp. I was regularly elected Secretary to the Cherokee Delegation we had in Washington. I know I worked hard. All the Secretaries to the other Southern Indian Delegations received their pay, much more than was allowed me. But I was formally elected Secretary. An account, originally in my name, was allowed for "clerk hire" for $1500. This money justly belonged to me. I have never got a dollar of it save the amount of $218 this day paid me by Maj Boudinot. I am very needy and destitute.

I hate to take it from Boudinot, "his part," as he calls it, of the $1500 allowed me. I write to you as the Chief of the South-

---

[40] Stand Watie was evidently returning from a trip to Washington.

250

ern Cherokees to see, if you can, that I get my due.[41] I ask for it to pay for meat and bread for my children. Maj. B. will tell you all. The boat is coming.

Yours truly,

Gen. *Stand Watie,*
Fort Smith, Arks.

J. W. WASHBOURNE

⋟ Stand Watie to Saladin Watie

Red River[42] June 6th 1867

DEAR SON,

Mr. John Fallen will call on you for corn. He is now on his way up, if you can do so let him have it, much as fifteen or twenty bushels. I will be good to you for it. I learn I am owing Jim Horsefly.

I am smashed up. A flood has swept my crop off. About a hundred acres of the finest corn is gone. I shall now of course move up sooner than I anticipated.

Your affectionate father,

Saladin R. Watie
Webbers Falls

STAND WATIE

⋟ Elias Cornelius Boudinot to Stand Watie

Maysville Ark.
June 9, 1867

DEAR UNCLE

I wish to purchase what remains of your old mill. Polson wants to get at something and thinks he can do something with the mill. Neither he nor I have any money. Have a few hundred, I have, and which will be needed in repairs; if you will

---

41 The title of "Chief of the Southern Cherokee" was hardly applicable after the Treaty of 1866. Washbourne evidently expected that Stand Watie's former official position would carry sufficient weight to guarantee the honoring of his claim as secretary of the Southern Cherokee delegation.

42 Stand Watie was still living in the Choctaw country. Saladin had returned some months earlier from Washington and had settled near Webber's Falls.

part with it, make any arrangements with Polson you like. He can tell you the condition of the machinery &c.

I understand the report of my infidelity to my friends and party is generally believed. Adair & Fields both *say* they have satisfied their suspicions were unfounded but neither have the manliness or generosity to correct the slanders they have set in motion.

One report is that I got $40,000 and that Saladin got $10,000. I hope *he* at least will learn from this how easy it is to slander and lie.[43] Love to all.

Affly,
CORNELIUS

Adair says Scales has your money.[44]

C.

W. P. Adair to Stand Watie

Webber's Falls C. N. June 20th 1867

GENERAL:

I arrived here on the 15 — left Fields & Scales in Washington to attend to some unfinished business respecting the feeding of our destitute and the removal of certain of our people to their homes, from the Choctaw & Chickasaw Nations. I send you our Report to show you what we did up to its date. I am looking for Scales in a week from this time. When he comes we will call the people together and report to them.[45] At this time I think our prospects in Washington are much better than they have been, provided we can beat Bill Ross for Chief which I feel assured can be done with proper management.[46] I will

[43] This of course, refers to the quarrel that had developed in the Southern delegation the year before, in which Boudinot had been accused by some members of the delegation of profiting at their expense.

[44] This evidently refers to Stand Watie's pay as a member of the Southern delegation.

[45] The Southern Cherokee maintained a delegation in Washington to look after the interests of their people, long after the treaty of 1866 had been signed.

[46] They were successful, for William P. Ross was defeated by Lewis Downing in the election for chief the following August.

go today & see Porum & others & consult them as to the course we shall pursue & let the people West of Grand River know our conclusion as they are awaiting our action in Canadian. Should the opposition to Ross act in concert and defeat him, I feel confident of our success in closing out Cherokee business in Washington.

Truly your friend,

Gen. Stand Watie
W. P. ADAIR

⋖§ Saladin Watie to J. A. Scales[47]

Webber Falls C. N.
Novem 4th 1867

DEAR FRIND, SCALES

I have concluded to write you a few lines but have nothing of interest to communicate you, when you started you promised to write me but I suppose you have but little time to fulfill such promises. I saw your sister and family yesterday. they were all well except one of the little boys who is troubled with the chills. My folks moved in a short time since and settled on Canadian, seven miles above Tom' Stars.[48] My mother is in bad health and has been for some time. I also saw Col Adair a short time ago and he told me that he expected you back in a few days; I since herd from you threw Sulaton who said that you did not speak of coming home until Christmas. Every body is very anxious to see you, more especialey the girls who are very affraid you will bring home that yankee wife, and if you do you need not expect to have any friends "here a bouts." My father told me to say to you to get his money which is due him for his services. He has all confidence in you. I suppose the letter which he wrote you will answer as a power of attorney for you.

---

[47] As stated in the preceding letter, J. A. Scales was still in Washington.

[48] This home of the Watie's was in Canadian District in the southern part of the Cherokee Nation. Probably only Mrs. Watie and the children moved in at this time, as later letters indicate that Stand Watie was still on the Red River in the Choctaw Nation.

253

Every body in this section of the country made plenty of corn. The man that is living on yure place made an abundance of it. Come and you can ride a fat horse. Write to your frind Scales, if you don't I will get mad at you and not claim you as such — tell me something of old 13th street. How I would like to be there about now.[49]

Your frind
SALADIN WATIE

ᎦᏏ Saladin Watie to Stand Watie

At home Near Breebs Town, C. N.
Novem. 16, 1867

DEAR FATHER

I will start my Waggon with the Boys tomorrow to assist you in moving. I have just got home from the Falls, where I have been for two weeks halling rocks and boards to finish my house. I also got in nearly all of Uncle Jim's corn and some of my own.[50] I would have finished in one week more if I had not to have had to send the wagon off. Since you left, I and Charles[51] has not been idle, but a part of our work was of no benefit to us; we cut a large amt. of hay and it was all burned up a few days ago.

I think we have got along very well so far, have had plenty to eat, except for the last week or so — we have been out of meat, that was in my absence. I will go out and buy a good beef from some Choctaw tomorrow,[52] and better than all mama has grown to be stout and healthy. She steps about like some young sixteen year old girl.[53] All of our horses are in

---

[49] Saladin Watie evidently enjoyed his stay in Washington as a member of the Southern delegation, since this was probably his first and only visit to that city.

[50] James M. Bell.

[51] Charles Webber, Saladin's cousin.

[52] The Waties lived very near the line between the Choctaw and Cherokee Nations.

[53] Mrs. Watie, at last in a home of her own and freed from the anxieties of former times, seems to have improved surprisingly in health and strength since the time of Saladin's previous letter.

good fix, the mule Peet has been found. The cattle is doing very well, so mama tells me. I have not seen them since I come back. I swapped my horse Bill off for a match to my kitchen horse, the finest looking span of horses in this country. Charles started to Ft Smith with a load of hides and went by the Falls and I stopped him to finish the halling, I would have had it done in case I had not sent the waggon off so soon. The wheel steers are very poor, but in good working condition and very stout, for they have had plenty of corn to eat, all that is necessary is to see they are well fed and they will pull all you can put on the waggon. If I was in your place I would much rather buy an ox team than any other kind to bring the large waggon you have, for oxen is ready sale, should you be compelled to sell them, and you can keep them with less expence than mules or horses. I think you ought to be able to buy steers at twenty dollars a head, young unbroke cattle, and they will bring you thirty two ½ dollars here (Green Backs) or you can use them for beef. I wish I was down to help you. I know I could be so much help in getting up your stock and bringing it out. I trust you will bring a good lot of hogs. Make Watica see to the five hogs I got from Stuart.[54] If you should need me and Charles and the Waggon, send us word by Stand Benge or Watica and we will go down and give you all the help we are able. Mama authorises me to say that we can do very well without old *"Sall* and Mrs. *Squirel."* we are all anxious to see you all roll in Dont let any one ride my mare and have good care taken of her for I hope she will be able to ride up to Grand River when you get back with her. Be sure and get my mule from Buffington and also have Watica and Stand Benge to get two Sows from him and half their increase for two years, but I will be satisfied if they only get the two which Boudinot let him have. I have give Boudinot Credit for the mule and the two hogs, and if you dont attend to getting them for me I will be eighty dollars looser, for Boudinot has give me hint enough if I did not get them I would not get anything. My House is getting going up

[54] Watica was Saladin's younger brother.

very fast now. I think you will be after me for a trade when you see it and of course I will trade with you, for I would rather see you live in such a house than to do so myself it would be more pleasure to me than anything in the world to see you and Mama in a good *comfortable* house.[55]

Nothing more just now make Uncle Charles write to me, for he can tell me about every thing on the place. You all can't imagine how anxious we are to hear from you all. If Watica was not so much help in driving Stock I would insist you would send him back to satisfy our thirst for news from the place.

From Your Son

SALADIN WATIE

P.S. It is with sorrow that I am called on to inform you of the death of our ill fated relative John R. Ridge, he died at his place of residence in California some time in September last[56] also the report of Lizzie's death has been confirmed. Foster Bell to came to an untimely end (as I suppose you have already herd) by some cowardly devils who waylayed and murdered him for what little money he was supposed to have had. It took place some whare in the Choctaw Nation and it is reported here that Johnson Thomas or Tuck Rider was the perpertrators of the bloody deed, if it proves to be the case it will be the duty of uncle Jim to report it to the Principal Chief and demand them. They are both Cherokees and I suppose it would come under the jurisdiction of our court.[57] I do not think the relatives of the ill fated youth ought to stop until the murders are caugh[t] and brought to justice — and to give such mean devils justice, I dont know how it could well be done unless it was given to me to desid. And I am pretty certain should it be the

[55] This sentence reveals clearly the generous heart of young Saladin.

[56] The death of John Rollin Ridge on October 5, 1867, at the age of forty, was a great loss to the State of California, where he was widely known and loved.

[57] Since these men were Cherokee, under the inter-tribal law, they would be surrendered for trial in the Cherokee courts.

[58] Just as this letter reveals the serious nature of Saladin, it also reveals his fiery temper.

case, they would meet with their deserts.[58] Write and send your letter to North Fork Creek Nation.

From Your Son
SALADIN WATIE

◄§ Saladin Watie to James M. Bell

Solitude, November 18th 1867

DEAR UNCLE JIM,

I have concluded to write you a few lines by the Boys, although I have nothing of interest to communicate you. I have been busy for the last two weeks getting in our corn and halling boards to cover my house. I got in four hundred bushels of your corn, from Mr. Horn's one hundred yet due, which I will hall and crib as soon as Charles gets back from Ft Smith. I put up a large amt. of hay as I told you I would do, but unfortunately some one set the prairie on fire before I had time to burn or plow around it, so it was all burned up. Two weeks as hard work as I ever done, did not benefit me one cent. The hay I put up would have been worth more than one hundred dollars to us in the way of feed to our stock this coming winter. I think you are loosing a great deal by not attending to your interest on Grand River, from what I have gathered your presents is absolutely necessary to secure what is justly due you from certain persons. Lon Lynch was down at the Falls hunting you some time ago. I also saw Mr. Richards who spoke very freely to me how things was carried on; I also learned from him that Brock still had your horse. The Jimmie Starr place has been valued and is now for sale. I think you should by all means buy it. I have learned that the rail road has been marked out and is to run in a few hundred yards of the House.[59] The place is only held at five hundred ($500) dollars, not the (1/3) third of its real value.

From Your Nephew
SALADIN WATIE

---

[59] Agitation for the construction of a railroad through the Indian Country began long before the outbreak of the war. In the negotiation of the treaty of 1866 the question was again raised and at this time, the Cherokee were hardly

257

P.S. Mr. Alberty sent for me yesterday to help him guard the supposed murders of our relative, Foster Bell. I am not well but will go and see what evidence they have against the men, and if good we can soon dispose of them according to *Justice* and say nothing about *law*.[60] SALADIN WATIE

Stand Watie to James M. Bell

Red River C. N. Dec. 28th 1867

DEAR COLONEL:

My waggon with folks of John Rogers starts today, thinking that they will overtake you I send this letter.[61] I do not hardly know what to say about the big waggons returning. I can make out myself with what I have here in moving, do as you think best with regard to the waggon should you think you'd need it, if Saladin is using the two horse waggon, tell him I can make out but if he is not busy and would just as soon drive down it will make it lighter on me. I have sold two of my mules; Beck & Pete, and Old Blue.

Nothing new has transpired since you left that I hear of.

Yours truly,

WATIE

I have had another chill. It's the third day — the Capt. is gone to see Majr Loren.

H. E. McKee to Stand Watie

Genl. Stand Watie Fort Smith, Ark 1867

DEAR SIR

We are directed by Major P. Fuller to request you to go immediately to Washington for the purpose of proving the time & manner of the Capture of the U.S. & Sutler trains at Cabin

---

in a position to refuse. Into the treaty was written a section granting right-of-ways to railroads.

[60] Saladin's spelling and use of English are surprisingly good, considering his lack of opportunity to secure an education.

[61] The return of the Cherokee to their Nation from their refugee homes required several months' time.

Creek in 1864 & to say that he will make satisfactory remuneration for the time and expense &c.[62]

Verry Respectfully &c
Your Obt Servt
H. E. McKee & Co

✑§ Elias Cornelius Boudinot to Stand Watie

Washington D. C. Jan. 9, 1868.

MY DEAR UNCLE:

I was so glad to hear from you and know that the arrangements concerning my tobacco business were satisfactory to you.[63] I believe we will be able to make a handsome thing of it this year, and so better and better every year. I calculate all expenses will be paid up in the spring and then we will have clear sailing. I wish to put up in conjunction with the factory a steam flour mill. What think you of it? If I save enough out of the treaty matter I will put it in a mill and give you an interest if you think it best. If I should fail here, however, we can put up the mill with our factory profits by the 1st of September.

I have drawn up and had introduced an important railroad bill. It is my own invention and I am entitled to a patent right therefor. The bill incorporates the Central Indian R. R. Co., the first directors to be apportioned to the several nations according to population, and the subsequent directors to represent the several nations in proportion to the stock subscribed. My plan is to allow the Indians to build their own road and own it. They have got the land and money to do it, and it will be their own fault if they dont. The bill takes well and is already printed.[64]

62 Evidently H. E. McKee and Company were the owners of the goods in the sutler's wagons, which were traveling with the United States Army wagons when the entire train was captured by Stand Watie. Watie's own report of this capture appears in the *War of the Rebellion, Official Records,* Series I, Vol. 41, pt. I, 787-88.

63 Boudinot had established a tobacco factory in the Cherokee Nation, the capital for which was partly furnished by Stand Watie.

64 Boudinot's plan to incorporate a railroad to be built with capital furnished by Indians of the various Nations did not materialize. It was hardly

Bill Penn has not yet arrived being detained by sickness of his wife in Kansas.[65]

I hope you will have the necessary buildings put up as soon as possible about the factory and move up and take possession.

I am hard pushed for means for the delegation has not provided for me.[66] Sometimes I get in excessive bad humor, when I think that notwithstanding all the hard work I *have* done, and *am* doing, for the Cherokees, they wish to throw me overboard.

But dear Uncle, keep my affairs straight at home and we will make money. Now with money and brains we can win in spite of family malice and prejudices.

Affly,

CORNELIUS

⊷§ W. P. Adair to Saladin Watie

Washington D C January 29th 1868

DEAR SALADIN:

We got here four days ago. I was quite unwell with cold and something like pluerisy of the side. I am much better. I am able to attend to business. Your father's money has been drawn by our friend Scales under the letter, or authority he (your father) sent him, of which I spoke to you. The am't is what I showed you, in the report made by Judge Fields as chairman of the delegation, to the commissioner of Indian affairs, and Scales will take or send the money soon to you or your father, or to both. He asks me to assure you that there is no wrong on his part so far as the money is concerned. I did not telegraph to you in regard to this matter as I promised, for

---

practicable, since the Indians did not have sufficient money to finance such a venture. The first railroad across the Indian Territory was the Missouri, Kansas and Texas, built a few years later.

[65] William Penn Adair.

[66] After the close of the war, each of the Five Civilized Tribes maintained a delegation in Washington to look after tribal interests. Boudinot, who was in Washington, had been appointed to fill a vacancy in the Cherokee delegation.

the reason that there is no telegraphic communication any further west than Little Rock; and I thought that a telegram under these circumstances would be very uncertain. We have not yet gone into any business. It may be some news to you to know that Boudinott, Judge Fields and Scales, and myself have all made friends.[67]

Mr. Brown did not come, as was expected on the Delegation — and the chief appointed Boudinott to fill the vacancy. Judge Fields has been appointed as special agent under the 22nd article of the Treaty of '66 to examine the accounts of the Nation with the U. S. Govt. &c. The claims of our Delegation (Fields, Scales and myself) is not quite through as yet. It has been audited by the department and I understand will be refered today to congress for an appropriation. As soon as I get my money I will send you a draft for what I owe you, to Fort Gibson, to the care of John C. Cunningham, Post Master there — Congress and the President are still quarrelling, with no definite results any way I will send you a newspaper to Fort Gibson in a few days. Our Delegation has visited the Commr. of Indian affairs — the Secretary of the Interior — and today we visited the President. He received us very kindly indeed. Col. Downing made a speech to the President and Mr. Ruse who is our interpretor being sick I had to interpret Downing's speech to the president.[68] You may guess I *did it up brown.* There were a good many ladies and gentlemen and some members of congress present who no doubt appreciated my knowledge of the Cherokee language. Tell Col Bell I will write to him in a few days.

Remember me to your Ma and Pa, and to Bell and all inquiring friends and believe me as ever,

Your friend and Cousin

Capt. S. R. Watie   W. P. ADAIR

[67] While the Southern Cherokee leaders frequently quarreled bitterly among themselves, their enmity towards the Northern group was so strong that any ill feeling toward one another usually passed away very quickly.

[68] Colonel Lewis Downing, almost a fullblood Cherokee, headed the delegation, since he was principal chief.

✑Mary F. Wheeler to Stand Watie

Gen. Watie,   May 7th/68
DEAR GENL,

My tenderest sympathy has been with you since your bereavement, and I have often wished that I could speake some word of comfort — but alas, what can I say — I cannot restore your noble boy.[69] I only know that I admired him much.

He was so high minded — so correct in his ideas of things, and grasous, and so magnanimous in his character. Then too he seemed so bouyant, so hopeful for the future that one's affection went out to him involuntarily.

But He who *cannot* err, who doeth all things well, has seen fit to afflict you, I pray that He will comfort and sustain you. He is able. He alone can heal, and that His presence be near you and yours, is my prayer.

My kind respects to Mrs. Watie.

I am Respectfully Yours,
MARY F. WHEELER.

[69] The writer is referring to the death of Saladin Watie. After the close of the war he had settled at Webber's Falls where he engaged in the mercantile business and in farming. His death, which occurred only a few weeks after that of his cousin and devoted companion Charles Webber, ended a very promising career. This letter, from an intimate friend of the family, indicates something of the deep religious faith of many of the Cherokee.

✥§ CHAPTER VII ﹅

THE LAST YEARS OF STAND WATIE

THE letters addressed to Stand Watie during the closing years of his life indicate that even when he was old and poor his relatives and friends still continued to the last to look to him for help in every emergency. He had not much left to give, except wise counsel but such as he had of material things, he gave freely. The task of making a living and of educating his children was not easy for a man of his years, especially since his health was failing, but his stout heart and boundless energy carried him on. He opened up his farm, purchased a little livestock, and worked early and late to supply the needs of his family. Before the war he had owned a large plantation on Grand River with broad fields of rich bottom land which he had cultivated with slave labor. This he revisited and apparently put part of it in cultivation again and planted crops.

The irrepressible Elias Cornelius Boudinot had half a dozen plans to make money and in several of them he sought to enlist Stand Watie's co-operation and aid. He urged that they secure farms along the line of the proposed Missouri, Kansas and Texas railway which was being extended south from St. Louis toward the border of the Cherokee Country.

Boudinot and Stand Watie also established a mill and eventually a tobacco factory. Boudinot was enthusiastic about this venture and was certain that it would make them both wealthy. Eventually he bought out Stand Watie's interest and carried on the business alone. He apparently had some reason for his optimism. He had consulted with officials of the United States government in Washington and had obtained from them an opinion to the effect that the internal revenue laws of the United States did not apply to tobacco manufactured in the Cherokee Nation. Fortified by this opinion Boudinot equipped his factory with excellent machinery and began the extensive manufacture and sale of tobacco. Much of it was sold for use in the adjoining states and since he paid no internal revenue tax he could, of course, undersell the tobacco manufacturers of Missouri. The latter protested vigorously to authorities of the United States government with the result that Boudinot's factory was seized and confiscated and he himself indicted for violation of the internal revenue laws of the United States. Apparently the criminal indictment was at last quashed but the Supreme Court of the United States to which he had taken an appeal affirmed, in the well known *Tobacco Case,* the judgment of the lower courts as to the confiscation of the factory. Boudinot not only found his property swept away but he was left liable for the payment of heavy attorney fees due the high priced counsellors that had been employed in the case.

As he had so often done before in time of need the despairing Boudinot turned once more to Stand Watie and implored his advice, and help. Boudinot asserted that the Tobacco Case was of vital importance to the Cherokee people as a whole since it involved a question as to the sovereignty of their Nation. If the United States could levy a tax on tobacco manufactured within the limits of the Cherokee country apparently it could levy other taxes there and the boasted sovereignty of the Cherokee Nation over its people was gone. Boudinot earnestly urged Watie to become a candidate for the office of councillor from the Canadian District. Once a member of the Cherokee council he might be able to secure an appropriation from that body to pay these attorney fees from public funds. Stand Watie was unwilling to seek this office, however, and there is no evidence that money was ever appropriated by the Cherokee Nation to pay these or other fees in connection with the Tobacco Case.

Boudinot later sought an appropriation from Congress to indemnify him for the loss of his factory, claiming that he had established it with the approval of officials of the United States but here he again met defeat. Eventually, however, he secured permission to bring suit in the court of claims and secured a substantial payment for his confiscated factory.

Both Stand Watie and Mrs. Watie were deeply concerned

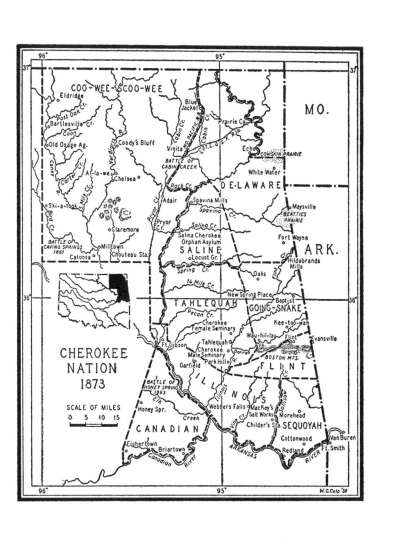

COO-WEE-SCOO-WEE

Eldridge
Post Oak Cr.
Bartlesville Cr.
Coon
Old Osage Ag.
Carter Cr.
At-la-we
Chelsea
Ski-a-took
Bird Cr.
Claremore
BATTLE OF
CAVING SPRINGS
1861
Milltown
Catoosa
Chouteau Sta.

Blue
Jacket
Prairie Cr.
Vinita
BATTLE OF
CABIN CREEK
Rock Cr.
Adair
Spavina Mills
Spavina Cr.
Pryor Cr.
Soling Cr.
Salina Cherokee
Orphan Asylum
SALINE
Locust Gr.
Spring Cr.
14 Mile Cr.
New Spring Place

Echo
COW-SKIN PRAIRIE
White Water

DELAWARE

Maysville
BEATTIES
PRAIRIE
Fort Wayne

ARK.

Hildebrands
Mills
Oaks

MO.

TAHLEQUAH
Pecan Cr.
Cherokee
Female Seminary
Ft. Gibson
Cherokee
Male Seminary
Park Hill
Garfield

GOING-SNAKE
Baptist
Kee-too-wah
Wau-hil-lau
Flint
Evansville
Barren
BOSTON MTS.

FLINT

CHEROKEE
NATION
1873

SCALE OF MILES
0 5 10 15

ILLINOIS

BATTLE OF
HONEY SPRINGS
1863
ETA
Honey Spr.
Creek
CANADIAN

Webbers Falls
MacKey's
Salt Works
Vine Cr.
Childer's Sta.
Morehead

SEQUOYAH
Cottonwood
Redland
Van Buren
Ft. Smith

Fishertown
Briartown
Canadian
River
ARKANSAS
RIVER

W. C. Culp '39

as to the education of their children. Their only remaining son Watica had been about eleven or twelve years old when the war broke out and the two daughters Minnie, better known as "Ninnie," and Jacqueline were about nine and five years of age, respectively at the outbreak of that struggle. The children had, of course, all accompanied their mother when she had gone south to Texas, as a refugee. Here they had almost no opportunity for schooling, though Mrs. Watie saw to it that they were given the advantages of what little might be offered. As a matter of fact, the disturbed conditions in the Cherokee Nation just prior to the war had probably affected the schools there to such an extent as to give Watica and Ninnie, who were both of school age before the outbreak of war, very little educational opportunities.

Once the family had returned to the Cherokee country, however, and a home had been established near Webbers Falls, Stand Watie and his wife evidently determined that no sacrifice was too great if made to provide their children with the education so long denied them in the past. Watica was sent away to school at Cane Hill, Arkansas. From here he wrote many letters home all showing clearly his lack of schooling up to this time, but all showing equally clearly his almost pathetic eagerness to take every advantage of his long delayed opportunities for education. These letters also show his deep appreciation of the sacrifices made by his parents in his behalf.

"I am proud to know I have a papa who will spend his last dollar to send me to school" he once wrote to his mother. A comparison of his early letters with the ones written later will show that he was learning rapidly, but the high hopes of his parents for their last remaining son were suddenly shattered. Later in the school year of 1869 Watica become suddenly ill and died a few days later.

The old general met this great sorrow with the same courage with which he had met so many misfortunes and disappointments that had come to him during his long and colorful life. His two daughters still remained to him and to provide them with a good education became his chief ambition. They were sent to boarding school at Fort Smith and also attended school at other places. It was at times very difficult to find the money for their tuition, board, and clothing but somehow it was always done.

Stand Watie's letters to these daughters indicate how deep was his affection for them and their letters to him and to their mother show plainly their love, admiration and respect for both parents. Jacqueline, the younger daughter, who seemed to have had an especially joyous and happy nature was particularly devoted to her father, which is shown in many letters filled with accounts of the little incidents of school girl life.

But the father who would "spend his last dollar" to send his children to school was not to be spared to them for much longer. The years of Stand Watie were fast drawing to a close. The hardships and exposure incident to war, the long days and nights in the saddle, and the heavy burden of misfortune and sorrow he had so often borne had at last taken their toll of even his iron constitution. Early in September 1871, he was taken suddenly ill and died on September 9th.

His death marked the passing of the last of the older leaders of the Ridge-Watie-Boudinot factions. Some younger members of the group were later to play a conspicuous part in Indian Territory affairs, but Stand Watie was the last of the earlier leaders, who had brought the Cherokee west to Oklahoma.

It seems particularly unfortunate that no son was left to carry on the traditions of so illustrious a father. It seems even more sad that within a very few years no descendant of his would be left to tell the story of a great ancestor. The two daughters Ninnie and Jacqueline both died in 1873. Ninnie was married but left no children; and with the death of these daughters and the death of their mother seven years later, the family of Stand Watie vanished from the earth.

But though no descendants remain he left a record of achievements that will forever keep green his memory in the hearts of a great number of people. Nor will his name ever be forgotten. Even in very recent years many a baby boy, born within the borders of the old Cherokee Nation, has been named "Watie" or "Stand Watie" in honor of the great leader, who contributed so much to Cherokee history.

ᴥᴥJ. W. Washbourne to Stand Watie

Millwood, C. N. Sep 27th 1868

DEAR GENERAL,

I was in hope that I should have seen you ere this. But I was not able to go down to the Council, where I suppose you went, and where you met Boudinot and the other delegates. I hope Boudinot and the others satisfied you that you would be better treated than you have been. If the treaty be ratified without any important amendments it will be a fine one for the Cherokees, and will give you and all of us a chance to rise again.[1]

I write to you to learn whether you have seen any of the Davis' folks yet and to beg of you to early strive for me to get the place, or in such shape that I can proceed. If I knew the parties I would not trouble you, and I believe you can get the place for me a great deal cheaper than I can.

Polson says you want some tobacco. There is none now at the Factory, being [all] sold or sent off.[2] But in a few days there will be plenty and I will try and have some for you.

Susan is better, the children are well.[3] Annie is doing finely. Flora & children are well.[4] Polson has bad luck all the time. He has got him a lawyer now and I hope he'll do better. Write me.

Yours truly,

Gen. Stand Watie   J. W. WASHBOURNE

---

[1] The treaty here referred to was never ratified by the Senate of the United States. A movement to abolish making treaties with Indian tribes was under way in Congress. The movement grew rapidly and in 1871 the making of further treaties with the Indians was prohibited by law.

[2] As previously noted, Stand Watie and E. C. Boudinot were jointly operating a tobacco factory.

[3] The writer's wife and children.

[4] Mrs. W. D. Polson, sister-in-law of the writer.

✑ Stand Watie to J. W. Washbourne

Webber falls Oct 3rd 1868

DEAR WASHBURN

Your letter of 27th Sept. came to hand by last evening mail. Am happy to learn of the improved health of Susan and good health of Flora and the rest. My wife and brother Charles have gone up and you will have seen them. I did not go to the Council neither have I learned the perticulars of the pending treaty as none of the Delegates have condecended to write or call on me. I hope that it will be as you say it "will be a fine one for the Cherokees and will give all of us a chance to rise again." I think we need rising again.[5] I have not seen the Davis family they are on Priors Creek near Albertys. I shall try to see some of them soon and then will try to get the place for you.

I am sorry that Polson has had bad luck all the time, but I am not at all supprised at it he will continue to have bad luck so long as he persists in the foolish ides he has of being able and competent to manage and run the mill himself. I saw when I was there how matters were working and advised to stop the mill untill he could procure a man competent to run [it], but suppose he thought I had no business to be concerned in his affairs — yet I consider it my business until I am paid for that is all my future dependence being flat broke and too old to work.[6] You promised to have some tobacco for me in a few days send word when I can get it if I had it I could hire work for it. write soon love to all.

Yours truly
S. WATIE

[5] Stand Watie, in common with many of the Southern leaders, had been a man of considerable wealth before the war. He was now poor.

[6] Evidently Stand Watie had sold an interest in his mill to W. D. Polson.

[7] Watica, the only surviving son of Stand Watie, at the time this letter was written was attending Cane Hill College. Mrs. Mary L. Pyeatle of Fort Smith, Arkansas, supplied the following information. "The first Sunday in September, 1868, Watica Watie, John Vann, John Drew and Jess Foreman rode up to my father's house and asked if they could board there and go to school. He told them they could. They started to school the next morning in the new school."

⮑ Watica Watie[7] to Stand Watie

Oct the 11th 1868
Cane Hill Ark

I Seat myself with the greatest of pleasure to Write to you. I am well and hope you and the family is enjoying the same blessing. I feal proud to think that I have a papa that take the last dollars he has to send me to Chool can I through my time away? no I dont think I can. I will try to lurne all I can. I hope I will be able to do better the next time so I will cloas.[8]

Good by love to all you most write to me.

I hope you all well.

You moust write to me.

from your soun
WATICA WATIE

⮑ Watica Watie to Jacqueline Watie[9]

Oct th 23 1868 Cane Hill
Washington Ark

DEAR SISTER

I recead your letter this morning as I was on my way to school.[10] I felt like a new boy. I was glad you know. We all made speeches to day. I don about as well as you might expect. You sad something of your teacher and I will say that I think we have a good teacher. now something about my boading place. I think that I coudnon bin suited any better. We are all well at this time. I would lik to be at home to night and See all the famly. it seem as if I had ben away from home year, but I can injorer myself on Cane Hill fine with the girl[s]. there are some Cerokee girls going to School about two

---

8 Up to this time Watica had had almost no opportunity to attend school, due to the war and the unsettled conditions in the Cherokee Nation just before and after that struggle.

9 Jacqueline, Stand Watie's youngest daughter, was about twelve years old at this time. She was attending school at Webbers' Falls.

10 Cane Hill College, chartered in 1852, served the students of Arkansas and the Indian territory until the outbreak of the war. In 1868 the college was re-opened in new buildings and prospered for many years.

miles from hear.[11] Callie Adair go to school thair. I have just bin to a debate to, and hear all the boys speak. This is all at present time. I will write agan when I have time you must write to me, and you must tell all the girls that Mr Watie is all that they can take about hear on this Hill.

You will excuse me this time perhaps the next time I will dow better. give my love to all at the Falls. you must all write.

from your brother

Jackeuline Watie   WATICA WATIE

COMPOSITION OF WATICA WATIE

Description of the Falls[12]

The Falls are situated about twenty five miles below Fort Gibson on the south side of the Ark. River. Two Storehouses a few dwelling houses is all it con[tains a]t the present time but from the beauty of [the] situation the richness of the soil and the advantage of navigation It promises at some day or other to become a considerable place. It is located upon the bank of the river above high water mark and has a beautiful view both up and down the river. Site of the place is exceedingly leavel and in the Sp[ring] when the grass is green there is no place [more] beautiful for there being no undergrowth the place presents the apperance of one continued lawn. It is also shaded by large trees and on account of the richness of the Soil It is the most productive portion of the Cherokee Nation. I have thus given you a gener[al desc]ription of the place which I call my home and though to others it may be a place of indifference but to me it is the best place: . . .

WATICA WATIE

Nov. th 12, 1868

[11] At the same time the Cane Hill College was chartered, a school for girls was established in this little town. It was known as the Cane Hill Female College.

[12] At the close of the war Stand Watie built a new home near Webber's Falls. This is the spot that Watica has described in this exercise in English.

✑ Watica Watie to Sarah C. Watie

Cane Hill Ark
Nov th 15 1868

DEAR MOTHER

I seat my self to write. I reseave a letter from Papa and when I saw it I was glad but you can gess what news he wrote — it was about five or six lines but it was grate pleaser to me to [get] it but I would like to hear all the news. I think I am doing very well. I feal truly proud to think that my parents will spend the last dollar to send me to School.[13] hope that I will be able to helpe my papa do bisness when I go to School a while longer. tell all famly howdy and kiss Jackye for me and tell Ninny that I will kiss her myself. I have no news at this time, but I say to send me a horse for Christmas and I will come home for as our School will have a week vacation and as I would like to see you all so much, you most try to send me som mony if you can. me and all the boy get along so well that I like to stay up on Cane Hill. I cloas my letter. I will tell you all when I see you all. all excuse my bad writing and hope I [do] better. love to all.

From your effectnate son

WATICA WATIE

P S be sure to send me a horse to come home on and foure dollars if you pleas for I am ner with out a hat.

✑ Elias Cornelius Boudinot to Stand Watie

Factory
Bondyville C. N.
Nov. 21, 1868

MY DEAR UNCLE;

The arrangment we spoke of is agreeable to my managers and foreman.[14] As soon as the expenses of removing the new

---

13 The eagerness of Cherokee youth to secure an education was only equalled by the willingness of their parents to make any necessary sacrifices to afford them the opportunity for schooling.

14 In this letter is told something of the previously mentioned tobacco factory operated by Stand Watie and E. C. Boudinot.

271

machinery to this point and putting it up are paid under the present arrangement, and the expenses of constructing the buildings and arrears I have yet to pay, you will receive an equal share of the profits with myself. A part of the machinery, 4 loads, arrived yesterday and is now unloading; the balance, some 10 loads, will be here early next month and be up for business; the cost of transportation will be something like $1,500. The cost of the new buildings with the arrears yet to be paid by me will amount to about $3,500. By the time you make your arrangements to come to your old place or at least by the middle of February these expenses will be paid, in other words your profits in the concern will commence the very day mine does. In the mean time if any delay should occur, you can draw for as much tobacco as you need, for you are a partner of mine, and the firm is known as and all manufactured tobacco, bills &c &c will be marked and branded &c &c — *"Boudinot & Watie."* We shall need a great many hands and must not be embarrassed by any change in the permit system or law which *will* embarrass us.[15]

Write to me at Washington City, care commissioner Indian Affairs, and tell me what has been done by the council and whether you are perfectly satisfied with our arrangement.

Love to all

Your aff. nephew,

E. C. Boudinot

⊷§ Watica Watie to Stand Watie

Cane Hill Ark
Nov the 27th 1868

DEAR PAPA

I reseve your kind letter it give me much pleasure. As Col Adair is go down thire I thought I would write to you. he tole me saw you and uncle Charles a fue day ago and sad you sad

---

[15] Boudinot evidently expected to employ a number of white laborers, and under Cherokee laws any citizen of the United States must secure a permit to reside or work in the Cherokee Nation.

all was well. I reseve a letter from Ninnie a day or to ago and was very glad. you can tell her that I will answer her letter next week. I think that I am don well as you could expect. I am getting along well and hoping that I will learn fast. I try to learn all I can. I am up with men that went to school last session and in Arithmetic I can lay over any of my class, at first any of them could best me but now only one or two can. I think in a week or two I can beat them, I will tell you all the [news] I know but I suspose you have hear it. We heard that the people in the south was in war thay had fouet one battle. I think we will hear all the perticlers of it in the next male. That is all the news. I cannot write much at the time but hopen that this fure lines will find you all well I will Cloas. you can tell uncle Charls to write to me. I would like to get a letter from him. tell him to tell me all the news and I will do the same as far as I can. you must tell the children to write to me. I would like to see all. we will have a fure day vacation Crismas. if you send me a horse up a fure day befor Crismas I can go home and see you all and get back in time school. Col Adair came from Talequah today and told us all the news.[16] I will cloas by tell you all to write to me soon.

From Your affectionnat son
S. W. WATIE

◄§Ninnie Watie[17] to Watica Watie

Webbers Falls
Dec. the 12, 1868

DEAR BROTHER

As I am going to Fort Smith soon I thought I would Write you a few lines to let you know that I have not forgotten my brother. you never write to me any more than if I was not you Sister. I have written to you four times and have never received but one short letter but it was [a] great pleasure to me.

16 Colonel William P. Adair.
17 Minnehaha Josephine, generally called Ninnie, was the oldest daughter of Stand Watie. She was at this time about sixteen years of age.

you must not think because I said a short letter that it did not afford much pleasure for it did.

I believe it is time to tell you the news. Major Scales is married you have heard that I know.[18]

Ellen is going to get married to Mr. Sam Foreman tomorrow by parson Heral.

I will try to tell some thing about this last race that was to be run by Mr Rayman and the Fishers. Mr Rayman got Mr Holt to train his horse and he played off on Rayman, he lamed the horse that it could not run and then he drew out and would not help to pay & they Forfeit and now all the blame is thrown off on Rayman. you ought to have been here and heard Mr Fisher curse and abuse Mr Rayman. It is getting late and I am cold and must close by saying write soon.

Stand Benge is very sick he has the pneumonia the doctor thinks that if he gets well it will be an accident.

When you write do as I have done tell all the news. do you ever get a line from Haram.[19]

You must write to him and tell him he must not forget me. I will say good bye for they are hurring me. Pa said he would send a horse after you christmas if he can. he will write soon and I think he will send you the money. Ma will send you clothes soon. she has got them made. that is all at the present.

From Your Most
affectionate Sister
NINNIE J. WATIE[20]

᭥Watica Watie to "Dear Sister"[21]

Cane Hill Washington Co Ark

DEAR SISTER   Jan the 8 1869

I received your kind [letter] and was glad. I would like see

---

[18] J. A. Scales had served as a major under Stand Watie.

[19] Hiram V. Blackmer, a friend of Watica.

[20] The writer's full name was Minnehaha Josephine Watie.

[21] Though the letter is addressed simply to "dear sister," Watica was surely writing to Jackie who was at home with her parents. Ninnie was, at this time, in school at Fort Smith.

you and mama, papa and can tell all the people I am try learn all I can. tell Hugh and Harrett I think of them ofene.[22] I hope you will excuse me for not writing of. I writen so when I first came hear and did not receive no answer I all most thought I was for gotten. I have no news to you but I would like to see you. you spoke of coming to examination. our Vacation will soon be hear a bout one month. you can tell Par Send the money to pay my boad it is $75 dollars. tell par I would write to him but I [haven't] time. Bollet did not tell me was going backe so soon and haden time. excuse bad writing for I am in a herry. I think of home but I think books mo. I dont bleave I want eny thing. I most close. Bollet is redy to go. excuse bad writing. all at the present

from your brother

W. Watie

❧ Watica Watie to Stand Watie

Cane Hill Washington Co
Jan th 25 1869

Dear Par

I seat my self to write to let you know how I am well and hope you all are well. I will tell you when the school is out it will not be out until Julie. we will have a examination the 5t of Febry. you can sean the mony to pay my boad. it will be 78 dollars. tell Jackquline I have got a good pen for her and when she get it she will write to me once a week. Write to me often or tell Jackey to write. I have writen to Ninnie sence she has ben at Ft Smith but have not reseve know answer tell all write to me. I would Write often but we live so far from the male it get old be[fore] it get home. I have know news so I cloas my letter. excuse bad write and I do better the next time.

From your Aff boy

S. W. Watie

---

22 Harriet Candy, Watica's cousin, who had married Hugh McPherson.

Sarah C. Watie to Watica Watie

Jan 29 1869

MY DEAR SON

I have a chance to send a letter to Fort Smith so that it can be mailed there, you know there is no office here. Your papa has gone to the old place on grand river[23] he has business to at the tobaco factory he may [be] gone longer than he expected. I did look for him home in time to go to see you in the next month but if I dont get there in time tell the gentleman that you bord with that I will come and pay up as soon as your papa gets home he has gone after money to settle all your dues. I hope after this that it will not be such a trouble to get money. you father has a good business now his income will be sufficient to support his family in good style and send his children to school to. what I would like is to be so as to live easy and that day has come so you shall have all you want next year. that is as soon as I can promis you much. I want you to study hard so as to catch up with boys of your age. I would be glad that you could go to school two or three years and longer than that if you will. it will *enable* you to do business in place of your papa he is getting to old to ride so much if he had some one that could take his place sometimes it would relieve him a great deal for that reason I want you to try hard. If I was not affraid I could tell you some funny things that has happined in the bottom since Jesse was here but I know that you and I could not keep it, not bad but funny but I will tell you when I come. I want to see you laugh at it. I will be there next month if possible. tell your friend not to be uneas about your board for if your papa has any luck I will be there some time next month. I cant say exactly what time for I got a letter since he left saing that he was needed at the factory so it depends on how much he is wanted there when he will be back. I suppose that he will have to stay there most of his time that will leave me here alone. I received a letter from Ninny she was sure there must

[23] This was Stand Watie's former home where, before the war, he had cultivated a large plantation by means of slave labor.

be a letter here for her from you but I wrote to her there was not. I wish you would write to Hyrum Blackmere and see what has become of him.

I will close so you can guess that we are all alive from this. Harriet is well and so is Hugh. All well in the bottom. I saw Emma Drew, Mrs Drew the other day all are well so is Mrs. Formans folks.[24] Will give you and Jessie a full history when I seen you.

your mama
SARAH WATIE

ᴥᎶ Nancy Watie[25] to Watica Watie

Fort Gibson C. N.
Jan. 30 the, 1869

MY DEAR COUSIN

I received your kind and well come letter the 27 of this month but the reason I didnt write any sooner I was very sick. I had a feaver and it didnt cool for five days I feel very weak. you said in your letter that I never would write to you but I have written two letters since Ive bin up here and never receive any answer from you and I thought I wouldnt write any more until I receive an answer from you. Ma is gone down to the Falls at her killing Hogs and as soon as she comes back Im going down to pay them all a visit we had a Dull christmas there was no body injoyed them selves very well Miss Sealie Mcdaniel and Miss Marthe Lee and Miss Cynthia Rider you cant guess what they done I will tell you but you mustnt say any thing a bout it the next day or two.

After Jessie left they all got Drunk. Watica that is more than any body can say a bout your little cousin. I would be so glad to see you but I couldnt do any more then to run and meet and kiss you. you said that you hope that I would think of you

[24] These were relatives of two of Watica's schoolmates who were with him at Cane Hill College.

[25] The writer was the daughter of Stand Watie's brother John, who had married Eliza Fields.

once a month. I will send you some of my hair and you must show it [to] your little sweet heart and tell her that is you Cousins hair. now I will tell you about Russel Bean he left his wife and took another woman and his first wife I got her to stay with me untill Ma come Home and last Tuesday Russel and his wife and Jack Griffon and his wife all come to whip him. old will Russells wife had a knife and the other woman had a six shooter but she stood her ground like a woman and they got mad at me because I tole her to stand her ground. they couldnt make a Hill of Beens offen her.[26] Surfronia Bean said to tell you that she had fell in love with you just by seeing you picture. the man is gone what makes pictures and his famlely is in town and when he comes back I will have one taking and send it to you you must write to me as soon as you get this letter. I will write every weeak to you so nothing more at the present time from your Cousin   NANCY WATIE

ᴥᔓNinnie Watie to Watica Watie

Fort Smith Ark
February the 9th 1869

DEAR BROTHER

I have been waiting and looking for a letter from you a long time and have almost come to the conclusion that you have forgotten me. I must try to tell you all the news. I have none though that will interest you. Miss Joe Harlan is here going to school. I believe you are acquainted with her. Yes I must tell you about the theatricals I went to last night. It was very fine indeed the most fool things you ever heard of in any little thing. it only lasted untill half after ten. I have been to two weddings and one party since I have been here. I have just returned from a wedding and I am almost too tiard to write if it was anybody else but you I would not write but I want to hear from you and so I write anyhow. Tell John Drew that Mary says he had not done as he promised to do, she wrote to

---

[26] Evidently there were occasional neighborhood rows among Cherokee, the same as among the whites in the rural districts.

278

him and has not received a line from him.[27] she is well and I suppose that she is doing well.

I am not going to school with her. She is going to the Convent and I am going to Sandles School. I have been to see her twice and she has been down to see me once that is all. Goodbye.   From your sister

P. S. Cousin Watieka   NINNIE WATIE

Excuse the Liberty I take in adding a few lines to lengthen Ninnie's Letter, also to inform you of the existence of a few important facts, which she has deemed *quite prudent* to omit. I believe she likes Ft. Smith exceedingly well and is *particularly attached* to some of the *inhabitants,* which here must be incognito, for I can't enlighten you any at present, for she is sitting by me looking at my writing, and of course I must write to please her fancy, but I *will tell*, she has several Sweethearts, should not wonder if Ninnie becomes a Coquette. Some time I'll reveal to you the names of these favorites. How are you progressing with your studies, better apply yourself with much diligence, for if you do not Ninnie and I will graduate before you do. Give a smile to all the pretty boys and compliments to friends and acquaintances.

I would be glad to hear from you at anytime, and as our Relationship entitles *me* to [a] little presumption I will say write me a long letter and tell me all the latest news.

SALLIE E. STARR[28]

ఇ§ Ninnie Watie to Watica Watie

MY DEAR BROTHER   Feb. the 15, 1869

I have just received two letters from you one was dated the 9 and the other the 12th of this month you can not imagine how much pleasure they afford me, your Sister. I hope you do

---

[27] The similarity of names leads one to believe that this was the son of Colonel John Drew of Civil War fame.

[28] The writer of this postscript was evidently the daughter of Nancy Starr, Mrs. Watie's sister who had died while they were in refuge in Texas during the war. Sallie Starr was in school at Fort Smith with Ninnie.

not think that I think more about Sweethearts than I do about you my only brother no I have enough to think about besides sweethearts. I have my books to think about but nevertheless I think of other things that I should not but you must not think that I am thinking of *marrying* for I have never saw any body that I liked well enough for *that* yet but I must change my subject this will not do but let me ask you what you have done with Miss Sallie Mackey.

Why is John Drew and John Vann not going to stay any longer dont they like the school and the teacher or are they to poor to finish the session. I think you and Jesse are sencible boy[s] to stay and try to learn all you can like you good sister is trying to do.[29] I think I improve rapidly my teachers say I do but of course I must be flattered a little. My teachers are very kind to me and that shows that they must be interested in my learning but I dont think I would like to board there, When you heard Miss Fannie Campbell was married did any of you cry. I heard one of you did, they say that helps. F took it very hard so miss Mary Mackey was telling *me,* some one of her school mates had a letter from Cane hill saying that J. F. Took it very hard. I told her he did not. I knew he was not so simple. So Mary Mackey is going to school to the Catholic School. She seems to like the bord there very well but you know that she would say that for there is always [one] of them Sisters there by to hear every word the scholars have to say. I am glad Pa did not send me there for I know I could not stand it they are too close but they are kind.

I had a letter from Mar yesterday. She told me to write to you and tell you that she was looking for Pa every day and just as soon as he gets home she will go to see you and take you what you need you had better write to her and tell her what you most need. I am looking for them every day. Mr. Wheeler[30] said he talked with a man that said they would be down

29 Jesse Foreman was another of Watica's schoolmates from the Cherokee Nation.

30 This was evidently John F. Wheeler, Ninnie's uncle. Before the war he had been a newspaper editor at Fort Smith. He may have still resided there.

in a few days but you know days are like weeks to me.[31] .....
... how do you get along in arithmatic. I have learned more
here in it than I ever did in my life but I dont think I could do
so well if Sallie was not here to help me sometimes. she is
mighty good to me and trys all she can to help me.

but it is near ten oclock and I am getting tiard and sleepy
and must clos for this time. you may let Jesse see this letter if
he will promise not to laugh at it correct my bad spelling and
excuse my writing. I will try to do better the next time and try
to write more. you may give my best regards to Jesse. Good
night dearest brother I am tiared and must Close. Write to me
soon give my compliments to Jesse Foreman.

From your most
affectionate Sister
Ninnie J Watie

ᴗ§ Sallie E. Starr to Watica Watie

February 15th 1869
Bell Grove Seminary, Ft. Smith

Dear Cousin Watica

I have just received your letter and will not defer answering
imediately. Minnie tells me she received yours yesterday. I had
hardly expected to hear from you so soon, knowing a School
Boy's negligence about writing. I hope you are making, rapid
strides, towards and Education. I would liked very much to
have been present at the Examination. Who was your most
advanced Scholar. I hope that our Indian Boys had as much
praise for excelling in their Studies, as for their good conduct,
which I heard so much about while I was up there.

You say you have several *Sweethearts*. I would be glad you
would captivate and bring off to the Nation one of the good
girls of Cane Hill, that is when you get old enough to marry,
of course you are too young to have serious thoughts of marrying yet. you must not let the girls have too much of your mind,
but my Dear Cousin, let knowledge, have all or nearly all the

---

[31] The original of this letter is very fragmentary and it has been necessary
to omit several lines.

sway in your mind. onward and upward climb high up in the ladder of fame, study hard, improve all your time, dont lose a moment, when you get tired and weary of studying then get some History and read, and try to remember what you read. Get the History of *Stonewall* Jackson and read. it is a good Book, and will be such an example of goodness and Greatness to you, that it will surely do you much good. Cousin Mary Starr has the Book and I know she will willingly lend it to you. I want to see you become the man your Father has been to his people and country.[32] I think Minnie is improving rapidly in Her Studies especially in Grammar. We are both studying Earls Grammar. I will not stay longer than until the first of March. I will have to go Teaching again.

Who are your several *Sweethearts* perhaps I know some of them. I know nearly all the girls up there. I suspect that Mary McCullock is the principle *one,* is Sam Perry up there. I saw his Mother a few weeks since and she told me she was going to send Him up there. What are the names of all the Creek boys up there. I know two of them. Charlie & Sam Smith, are they still there?

Give my regards to all inquiring Friends.

Be a good Boy and Study Hard.

Write to your Friend

SALLIE E. STARR

P.S. Dont be afraid to write to me, Watika. I will not criticize Either your Writing or Spelling, but all mistakes are overlooked and excused.   SALLIE

◄§ Sarah C. Watie to Watica Watie

March 22 1869

MY DEAR SON,

I have a chance to send this to you by hand so I must not neglect the opportunity. Mc pherson is going up to morrow. I

---

[32] The Cherokee boys and girls, in common with their elders, fully recognized Stand Watie's qualities of greatness and the debt the Cherokee people owed him.

want you to improve your time you will be a great help to you father. I want you to be a good boy and try hard to learn so that you will be a useful man to your country. you papa is gone up to the old place he will be back in a few days, our town is going up fast there is *one* new house in it. you papa will have a new house before you get here that is for good, when he gets his goods I will send you all you need. you can tell me what you need when you write. just as soon as you can, write and tell me all you want. I will send you money as soon as I get it. you must do the best you can for the present. your papa will be able to do more next year, his business will be more and better so that he can do better for you. do try to learn for I feel ancious that you should be a good scholar and I feel proud of you. I know that you are a good boy and will try to please your teachers and parents. how did you do at you examination I want to hear. Hugh will tell you all the bottom news.

from you affectionate mother

S. C. WATIE

⊷§ Watica Watie to Jacqueline Watie

Cane Hill Washington Co. Ark
March 31st 1869

DEAR SISTER[33]

I take the pleasure to write to you. Mr. Mack Austin is going to the falls, he came up today and I have the cance to write to you. I wrote to Mar about a week ago. I have know news that will interest you but I know you would be glad to hear from you Brother and to know that he is well and dooing well.[34] I received a letter from Ninn a day or two ago. She is home sick. she cannot stand staying away from Mar like me but I get home sick sometime and want to see my old Mar and Par and little sister, but we will have our fun when I get home.

[33] Jackie and Ninnie were both at home. The latter had returned from school at Fort Smith shortly before the date of this letter.

[34] Watica was indeed doing well in his studies. This is clearly seen in comparing this letter with those written five or six months earlier.

283

Par will be so glad to see me he will not send me to work so we can go berry hunting and ride about and see the people. I think of a great many thing to do when I get home. Well I will hafter quit I have a hard sum to work out to night. So good night to all.[35]

From your Aff Brother
S. W. WATIE
to his little sisters

❧ Hiram V. Blackmer to Sarah C. Watie

Springfield Mo.
April 22th, 1869

Dear friend after my respects to you all I take the Pleasure of Writing you a fiew lines to Let you know that I am well at present time Hoping that this Letter May find you all well & Doing well.

I received a letter From one of Wattica School Mates. I was Sorrow to hear of his Death but I could only thinck Back when i and him was school mates & the menny happy Days that we Spent to geather. thoe no Relatives he Seemed to me like a Brother. I wrote a letter to him & was wating for an ancer when the letter come Relating the news of his Death. he had rote Several letters Before he took Sick.

he said that he was getting along verry well and hoping that he would See me Soon & at last of his lines Biding me fairwell. I have bin Reading his letter this morning & Sheding tears over it. tho i Did not get to See him I hope to meat him on that Shore. as it is getting late I will close my letter for this time hoping to hear from you soon.

[35] Late in the school year, shortly after the date of this letter, Watica was stricken with pneumonia. Mrs. Mary S. Pyeatle, in whose home the Cherokee boys were living while they were at Cane Hill, wrote the editors: "Father at once sent for his (Watica's) parents. They were here some days before his death. They took the body home with them for burial. I was only 14 at the time but I remember how broken hearted the old general was over the loss of his last son. Wat was a quiet, well behaved young man as were his companions."

Tell Ninnie to write. give my Respects to Jackeline. I am Staying in Petter Imlers Store at Present time & Expect to continue until fall.

Give my respects to Par and all of my friends. Dont forget to write.

I would like to see you all Verry well & to know how times is there & to know where you ware going back to Grand river or Not or when you had Heard from henry or william.

So I Will Close for This time.
                                                    Respectfuly
To Mrs. S. Watie   HIRAM V. BLACKMER
Direct your letters to Springfield Mo.

ᴥᔞ Stand Watie to James M. Bell

Col J. M. Bell   Webbers falls April 24th 1869
DEAR SIR;

Your note is received. I send by Heaton one box of tobacco the best I have 25 lbs @ .80 — $20.00. You can take the place and settle with Porum. I intended to return it back to him there is a claim against him about to the amt of the price of the place. when I saw him last he seemed to be disposed to shuffle out of the contract. There are some cattle on the place or near there which you can have at whatever they may be worth. I will take your stock hogs here for as many of the same kind there. I am glad you have come so near in telling me what I am behind with you, make out your figuirs and I will come up to them soon as possible. I want to settle. Soon as Sallie comes home I will come over we then can settle and talk over other matters.   Yours
                                                    STAND WATIE

ᴥᔞ Elias Cornelius Boudinot to Stand Watie

                                                    Fayetsville Ak.
DEAR UNCLE   Aug 15 - 1869

I visited my tobacco establishment the other day and found things in a prosperous condition. Owing however to the un-

285

precedented rains in the winter & spring and the amount of my liabilities exclusive of the machinery & buildings, I find I shall not get out of debt so soon as I expected. I shall go to Ft Smith this week & return next. After I get back I shall give my personal supervision to my affairs at the factory: In the mean time I think we can agree upon some combination to make money which will suit you better than an interest in the factory in the future.[36] I think we should lose no time after the hot season in securing claims in the nation along the lines of the R. R. which *will* be built.[37]

I am glad to hear from Perry that you have a prospect of a good cotton crop. I hope your profits will relieve you of all your embarrassments. The delegation treated me very badly as you may have heard. Love to Aunt Sarah & all the family.

As ever

Yr. aff. nephew

E. C. Boudinot

Alice H. Rucker[38] to Sarah C. Watie

Lake Providence La

Sept 27th, 1869

Mrs. S. Waittee,

My friend having received your letter dated the 10th of Feb, I have now an oppertunity to answer it. I am very sorry to hear of the death of Charlie & Saladin,[39] But I can sempathise with you for we have lost our Little Nissie on the 6 of Aug

---

[36] Boudinot had evidently acquired Stand Watie's interest in the tobacco factory.

[37] The railroad referred to was the Missouri, Kansas and Texas. The steel had been laid from St. Louis to the border of the Cherokee Nation by June, 1870. Since Cherokee lands were held in common, any citizen of the Cherokee Nation could settle or improve a farm anywhere on the tribal domain. Boudinot was suggesting that farms be taken up and improved along the survey of the proposed railway.

[38] The writer was evidently a friend that Mrs. Watie had made while living as a refugee in Texas.

[39] Charles Webber died about a fortnight before the death of Saladin Watie, in the winter of 1867-68. They had been friends since boyhood and it has been said that Saladin died of a broken heart.

1867. She died very Sudently with spasams & lock Jaw. Mr. Oaks has allso lost his little son & baby, his son died the same week Nissie died, his baby died last spring, he has none left but Ninnie, We have a little Daughter & call her Alice, born the 1st day of Janyary /69. Our little General is a man in ways he is the size that a 6 year ought to be and thinks he's the greatest reb in the state that's what he calls him self.[40] I hope you are doing better than we are, for we are doing badly we are trying to live honest as southern people ought to do, so you can judge by your self how slow we improve in money matters. We have no news to write for times are very dull, only we are going to have a liviee put by the yanks made of earth, wood & iron, so they say. Now if you wish a home in the mississippi bottom, now is the time to purchase. You can get land cheap; good improved land for 5 to 10 per acre with or without houses. Just as you like or chose. You can get land by buying larg tracks from 1 to 5 dol per acre. Stock are selling very high hear, are they selling high with [you] or not. You must write and give me all the particulars of your country and let us know if there is any opening for a poor old *Reb* to get a home with the *rebs* and mak a living. I do wish you would come down and see us & get a home hear so we could be to gether. I do want to be with you as we use to be in good old Texas. Mr. Rucker sends the General a piece of poetry to laugh & sleep on for a week or two. He says it suits the General so well we must send it with out fail.

Give my respects to all acquainttences, ask them to write and if you can hear of an opening for a tradeing man let Mr. R. know. Mr. Rucker says send him a confederate man down to live with him & hunt. there is more dear hear than ever was known. any one person to follow the buissness of hunting & dressing the hides can make a fortune at it in a short time. Venson is worth from 15 to 30 cts. Bair meat is worth from 25 to 50 cts, other game in propotion, all high. dress Bucksskin is worth 2½ to 10 dollars, if he will come and live with us, it

---

[40] Their son was probably named for General Watie.

will not cost him nothing, and you can say you now know us well. We want a recomendation from you for him. This is the country for Cherokee hunters and stock raisers Mr. R will give them all buisness Just to get some honest men in hear with us. my paper is scarce so I must close. write soon & give my love to the children and keep a large potion for yourself for you know me. ALICE H. RUCKER

✤ Elias Cornelius Boudinot to Stand Watie

Washington D. C.

DEAR UNCLE — Mch. 3 1870.

Henderson writes me that you have drawn on me in his name for $250. I am surprised at this. I am in a death struggle; have pawned my watch & rings and now want you to send me the $30 I let you have at Tahlequah if you have not already disposed of it. I am in a terrible strait; all my business affairs are broken up of course;[41] when I get over this trouble, we can make a combination which will be mutually advantageous. I have written Nathan to send me $25 I let him have at Tahlequah. I have just $10 left; have borrowed $200 & my watch is to redeem; for Gods sake help me out! if you can spare the money send it to me; I cant honor any drafts on me.

I am crushed to the Earth. The delegation look on with delight. By God I will be avenged!

Yours

E. C. BOUDINOT

✤ Elias Cornelius Boudinot to Stand Watie

Ft. Gibson

DEAR UNCLE, Monday Oct. 3, 1870

I hurried down to see you. Had you come on to Creek agency would have met you yesterday.

---

[41] The United States district court had affirmed the confiscation of Boudinot's tobacco factory but he had appealed the case to the Supreme Court.

I shall be at factory this week for a few days; shall go from there to Van Buren to get every thing ready for my trial in Nov. Unless I can get a continuance of my case, until the Supreme court decides the law, I shall be convicted I fear.[42] Clem Vann now is willing to help. The council should pass a resolution setting out the importance to the nation of the case and close with a request to the U. S. court that the criminal side of the case be not tried until the law is decided by Supreme court. That with what I can do will force a continuance. Dont fail to meet me at factory.

Yours affly
E. C. Boudinot

Elias Cornelius Boudinot to Stand Watie

Chetopa — Dec. 11, 1870

Dear Uncle,

I see from the telegraphic dispatches that Senator Harlan introduced on the 6th inst "a bill to authorize the Indian Grand Council to elect a delegate to Congress;" & that on the 10th the bill was reported on favorably; there is little doubt but such a bill will pass; but I hope it will not until after the holydays.[43] I have written to have it held back till then; the bill can be passed then authorizing the calling of the council in extra session. With the help of Maj. Geo. Reynolds & friends of ours among the Creeks & Seminoles I think I could get a majority of their votes; if you could be in your seat at the time of Election I would not exchange my chances with anyone. I will go to Washington this week & if the bill passes *before* the holy-

42 Boudinot had not only lost his tobacco factory but was facing trial on a criminal charge of having violated the internal revenue laws of the United States. Evidently he secured a continuance of his case as the matter seems to have been dropped until the following May.

43 This has reference to the inter-tribal council held at Okmulgee. The treaty of 1866 had provided that the Indians might hold such councils and, if they so desired, might eventually form a territorial government. Boudinot, who had been a delegate to the Confederate Congress at Richmond, evidently felt that if the tribes of Indians were united to form a territory of the United States he might be elected as territorial delegate to the United States Congress.

days will return at once; let us be stripped for the fight for now is the time when our family, so long under the ban, may assert its just position of honor among our people. Should anything important occur, I will telegraph you at Baxter Springs to be forwarded to Oseuma by mail.

Your aff Nephew

CORNELIUS

Destroy this letter after reading for we dont [want] our plans developed prematurely.   **C.**

~§ Ninnie Watie to Stand Watie

Webbers Falls C. N.

January 1st/71

MY DEAR PAPA

Mamma and I arrived yesterday morn "Safe and sound." Cousin Argile Quisenbury brought us up in his Spring wagon.[44] He Argile is quite sick. We were very much disappointed at not finding you at home. Spent Christmas in Fort Smith had quite a nice time. Mamma says that she is very sorry that she did not come back the way she went but I had started when she got there. Started home on the 6th of Dec. and she got there on the 8th. We found all well and I believe doing well— considering. Mr. Foreman I believe gave a dinner last Friday (the 29th). I believe everybody was there —excepting Mamma and myself — who had not as yet arrived. Papa do come home just as soon as possible. Mamma says she is very sorry that you waited for her so long. If you are not coming home soon write to us.

As ever

NINNIE

P.S. Cousin Argile Q. is going up to Grand River to get him a place just as soon as he gets well enough to ride. Bring Mr. Mc. when you come.

N. J. WATIE

[44] Argyle Quisenbury was the husband of Stand Watie's niece, Harriet Boudinot (Wheeler) Quisenbury.

❧ Jacqueline Watie to Stand Watie

Webber Falls C. N.
March the 15th 1871

DEAR PAPA

Col Henderson is starting. I did not know he was going to day and have not got time to write much. David has got better. Mrs. Downing has been sick but is better now. I have not started to school yet on the account of not haveing shoes. Write & tell me whether you will be able to send me off or not, I hope you will.[45] Tell Stand, William & Tobaco, houdy for me. Ninnie is going to school now.[46]

From your little girl
JACK W. WATIE

P.S. I want you to bring me one box of stockings when you come.

Mama says she had to hier a white man to plow and plant the oats, he charges $20 a month, he is a good hand too.

❧ Ninnie Watie to Jacqueline Watie

Webbers Falls C. N.
April 17th 1871

MY DEAR SIS —

Near three weeks has passed and yet not a line have we recvd from you, I am expecting every day to hear from you as I feel very lonely since you left home.[47] You are well pleased with the place I suppose, and have not taken the time to drop a line to me, Mama, or any one else on the place. Papa came home and stayed a week. I don't know how long he will be gone, as I've not heard from him since he passed through Tahlequah, on his way to Grand river. Oh! I've some news to tell you. Jess has broken my Pony for me. I have rode it once. If you should see it, you would want it I know. So I don't have

---

[45] This refers to Jacqueline's desire to go away to boarding school.

[46] Ninnie was attending school in Webbers Falls.

[47] Stand Watie had found it possible to send Jacqueline away to school and she was now at Clarke's Academy in Berryville, Arkansas.

to borrow all the time now. Tell Miss Emma that Billy is poor and his Shoulders hurt very badly but Traveler is fat and Saucy, and no one at home to ride him.[48] Everybody and Everything seems lively in the bottom and I really think they will all be glad to see you and Miss Emma when you come. I mean to say some of the boys, not the girls, for I believe they are all glad you are gone. No news of importance, in the bottom, and as you have not written to me I will close by asking you to write soon to your ever affectionate Sister.

NINNIE J. W.

✌️ Jacqueline Watie to Stand Watie

Berryville, Ark.
MY DEAR PAPA   April 22ond 1871

This eaveing is still and I will have no other chance to write to you, and I will give you as good a history of Berryville as I can. Well Cap. Clarke[49] has a very full school I dont believe I ever went to any better school than he has; for he makes his scholars study now just rite. He dont allow any sweet-hearts to be claimed so I just think he is rite about that. For I dont think it is rite for students to have such things as they call sweet-hearts. The students are some of them very far advanced. Oh! I think Capt Clarke is a splendid teacher. This place dont carry fashions to such an extent; for povity will not let them. But at the examination time we will have big to do. You will come wont you; I would rather you would come than any one else. I will need some money too, for I will have to get some things for the examination, for it will take me from now to get ready. Those folks carry fashons to an extence then; for they go well evry Sunday. But evry day as I told you above they go plane and I can keep up with them then. Papa you must send me some money; if it is not but $5, for I need it very bad and have been needing it a long time. But if you have $25. send it; for

---

[48] One may wonder if this horse had not been named by General Watie for the famous "Traveler" of Robert E. Lee.
[49] Professor Isaac A. Clarke, founder and principal of the school.

it will take that much to fix me for the exhibition, and more too I expect. And I will need some between *now* and *then.* You told me to let you know what it cost: I will send you a cirseler and then you can setle with Clarke. Sister told me you all was surprised to here I had come on to school with Miss Emma; Why! Mama baged me to come after I had given out coming, then she told me to just go as far as Uncle George's. And then she did talk to me awfull that morning before I started. Mabe she thinks diferat now but mabe not. I would hate to think she would think that, always. Well Papa I think this is a very cheap school and good too. I would like to come back here if possible next session; but if it is exposing your povity I will not ask any more, but I think the boading place cant be beat for we are treated just like home folk. We are not treated like strangers. Capt Clarke has the best mother or as good as ever was, for I like her as if she was kin to me. I am taking music lessons and hope to be able to play some for you if you come after me. You must bring Sister with you if you come. The school will be out in July. About the 3rd of 4th. You come about the last day of June and the you will see and here all that is to be heard. But you must be dressed now I tell *you.* For these people are mity sprucy them times.

Well Papa I expect you are getting tired reading my letter it is just filled up with nonsense. You may tell Stand, William and Tobaco houdy for me. And David too. Well Papa send me some money just as soon as you get it if you have it now send it as soon as you get this. Good bye Papa answer this when you receive it. These people dont like to call me Jack.[50]

Your affectate Child

JESSIE WATIE

I have got read of that name at last. But it was a long time wasent it. You direct your letters to J. W. Watie. Miss Emma and Frank is both well.[51]

[50] While in school at Berryville Jacqueline was known as "Jessie." At other times she was called "Jackie" or "Jack."

[51] Emma and Frank Vore, whose father was Major Israel G. Vore of Webber's Falls, were in school at Berryville at this time.

✌ᔒ Sarah C. Watie to Jacqueline Watie

April 25 1871

MY DEAR DAUGHTER

I went to flint and did not find you. you pa come monday after you left and I just got home in time to see him. I was glad that I did not go with you as Mr. E said he had hard work to get throug the roads were so bad. write and tell me when the school will be out. Mr. Effort said that the Fayetteville school was a great deal better than the one you went to. I was sorry you went when I found it was so far but I hope it will be a blessing to you as long as you live and I [hope] you will live for the service of God. dont forget that you have an account to give of all you idle time. improve while you can for old age will creap on and there will be other things to claim you attention besides study. the bottom still continues soddon like. there is not much repentance in it. every week there is one or more new lies so all I can tell you is to keep you toung inside you mouth. dont be writing to Fanny Griffin. I told you not to and I heard a great story about you letter so you made nothing in writing to such folks. I tell [you] a liar is worse than any body. there is no good to be gained from them. I have staid at home for the last two years and almost isolated myself from the world so that people could not find any thing to say about me but with all it did no good so far as my children is concerned. so you can be careful not to write to any except you sister and May Starr. she said that if she had been at home you should not went on but all is well that does well. love to all.

S. C. WATIE

To Miss C. Vore

Please take good care of my baby for if I had known that it was half so far she could not have gone you must all make up you mind to go to Fayetteville next term it is a good school so says Mr Effort. love.

S. C. WATIE

❧Elias Cornelius Boudinot to Stand Watie

Mrs. Trotts May 10, 1871

DEAR GENL—

The Supreme court has decided the tobacco case against me; it is the Death Knell of the Nations; I am totally ruined if you do not run for the Council; for Gods sake do not delay to declare yourself a candidate from Canadian Dist; the retaining fees $1500 to Pike & Johnson — $2500 to Key, $500 to Jones & Wilcot & $500 for printing ought to be paid by the Nation.[52] I must be at Van Buren by next Monday ready if they require it to stand my trial as a Criminal.[53] Write home a line at Van Buren telling me that you have given notice you are a candidate; I shall then feel easy.

Affy
Your Nephew
CORNELIUS

❧Stand Watie to "My Dear Daughter"[54]

Grand River, At Old Place,[55]
May 10 1871

MY DEAR DAUGHTER

Your most affectionate & loving letter has reached me. I am happy & delighted to hear from you. You cant imagine how lonely I am up here at our old place without any of my dear

---

[52] This tobacco case (11 Wall., 619) was of great significance to the Cherokee Nation, since it involved the question of the right of the United States to levy a tax on manufactures within the limits of the Cherokee country. Boudinot felt that the attorneys' fees and other expenses incurred in the case should be borne by the Nation and, if Stand Watie were elected to the council, he might be able to secure an appropriation for that purpose.

[53] Boudinot was under a criminal indictment for violation of the internal revenue laws of the United States but this was evidently quashed as there is no evidence that he was ever brought to trial.

[54] This letter was written to "My dear Daughter," but the content shows that Stand Watie was writing to Jacqueline who was in school at Clarke's Academy in Berryville.

[55] As explained in this letter, Stand Watie was making improvements on their old Grand River farm where they had lived before the war. This was to be their new home.

children being with [me]. I would be so happy to have you here, but you must go to school. I am glad you are pleased and like the school and your teacher. I am well acquainted with Capt Clark, he is a fine man. I have been at home since you left. Staid only a few days. "Mama" was then gone up to Flint, came home only day before I left. I am going to start back tomorrow, will be gone about two weeks. Had a letter from Mamma. They were all well on the 25th date of the letter. I must try to come to Berryville at the examination. I shall do my utmost to send you back again next term. While you are home on vacation you can vissit our old home, it [is] now two years since we came up here. you know it's Strawbery time and it was on the 7th when we were coming up on Green Leaf when you wanted to know whose Saturday that was. I think of you every time I pass the place. I have done great deal of work on this place. I am staying at the Cricket place. the boys are still with me. they are good boys. You would hardly know the place, although I have not built any houses yet. The Grand Council will meet the first Monday in June.[56] I may have to attend but will be back in time to go to your school. I will try to send the money you require. I will write you again soon as I get [back]. I start this morning will be gone two weeks.

Your affectionate father
WATIE

◄§ Sarah C. Watie to Jacqueline Watie

May 28 1871

MY DEAR CHILD

I think often of you and wish that you was not so far from home but I hope it may be a great benefit to you in the end. I

---

[56] The inter-tribal grand council, previously referred to, met annually for several years in an effort to bring the Five Civilized Tribes under one government. It was not able to accomplish anything of importance, however, so Congress at last refused to make further appropriations for it with the result that it ceased to meet.

hope that you will improve you time and make a good and useful woman to you country.

I want you to lay all selfishness aside and attend only to you book dont be writing to this one and that one that you have captivated this one or that one, you are too young to be thinking of any such foolishness. you will find when ever you change from childhood to womanhood that you have only changed from pleasure to trouble. always obey you supiriours in all things that is right and read you bible and be guided by that and then you will not fail to be right. you papa has gone to his home, you asked him to send you some money. he has not got any yet but will try and send you some as soon as he gets back from the grand council. I will send you what I have on hand, it may answer you present wants. in my next I will send more, you know that my means are but slim. I have a very poor way to make any thing just now. you papa business this year is not as good as last year. study hard and you will be able to help yourself in one more year and papa to. as for me I always try to keep up good spirits and that is half the battle. you know that I always try to do the best I can for all. I do my own work so that you and N. may go to school. Betty has gone to her brothers to stay. she was sick all the time and could not be much help that I kneeded though she was the best help that I ever had when she was well. God grant that we may all meet again. all well in the neighborhood and good luck to you and you friends. tell E that if I had known that it was so far you could not have gone.

S. C. WATIE

June 1st

we are all well at present papa has gone to the grand council. I will be glad to see you when school is out. do you ever think how you was mad at papa and do you ever ask God to for give you for it. I am not angry with you for going. study you book and keep foolishness out of your head. I find that you have a great many foolish things in you head. I find that from you letters. be careful God knows you cant be to strict. think twice before you speak once. I send you ten dollars in this letter.

COMPOSITION OF JACQUELINE WATIE
Clarkes Academy
June the 1871

Lettuce

Who would object to eating such a vegetable as this? If evry thing that grew in the garden was as good as lettuce I would not mind helping to make a garden once in a while. There are various kinds of lettus; they are not to tedious to mention if I knew them all; but it is no use for me to comence and then not finish. I love lettuce nearly as well as onions; and equaly as well as potatoes — and better than turnips. This vegetable does not last long, I expect that is the reason I love it so well. it does not stay long enough for me to get tired of it.

We have lettuce here some-times. But not as often as Miss Emma would like it. Miss Emma says it will put her to sleep if she eats it during school day. It does not affect her when she eats [it] on Sunday. I think Eva Bobo loves lettuce as well as any one I ever saw. Donie Bunch [dont] love any one as well as Miss lillie does. Sue Sanders loves potatoes too she says, but not as well as lettuce. Edna Scott loves lettuce as well as she does the boys. Jane Gibson loves peas as well as she does me.[57]

JESSIE WATIE

✒️ Ninnie Watie to Jacqueline Watie

At Home
June 26/71

MY DEAR SISTER

Mr Carlisle is here just starting after you.

Here is fifty dollars to pay your teachers, if it is not enough Papa will send the ballance just as soon as your school is out.

Some of our family would go but it is imposible.[58] Glad

[57] This composition has been included since it shows that school girls are essentially the same at all times and places. It was probably begun as a serious English exercise and ended as a burlesque for the amusement of her schoolmates. It was perhaps such frivolous things as this that caused Mrs. Watie to urge her daughter to take her school life and work more seriously.

[58] For the closing exercises of school.

you are so near home. I have no time to write news F & B G is at home —

Your Sister

Excuse haste   NINNIE

◁§Mrs. Hardcastle to Sarah C. Watie

Mrs. Watie

Jacksonville, Pulaski Co. Ark

Friday Morning. Oct 27th 1871

MY DEAR FRIEND,

A long time has elapsed since I (the Arkansas School-teacher) gladly received your interesting letter of May 16th.

Many times I have thought of *our* interesting and amusing trip from Memphis to Little Rock.

I read with sadness of the death of your much esteemed husband.[59] My tenderest sympathy is yours. I trust you have consolation from a *Higher Power* than earthly friends for the loss of *one* so dear to *you.* His labors on earth have not been in vain, he has done much lasting good for his country and country-men, that will never be forgotten but handed down to the future generations in the book of history for *them to follow* in his foot-steps and *to aspire* to leave *their* foot-prints on the sands of time as well as he.

With you, I say, would that *such spirits* as the *True Patriots* of *"by gone*-days" possessed could be found to fill the *Chair* of *State."* Would that a Washington or Jefferson could *now* be brought forth to be a *leader* once-more, for this *once* happy and prosperous land. I look forward to the Presidential Election as a *time of* excitement, never before known. Every *voice* will strive to be heard, the faint-hearted as well as the *"Strong-minded women"* will feel that they must throw in their "mite." *"The Young Americans"* will let *their eloquence* have *full show-*

---

[59] The death of Stand Watie occurred on September 9, 1871.

299

ing in the school-room and on the play-ground. The *prayers* of the pious will be earnest and deep the *curses* of the wicked loud and long. All, *all* will feel that they must be *up and doing* for the *day* is *far spent* and the night, dark with fore-bodings of coming evils, is nigh at hand. "Truth crushed to earth *will rise again.*" I can not believe but that this Government will rise again to its *former standard* and be such as it promised to be to its *Founders.*

The burning of Chicago, and other fires of the North and West are now on every tongue. No pen can write nor words express the suffering of the poor and helpless robbed of their homes and wordly goods by the devastating work of *fire.* It has made the poor and rich, the innocent and wicked alike its victims.[60] The *fall* thus far has been very pleasant and delightful. The farmers are busily engaged picking out their cotton, which seems to be the main-spring to their prosperity.

You doubtless have heard, that I have given up *my mission* as an Ark. School-teacher and have now a *life-long* Mission to perform, the highest *one* that woman kind can aspire to, that is to be a *true, devoted wife.* Make home and life happy for both.

We do not intend remaining long in Ark. Think to find farther West-Ward a place to spend our life-time, that will be more to our liking than here.

There is no *society* here, not such as I appreciate at least. No intelligence with many of the people. I have many thoughts, many bright hopes for the future, that I will enjoy better when realized, in a different place from this.

My Aunt is still here teaching, is liking Ark. much better than she thought to, at our coming. She will return to Ohio in the Spring if not before. I shall in time go on a visit. I would like very much to see you, hoping I may some time in the future and assuring you of my good health, happiness, and kindest love to you, I close.

60 The Chicago fire started on October 9, 1871.

Will be much pleased if you favor me with a reply. Yes *do* write me soon.

Kindest regards to you I am still

Your young friend

A. K. Hardcastle[61]

David L. Nicholson to Sarah C. Watie

	Lebanon Ala
Mrs. Sarah C. Watie	Oct. 22nd 1872

Dr. Cousin,

Looking over the "Cherokee Advocate" the other day, my eye was caught by the name I address. The writer is a son of Evan Nicholson and your Aunt Sallie, formerly, Vann, I am told you are my cousin. I am coming to the Cherokee Nation. I will be there about Christmas next. I have a small family, a wife & a few flaxin haired children. I go, because I think it my interest to do so.

When I get there & see you, we will talk about National affairs freely. It strikes me that Rail Road Combination & their accomplishments threaten to overwhelm your Nationality.[62]

I humbly concieve this to be wrong, from my present standpoint. I come to make my destiny that of my People, from whom I have so long been estranged. I close by assuring you, that I deeply condole with you in your bereavement, in the loss of your distinguished husband Gen. Watie.

Respectfully

David L. Nicholson

61 The writer was evidently an old friend of Mrs. Watie. Her letter furnishes another evidence of the high esteem in which Stand Watie was held by so many people.

62 The Cherokee had long opposed the introduction of the railroad across their tribal domain, on the ground that intruders would soon fill the Nation and the tribe as a separate political entity would cease to exist. The charters granted to railroads also provided that they should receive land grants if the tribal title to the Indian lands were dissolved and they should become part of the public domain of the United States.

N. B. Will you write & give your views on the main point herein touched upon?

P.S. When I tell you I do not know how to pronounce correctly *Oklahoma* I feel assured you will laugh. Mr. Parker's Territorial Bill to my mind is the Trojan Horse: filled with Soldiers inimical to the Red Man. Beware of it![63]

> Breathes there a man with soul so dead,
> Who to himself hath never said,
> This is my own, my native Land!
> If such there be, go *mark* him well,
> For such, no Minstrel (raptures) swell!

My Dear Cousin:—Write me fully. I expect to be at Tahlequah on 10 Jany next.

D. L. N.

[63] Numerous bills were introduced in Congress providing for the allotment of Indian lands in severalty and the formation of a territorial government to embrace all of the Five Civilized Tribes.

GENEALOGY OF THE RIDGE-WATIE-BOUDINOT FAMILIES

CALENDAR OF LETTERS

CALENDAR OF LETTERS

CHEROKEE CAVALIERS

CALENDAR OF LETTERS

INDEX

309

Chisholm Trail, probably named for Jesse Chisholm, 214n.
Choctaw Indians, xx, 151, 165, 224
Choctaw Nation, 161, 182n., 233, 240, 253n., 254n., 256; permit to export cotton, 176
Choctaw troops, use of, 116
Chouteau, Capt. Augustus, 209; commands company of Osage Battalion, 186
Chouteau, L. P., 187, 209, 210; Adjt. of Osage Battalion 1852, 185
Chunestootie, killing of, 112, 112n.
Clark, Tom, 34
Clarke, Isaac A., 293, 296
Clarke, Isaac A., school of, 292, 292n.
Clarke, P. D., in Canada, 94
Clayton, J. W., 117
Cockrall, Alex, arrest of, 48
Colbert, Winchester, 176, 177; Governor of Chickasaw Nation, 176n.
Comanche Indians, 225n.; desire to fight North, 209; at Council Grove, 224
Commissioner of Indian Affairs, the, 260
Compere, Chaplain E. L., 196, 197n.; collects supplies for Watie, 196; collects articles for refugees, 183, 183n., 207n.
Confederacy, desire for alliance with Five Civilized Tribes, 98
Confederate Congress, advances money to Cherokees, 150
Confederate Indian Nations, 219
Confiscation Laws, repealed, 246n.
Conner, Jim, 96
Conscript Law, 130, 161; provisions of, 130n.
Cooley, Dennis N., Commissioner of Indian Affairs, 229, 239n.
Cooper, Gen. Douglas H., 104, 111, 121, 131n., 136n., 137n., 140, 141, 145n., 165, 204, 217, 220n.; order to raise Choctaw and Chickasaw regiment, 105; becomes colonel of Choctaw and Chickasaw Rifles, 105 n.; marches against Fort Smith, 142; Indians' opinion of, 151n.; replaces Maxey in command of Indian Ter-

ritory troops, 193; brings Creeks and Seminoles to Little Boggy, 203
Corntassel (Cornsilk), murder of, 30, 32
Cotton, profiteering in, 177n.; taken to Mexico, 222; price in 1865, 208
Council Grove, council at, 224, 224n.
Council of Fort Smith, 229
Crawford, John, 152, 152n.
Crawford, T. Hartley, 19
Creek Indians, xx, 28, 127, 156, 164, 227, 289; kill white man, 26; Northern and Southern factions of, 113n., 185n.; cotton arrangement of, 207
Creek Indian Agency, 156
Creek Nation, 213, 257
Creek refugees, 100
Creek Treaty of March 24, 1832, 10
Creek troops, kept in own country, 116
Cudjor, Billy, arrest of, 33
Currey, Major, 13

DAUGHERTY, Stand, murder of, 29, 29 n.
David, Samuel W., prisoner of dragoons, 44
Davis, Jefferson, 103, 166, 189, 226, 226n.; guarantees integrity of Indian Territory, 159; admiration for Watie, 189n.; reported at Shreveport, 193
Davis, Tom, 34
Deer, Standing, death of, 96
Deupree, Mrs. Charlotte, 125, 179, 188; sister of Sarah Watie, 123n.
Deupree, Dr. W. J., 122, 134; made surgeon of Watie's regiment, 123n., 133
Doaksville, 165, 189
Dorn, A. J., 186; Osage agent, 186n.
Downing, Col. Lewis, 249, 252n.; elected chief, 249n.; speech to President, 261; heads Cherokee delegation, 261n.
Drew, Col. John, xxi, 116, 214n., 218, 236, 268n., 278, 279n.; becomes colonel in Cherokee Guards, 109, 109n.; on Chunestootie mur-

INDEX

der, 112; on murder of Arch Snail, 113
Duncan, Caleb, 35
Duncan, W. A., 93; circuit preacher, 93, 93n.

Eagle Pass, 177
Elk Creek, 155
Elk Creek, battle of, 140, 140n.; officers engaged in, 141
Elliot, Jack, murder of, 41
Emancipation Proclamation, 120

Farley, B. F., 216; "scout" of, 216
Faught, Wheeler, hanged for murder of Stand Daugherty, 29, 33
Fayetteville, 130
Federal Commission, 229
Fields, Richard, 31, 152, 226, 230, 237, 242n., 260; kills Nave, 144; in Creek country, 227; in Washington, 252; appointed special agent, 261
Five Civilized Tribes, 296n., 302n.; reasons for Southern sympathy, 98
Foreman, D. M., 238
Foreman, Jesse, 268n., 280, 280n., 281
Foreman, Stephen, leads fifth removal detachment, 14
Foreman, Thomas, conducts second removal detachment, 14
Foreman's Landing, murderers at, 26, 27
Fort Arbuckle, 116
Fort Cobb, 116
Fort Davis, 114, 115; location of, 114n.
Fort Gibson, 49, 122, 127, 131, 131n., 139n., 142, 148, 156, 158n., 162, 164, 185, 227, 261, 270; captured by Phillips, xxi
Fort McCullough, 234
Fort Smith, 62, 72, 115, 116, 117, 118, 122, 129, 137, 137n., 148, 155, 156, 164, 165, 175, 184, 217, 217n., 218, 229, 250, 255, 257, 273, 274n., 276, 279, 280n., 283n., 290; council at, xxii; Southern Superintendency administered from, 98; disorder at, 120; commission at, 231; Commission of, 236n.; failure of peace council of, 240
Fort Scott, 131n.
Fort Washita, 182
Fort Watie, 28n.
Fort Wayne, xviii, 4; armed men at, 25
Fry, Moses, commands battalion, 145
Fuller, Major P., 258

Garland, Samuel, Governor of Choctaw Nation, 176n.
Gaynes Creek, 180
Georgia, offensive acts, xvii
Georgia Compact, xv, xvi
Gettysburg, battle of, 145n.
Gold, Col. Benjamin, 61n.
Gold, Mrs. Benjamin, 61n.
Gold, Franklin, 6n.; visits Elias Boudinot, 6
Gold, Harriet, married Elias Boudinot, 4n.
Grand Council, 228, 297
Grand River, 236, 253, 255, 263, 291
Grand Saline, 118
Gunter, Edward, 18n.

Hamilton, Charles A., 207; cotton proposal to Watie, 208
Hardcastle, Mrs. A. K., 299
Harlan, N. R., 26, 27, 29
Harden, T. R., 162, 162n.
Harnage, John, 161
Harney, General William S., 229
Hawkins, Jack, assault on, 18
Hendren, Capt., military activities of, 163
Hicks, Daniel, capture by Watie, 144
Hicks, Elijah, leads first removal detachment, 14
Hicks, George, 15n.
Hildebrand, Captain Isaac N., 113n.
Hildebrand, J.M., 249
Hildebrand, Peter, 15n.
Holt, W. L., 238
Honey Springs, Battle of, 136, 136n.
Hopotheyohola, (Opothleyoholo), 114
Huff's Mill, 162
Hunt, Henry J., 238

INDEX

May, Ben, 34
Mayes, Joel B., 89n.
Mayes, Samuel Houston, 89n.
Meade, George G., 144, 144n.
Missouri, Kansas and Texas Railroad, 260n., 286n.
Monroe, Tom, shooting of, 96
Moore, E, 18, 19
Mountain Feds, 216, 216n.
Murieta, Joaquin, John Rollin Ridge's life of, 82, 82n.
Musgrove, William A., 221; secures cotton, 216, 222n.

NAIL's Mill, 228, 248
National Intelligencer, 10
National Journal, defunct, 10
Nave, Andy, killing of regretted by Watie, 144
Neosho River, 114
Neutral Lands, xviii, 10, 11n., 114n., 233; whites evicted from, 85; intruders in, 85n.
New Echota, treaty of, xvii, 4, 5n., 12n., 20n.
Nicholson, David L., 301
Nightkiller, David, arrest of, 33, 37
North Fork, 115, 226, 257
Northrup, Sarah Bird, marries John Ridge, 7n.

OGDEN, John B., 75
O-hop-ey-a-ne, 213; second chief of Comanches, 215
Okmulgee, intertribal council at, 289, 289n.
Old Settlers, xviii
Oo-watie, David, 4n.
Opothleyoholo, 111n., 113n., 114n., 116; leader of Northern Creeks, 100; defeat and flight of, 100
Osage Battalion, 185n., 210
Osage Indians, 185, 185n., 186
Osage Prairie, 66, 68, 71
Owen, Narcissa Chisholm, 170; mother of Robert L. Owen, 170n.

PARK HILL, xx; capture of, 144
Park Hill Mission, 5n.
Parker, Colonel Ely S., 229

Parks, Lt. Col. Robert C., death of, 156, 156n.
Paschal, George Washington, 38n.
Paschal, Sallie, 145
Pawnee Indians, 224
Pea Ridge, Battle of, 114n.
Pegg, Tom, Lieutenant Colonel of Cherokee Guards, 109, 109n.
Petersburg, 166
Phillips, Col. W. A., captures Fort Gibson, xxi; leads second expedition into Indian Territory, 101; takes Fort Gibson and Tahlequah, 101
Pike, General Albert, 116n., 117; Confederate Commissioner to Indians, xix; visits Cherokees, xx; makes treaties, xx; commissioner to Five Civilized Tribes 1861, 98; forms alliance with Five Civilized Tribes, 99; assumes control of troops in Indian Territory, 100; commissioned Brigadier General, 114n.; plans of, 115; location of forces of, 117n.
Pins, xix, 57, 121, 123, 123n., 127, 156, 164, 236, 242, 249, 250; killed at Tahlequah, 144; activities of, 162, 162n.
Plains Indians, trouble with, 155; activities during war, 210n.; visit to Creeks, 213; North councils with, 213; at war with Federals, 224
Polson, Dr. W. D., 267, 268n.; marriage and family of, 121n.; letter of, 194; staff surgeon in Stand Watie's regiment, 194n.; ill fortune of, 268
Polson, Mrs. W. D., 267, 267n.
Price, Gen. Sterling H., 114, 151

QUANTRILL, W. C., kills Creeks, 156; raid of, 156, 156n.
Quisenbury, Argyle, 290, 290n.
Quisenbury, Harriet Boudinot, (Wheeler), 290n.

RAILROADS, 257, 257n.
Ramsey, John, shooting of, 96
Rector, Elias, xix, 194, 194n.; superintendent of Southern Indians, 98

INDEX

317

Vore, Emma, 293, 293n.
Vore, Frank, 293, 293n.
Vore, Maj. Israel G., 152, 152n., 206, 207n., 293n.

WALKER, Col. John, 9; takes Creek murderers to Little Rock, 28
Walker, Leroy Pope, Secretary of War of Confederacy, 104, 104n.; plans defense of Indian Territory, 105
Washbourne, J. Woodward, 67n., 69, 77, 106, 122, 158, 159n., 243, 245, 267, 268; urges organization of Southern Cherokee Government, 232, 244, 245; returns to Little Rock, 245n.; complains of treatment, 250; secretary of Southern delegation, 250
Washburn, Rev. Cephas, 67n.
Washington Conference, 236n.
Watie, Charles Edwin, 50, 50n., 51, 56, 58, 77n., 90, 147, 179, 268
Watie, Cumiskey, death of, 121, 121 n., 147n., 234
Watie, Mrs. Eliza (Fields), 277n.
Watie, Jacqueline, 134n., 135, 147, 173, 175, 265, 269, 283, 283n., 285, 291, 292, 293, 294, 295n., 296, 298; character of, 266; death of, 266; in school at Webber's Falls, 269n.; attends Clarke's Academy, 291n.; called Jessie at school, 293
Watie, John Alexander, 18, 18n., 19, 41, 52, 56, 73, 75, 277n.; in command at Fort Wayne, 26n.; in California, 73
Watie, Nancy, 277, 277n., 278; on neighborhood troubles, 278
Watie, Ninnie (Minnehaha), 135, 189, 265, 273, 273n., 274, 274n., 278, 279, 281, 282, 283n., 285, 290, 291, 291n., 292, 298, 299; death of, 266; on Catholic schools, 280; illness of, 283
Watie, Saladin, xxii, 23n., 58, 95, 128 n., 143, 143n., 145, 147, 173, 179, 180, 188, 222, 234, 241, 242, 242 n., 246, 247, 251, 253, 254, 256, 257, 258, 258n., 260, 261; serves as soldier, 149; illness of, 165; at-

tends Washington Conference, 230, 254; death of, 234, 262, 262n., 286, 286n.; farming operations of, 255; new house of, 255; generosity of, 256, 256n.; loses hay, 257; character of, 262
Watie, Mrs. Sarah C. (Bell), 29, 37, 38, 45, 49, 50, 52, 58n., 79, 81, 81n., 85n., 93, 94, 95, 121, 124, 128, 129, 131, 136, 142, 155, 163, 163 n., 164, 175, 177n., 178, 180, 187, 189, 190, 200, 202, 208, 227, 228, 253n., 254, 255, 271, 276, 277, 282, 284, 285, 286, 294, 296, 299, 301; seeks refuge in Texas, 124n.; life and plans of, 125; on conditions in Texas, 132, 135, 201; on rumored Southern successes, 133; hardships as refugee, 146; worries about children, 146; refugee in Texas, 149, 193; hardships and illness, 163; plans of, 172, 179; business activities of, 173; illness of, 174; feels Federals will be punished, 188; dispiritedness of, 189; children of, 201, 201n.; on rumors in Texas, 225; health at end of war, 234, 253, 254, 254n.; lives in Choctaw country, 240n.; concern over children's education, 263, 265; advice to Watica, 276, 282; advice to daughter, Jacqueline, 294, 297
Watie, Stand, education of, xvii; becomes head of treaty party, xviii; collects troops at Fort Wayne; becomes colonel, xx; military activities of, xxi; in peace negotiations, xxii; death of, xxiii; becomes leader of treaty party, 4; life of, 4n.; elected to National Council, 5n.; in charge of Cherokee Phoenix, 7 n.; collects troops at old Fort Wayne, 4, 25n.; goes to Washington, 26n.; becomes Colonel of Second Cherokee regiment, 101; falls back before Weer, 101; on Chunestootie murder, 112; on murder of Arch Snail, 113; elected colonel, 114n.; chosen principal chief by Southern Cherokee, 121n.; Cabin

INDEX

Creek battle, 131; to be made brigadier general, 122, 122n.; raids Tahlequah and Park Hill, 144; in command of Indian troops, 145; captures steamboat, 148; captures wagon train, 148; in Choctaw country, 148; made brigadier general, 151n., 166; military aptitude, 151n.; opinion of self, 157; Biblical knowledge of, 165n.; raids across Arkansas River, 184; capture wagon train, 189, 190, 191n., 195, 195n.; goes into winter quarters near Boggy Depot, 192; refuses to advance cotton speculators' schemes, 192; takes the field spring of 1865, 193; rumored capture of, 193; surrender of, 194, 229; helps Southern Cherokees, 194; principal chief of Southern Cherokees, 194; high sense of honor, 208n.; requests his wife to send goods, 209; suppression of lawlessness along Red River, 212, 212n.; receives orders from McCulloch, 217; pleased at friendly disposition of Plains Indians, 218; thanked by Confederate Congress, 223; sends troops home on furlough, 227; aids refugees, 230; at Washington Conference, 230; assists Cherokees to assemble property, 234; attempts to restore fallen fortunes, 234; settles near Webber's Falls, 234; appoints commissioners, 237n.; plans to return to Cherokee country, 258; concern over children's education, 263; friends look for aid of, 263; post war activities of, 263; aid sought by Boudinot, 264; urged by Boudinot to run for Councillor, 264; meets sorrows bravely, 265; affection for daughters, 266; death of, 266, 299, 299 n.; tobacco factory of, 267n.; financial condition of, 268n.; builds new home near Webber's Falls, 270n.; trip to former home, 276, 276 n.; recognition of greatness by Cherokees, 282, 282n.; grief at Watica's death, 284n.; visits family,

291; plans and activities of, 296
Watie, Watica, 134n., 135, 175, 255, 256, 265, 269, 270, 271, 272, 273, 275, 276, 277, 278, 279, 281, 282, 283, 284; appreciation of parents' efforts, 265; educated at Cane Hill, Arkansas, 265; at Cane Hill College, 268n., appreciation of father, 269; on life at school, 269; previous lack of schooling, 269n.; plans of, 271; progress in school, 273; does well in studies, 283n.; death of, 284; behavior of, 284n.
Webber, Charles, 128n., 134n., 147, 254, 254n., 255, 257; charged with killing Chunestootie, 112; death of, 262n., 286, 286n.
Webber, Elizabeth, 21, 21n., 22, 29, 50, 52, 58n.
Webber's Falls, 141, 234, 249n., 251, 251n., 252, 262, 265, 270, 270n., 291
Weer, Col. William, 121n.; invades Indian Territory, xx, 101
West, George, killed, 127
Wheeler, John F., 72n., 175, 175n., 181, 182, 280, 280n.; letters to, 204
Wheeler, Mary F., 262; condoles Stand Watie on death of Saladin, 262
Wheeler, Sarah Paschal, 38n.
White River, 120
Wickett, Susie, marries Major Ridge, 12n.
Wichitas, 225n.
Wilderness, Battle of, 159, 159n.
Wilson, A. M., 84, 84n.; urges Stand Watie to organize Cherokees for border defense, 106
Wilson, John, 209
Wilson, Thomas, 15
Wistar, Thomas, 229
Wool cards, 165; need for, 165n.
Worcester, Rev. Samuel A., 3, 4, 10; life of, 5n.
Worcester v. Georgia, 4, 5n., 8n.
Wyandotte Nation, emigration of, 95

YELL, Governor Archibald, 29, 29n.
Yellow Tavern, Battle of, 169
Yopothleyoholo, (Opothleyoholo), 112

319

CHEROKEE CAVALIERS

BY EDWARD EVERETT DALE AND GASTON LITTON

HAS BEEN COMPOSED ON THE

LINOTYPE IN 11 POINT GRANJON. THE

PAPER IS ANTIQUE WOVE

UNIVERSITY OF OKLAHOMA PRESS

NORMAN, OKLAHOMA